Land Investment

Land Investment

Maury Seldin
Professor, Real Estate and Urban Development
School of Business Administration
The American University
Washington, D.C.

D.J-I. 1975
Dow Jones-Irwin, Inc. Homewood, Illinois 60430

First Printing, July 1975

ISBN 0-87094-094-5
Library of Congress Catalog Card No. 74-25813

Printed in the United States of America

to
Rachel, Susie, and Judy

Preface

This book is written for real estate investors and potential real estate investors to assist them in making better investment decisions. This book will explain not only the risks and rewards of land investment but also the nature of the contemporary problems of land use and how those problems present opportunities for profit.

The intended audience for this book includes everyone associated with real estate, as well as persons who are interested in land as an investment.

Because the book explains how things work, it will be a valuable aid to a large segment of public officials, especially those involved in local government and with environmental control at all levels of government. The issue of land use and control has such importance in the political scene these days that the astute politician will see the merits of better understanding how the land markets are operating.

Two more major groups (in addition to investors and public officials) will find the book of interest. One is a general public readership interested in the land controversy. While some aspects of the book may be too technical for their interest, the format permits them to read this book and get the concept without having to follow a great deal of detail.

The final group would probably prefer more detail, since it is an academic group. Although the attempt is to write a book of general interest rather than a text book, this treatment of the subject can provide a valuable aid to academicians in understanding and explaining our system of land use and control.

The impetus for this book has come partly from the author's need as a professor to explain how things really work and partly from the author's work as a consultant. The catalyst was an assignment to develop a course syllabus for the NIFLB (National Institute of Farm and Land Brokers) focusing on the needs of the real estate agent who wishes to specialize in land. That work combined with the regular development of materials for teaching at The American University provided the start to the work.

The list of persons to whom the

author is indebted is long. Included are Alan Inbinder and Dwight Jundt of the NIFLB with whom the author worked in developing the syllabus, and Ina Bechhoefer, Janice Stango, Michael Lipson, and John Urciolo who provided research support. Early typing was done by many including Bernadine Haber. The heaviest typing burden was carried by Beverly Unsworth with an amazing turnaround time. The editing was done by Doris Tennyson. Among those who reviewed parts of the book and provided help in research and/or review for specific chapters were: John Wetmore, Chief Economist, Mortgage Bankers Association of America; Robert Suter of Purdue University; William Crowley of the U.S. Department of Agriculture; Michael Sumichrast, Chief Economist, National Association of Home Builders, and Homer Hoyt. Some of the professors under whom I studied were of substantial influence in my perception of the discipline. While there were many, the key figure is Arthur M. Weimer. Additionally, one nonuniversity colleage, Lyle Bryant, was instrumental in a series of projects which developed the research basis for some of this book.

The responsibility for such errors as there may be are, of course, the author's.

As a final acknowledgment, the book is dedicated to Rachel, my wife, and Susie and Judy, our daughters. It is, of course, in some measure their time which has been used for this book.

MAURY SELDIN
June 1975

Contents

List of Figures and Tables

Part one
Land as an Investment

1

Perceptions of Land

Land is for making money!

Land is for living!

The battle is on. The struggle between these two points of view is being fought in the zoning process, in the courts, and in the electoral campaigns.

The investor may improve his investment results by increasing his understanding of the battle. The first step is seeing land from the different points of view, which is what this chapter is about.

THE "ONLY WAY" SYNDROME

The cliches of real estate are legion, starting with "Real estate isn't the best way to make big money, it is the only way." As with most cliches, the simple statement has an element of truth.

Among the several ways of accumulating great wealth are: cornering the market in a natural resource, dominating the market with a superior good or service, and selling future expectations at a favorable price.

Cornering the Market. Cornering the market in a natural resource was most popular in the era of "robber barons" (or captains of industry, depending on the point of view). The diamond cartel still does well, and at this writing some questions are being asked as to whether the captains of the oil industry utilized the 1974 fuel shortage to further restrict competition and raise prices. These cornering schemes can be especially difficult to pull off because of the vast amounts of capital required and because they generally involve conspiracy in restraint of trade.

While conspiracy in restraint of trade is illegal for business in the United States, it is not so in all countries. International cartels are acceptable in many quarters. In the United States agreements among local governments about sharing markets or other economic or development interests are considered cooperative efforts, not conspiracies.

Landowners may conspire, or rather cooperate, to limit the availability of use of land for various types of purposes. For example, a group of owners may pool their interests by assembling a very large tract of land, perhaps suitable for a new community. The land may then be developed for residential uses with one section set aside for a shopping center. By judicious planning, that shopping center may be placed so no competing center can have good access to the spending population.

Pooling the ownership of land is not the usual method of conspiracy. Rather, the individual owners get together to influence the regulation of land use. Zoning, for example, provides manipulative opportunities to owners of land who seek to obtain for themselves the highly restricted categories of permitted use. The value of such zoning may become so great that the usual or rather acceptable political processes are bypassed, and inducements are given to persons in office to vote the right way. Sometimes a great deal of time and money are expended to replace honest officials with corruptible ones.

Attempts to gain control of the political machinery by private interests are really nothing new. However, attempts by the general public to protect itself against such abuse of power are of recent vintage. There seems to be no way to keep profit entirely out of the political arena, just as there seems no way to keep politics completely separate from profit-making enterprises.

When profits find their way into a segment of the economy they eventually, aside from what is skimmed off up front, flow back through the marketing and production process to the owners of land or raw materials. Changes in gold prices do not significantly enrich the gold distributor who sells to dentists and jewelers. While some speculators may profit by holding gold in some form, the big gains go to the owners of gold mines. The price increase filters back to the mine owner. It is the same with land. The sharp rise in the price of housing may provide a one-time benefit to the home builder, but it is a real boon to the land investor. Many builders make more money on their land than on building houses. Those who sell them the land may make more from land investment than the builder makes from building. And it is quite common for farmers to make more profit from the sale of their land than they have earned in all their years of farming if they have farms on the urban fringe.

The mechanics of it are simple. The price of a good may go up, with or without conspiracy. The retailer or builder gets a windfall, but it does not take the supplier of the raw material long to figure out that he can raise his price without significantly affecting the quantity he can sell. The raw material in the case of diamonds is the uncut diamond; in the case of oil it is the crude oil as it comes from the ground; and in housing it is the land.

So far the discussion has emphasized cornering the market in a natural resource. In these cases, with the exception of land, the commodity is fungible —that is, one unit of it is pretty much like another except for differences in grade, quality, and other characteristics of subclasses. The cornering of the market in such commodities is difficult because they are substitutable and mobile. Land, of course, is different.

One cannot move it and each parcel is unique, at least by virtue of its location. Thus one parcel of land may be considered of superior quality and substitutes can not readily be brought to the market at that location. The restriction of competition enhances the price. That is what is meant by cornering a market.

Dominating the Market. Xerox has enjoyed the fruits of a superior product in the market, as have Polaroid and numerous other producers of goods. While some inventors get rich, the facts are that in the business world the big money is made in the implementation of an idea, not the conception. An inventor who conceives and demonstrates the usefulness of some labor-saving device will not fare as well as the businessman who gets that device produced and distributed to the people who need it. No matter that they did not know they needed it until it was invented and marketed; so long as they prefer it to other goods or services they could spend their money on, the profits will flow to the businessman.

The big profit in this case arises from the competitive advantage of getting to the market first at prices well above costs of production (including royalties to the inventor). In a competitive situation, others will enter the market and drive down the price to margins theoretically just enough to make it worthwhile. Actually, the dynamics of the market may drive prices below that point and run some producers out of business because of temporary oversupply. Good oligopolists (the small group of would-be monopolists who cannot get everybody else out, but are close) understand such ruinous competition and look for subtle ways to keep prices at comfortable levels. The check on one oligopolist who would cut prices is the retaliation of the others. Profits are maintained in this way without collusion. In the United States, conspiracies among oligopolists are illegal. However, action may be harmonious without being concerted. Thus many play the game without conspiracy.

The easiest industry in which to gain monopoly profits is real estate. Every parcel by virtue of its location has some element of monopoly; the only question is how large an element is present by virtue of the size of the parcel or the zoning regulation of the local government. Land zoned for high-density use in a low-density area of heavy demand for moderate-priced housing enjoys a monopolistic advantage. The rents will be higher than those in other areas not so well located. And resale prices will rise rapidly because housing is a product or service that people want and for which they have relatively few alternatives. Owning the only land zoned for a shopping center provides a tremendous advantage in pricing rentals. The investor will do well because no one can come in and provide ruinous competition. No land is available for a competing shopping center. The investor dominates the market.

Thus far, real estate investments including land have fared well among the several ways of achieving great wealth. Land lends itself to cornering the market because it is a natural resource, and competition at a specific location is physically limited. Land also lends itself to monopolizing or dominating the market with a superior good or service because its location has an element of competitive advantage which may be strengthened by zoning or by building—for example, by building houses on all of it except on a space left for one shopping center.

Selling Future Expectations. Now consider the third general way of achieving great wealth—selling capitalized future income at a favorable price, as in the stock market. All the stock investor gets is the stream of dividends, plus the net sales price when he sells his stock. The buyer of the stock gets the same thing, income while he owns it and the proceeds when he sells.

The prices paid for stock at any time are based on expectations as to the future. Some investors have a resale price expectation, but the more astute evaluate both the earnings expectation and the market's assessment of the value of those earnings. The market assessment capitalizes earnings, that is, it converts future earnings into present value. When a great many buyers are in the market and their expectations are high, prices are inordinately high. When pessimism prevails, prices are low. At that time excellent buys are available for those who can wait for expectations to change. Of course, the actual earnings performance of the company is of considerable importance.

While some stock investors do well, most have a difficult time of it because they did not start from the right point. Investors who get in on the bull markets, the upswings, generally do well. But a bull market is not the right starting point. The right starting point for a particular stock is before it demonstrates fantastic earnings and before it sells at incredible price-earnings multipliers. The biggest winner of all is the businessman who builds a business, takes it public, and then rakes in the "super money"—the capital gains that he gets from selling the future expectations.

The stock market is a relatively recent phenomenon. It has magnified the opportunities for making money because it introduces an organized market for the ownership of the companies that produce profits. It is one of two tiers in the capitalization of future income; one tier is the income-producing entity itself, and the other is the market for buying and selling ownership of it.

As for the income-producing entity, what kind has the greatest potential? Mining and other extractive industries are profitable, but they use up the resources upon which they depend. Manufacturing is profitable, but companies have to change with the times or go under. Service industries have been doing well, but they are at the mercy of competition for a consumer who does not seem to know what he really wants out of life. What about land and real estate? (Real estate differs from land in that it includes buildings and all other improvements as well as the land.)

As an income-producing entity, real estate is marvelous. Any improved piece of real estate may be looked upon as a business. Its rents are its gross receipts. Its operating expenses are much the same as any business's operating expenses. Its profits, however, are hard to calculate, and this difficulty has given rise to an added benefit—the tax shelter.

As a business, its various risks are generally comparable to those of the other industries mentioned, and they may be even greater. But unlike the others, land can go on producing income forever. When one building is torn down, another can be put up. Moreover, the price paid for the use of the land keeps going up.

The value of land derives from its potential earnings. Changes in potential earnings change the value. Much of this change does not stem from any effort on the part of the investor. If he owns land in the right location at the right time, the growth of the community and the efforts of others can make him rich without his having to move a muscle.

LAND AS THE WAY

The promise of riches sometimes entices investors to follow principles that may be categorized as "Get what you can while you can," and "You can make it by rigging it." This kind of outlook is not found only in the field of land development, but it is here that the results are most conspicuous. Everyone has seen the strip commercial developments with a confusion of signs that do violence to sight, the wall-to-wall roof tops of barrack-like subdivisions that deny individuality, and the suburban sprawl that sacrifices society to making life one big highway. These are what happen when land is developed solely for the purpose of profit.

What happens to be profitable depends on what is available for development in needed uses. That in turn may depend on zoning, the decision of an owner to sell, or the passing of land into an estate. The development decisions are opportunistic.

Individuals in a free society presumably have an inalienable right to make money on land. That philosophy leads entrepreneurs to build where they can, when they can, according to what looks most profitable to them. No criticism is intended. They are doing what comes naturally, and idealistic hopes that they will do otherwise are idealistic hopes.

The participants in the process, including the developers, might conceivably take a longer view. They could have a better understanding of what they are doing—that it is deleterious to the environment and that they could find a better way to develop land. But the industry structure does not accommodate much research and development with regard to which land should or should not be developed.

One can argue that local governments are responsible and should provide more effective regulation of land. One could also argue that state governments should have an urban development policy, and that the federal government should have an urban growth strategy. One can go further and argue that many federal policies, for example FHA lending, only serve to aggravate the situation. But, justifiably or unjustifiably, the land speculator has been cast in the role of principle villain.

This book does not focus on the issue of who is responsible and how to improve the situation. Rather it is about how to make money by owning the property rights to land. Nevertheless, the investor would do well to understand why many people perceive the landowner as principally responsible for what has gone wrong in land development. It is also important to understand where the problems in development really lie, and that requires some understanding of how the system operates.

WHERE THE PROBLEMS ARE

Sooner or later most land investors are confronted with the ghost of Henry George, the 19th-century American reformer who proposed that the government tax away all of the increases in the value of the land. Henry George perceived that land increases in value because of society—partly because of public investment in facilities. He reasoned that since society gives the land increased value, society should have the right to tax away this "unearned increment."

Some Georgeists are still around, and the argument does have some merit. But investors have no cause for alarm. The changing value of land is an essential part of the market process, and the market process as a discipline is too good to give up.

In a market system, who gets to use the land is generally determined by who is willing to pay the most. The market system may be contrasted with non-market systems of allocating land. according to who gets there first, or by the fiat of some commission or military authority. One non-market system is rent controls, which have been tried on a temporary basis during wartime and severe inflation. Under that system whoever gets there first gets to use the property with the rent levels fixed or closely regulated.

New York City has kept rent controls, and they do not seem to work well. The same is true of Paris and other cities. They work for a short time, but they lower the incentive to economize on space and discourage the production of new housing. The incentive to economize on space is lowered because the prices paid in rent-controlled space are cheaper than market prices and some renters would manage with smaller units if prices were competitive. New housing is stifled because of expected effects on profits. Both factors tend to reduce the potential amount of space available.

The market system, however, prompts people to economize on space and stimulates an increased supply of housing by offering prices that make adding to the supply attractive. In order for the system to operate, new construction has to be exempted from rent control. Even this is not enough, since a freely floating price of land is essential for the process of adding to the supply of developed land. Not all land is equally desirable, and differences in prices reflect differences in desirability and availability. Thus, the choice of which land gets developed is influenced by the price system.

The market system for land is often closely regulated through zoning laws, which determine how a particular parcel of land may be used. But within the limits of such control, the market still determines how the land gets to be used because whoever successfully bids for the land gets to make that decision.

The choice of course lies within the constraints imposed by zoning. If the zoning can be changed, some value may be created. This possibility has given rise to the "you can make it by rigging it" philosophy alluded to earlier.

Under that philosophy, rezoning is applied for but the case does not stand on its own merits. The "lucky" landowner who obtains the rezoning he seeks may be the one who retained the right zoning attorney for a large contingent fee (a fee to be paid in the event of success). Inquiry as to the full use of that fee may produce some surprises. Some of it might be used to pay for past political support or for the next election – or to line somebody's pocket. Payments may be cash on the barrelhead. And sometimes the result is indictment and conviction of applicants and public officials for bribery or attempted bribery or solicitation of bribes.

Rigging the system can be illegal, but it need not be. Sometimes unethical is enough. And sometimes nothing is really wrong; the person involved just happens to be aware of pending public action which will result in changes in the value of certain land. Or an area may be so underzoned for modestly priced housing, mobile homes, shopping, or any relatively intense use that making a case is easy.

Not only rezoning is involved. As will be explained later, the developability of a site is critical. And, the developability may hinge on the availability of public sewer lines. The decisions as to where the sewer lines go can be corrupt, but they do not have to be.

So much of the political process involves being responsive to public desires that political support for pro-development government officials is no less holy than support for no-growth officials. But, the point is, participation in the political process has given the land investor and the public official a poor reputation and sometimes it has done so with just cause.

As mentioned above, efforts à la Henry George to tax away the value of all private land are not likely to come to fruition in this century, and the market system as a discipline of land-use control is too good to give up. The political system as an alternative discipline in land-use control really has not fared any better than the market system and probably much worse.

What has happened has been a shift toward greater control by the body politic. The method is basically a staging of land development, i.e., influencing when the land will be developed. That means that the range of choice in the market as to which land gets developed and where is severely restricted by local government in addition to the zoning regulations. Some no-growth people and those concerned with adequate public facilities provide the strongest impetus behind such staging plans. Adequate public facilities is the rationale for such regulation.

Development requires a balance of facilities including roads for access, pipes to bring in water and pipes to take it out, treatment plants to purify the water, and a whole host of services ranging from police and fire protection to libraries and schools. Scattering development all over the landscape simply does not make sense. Making facilities such as schools available in one part of the county, with sewage treatment capacity in another part of the county, and roads in a third part makes even less sense. Yet that is what often happens because of the division of local government authority among different governmental and quasi-governmental agencies that provide those facilities without adequate coordination.

Development planning and the environmental issues can be used in guiding growth. They also may be used to stifle growth. Some people would stop urban growth under the guise of working for clean water, while in reality they just do not want more urbanization near where they live.

One can argue that the present system is not working. The air is so polluted that on some days one can hardly breathe; the water is so polluted that it is not only undrinkable, it is not even safe for swimming and boating; noise is ever present, and to get to a quiet place often requires a long journey. The environment in a physical sense is being destroyed. Seeing growing greenery becomes more difficult and one sees no live animals other than cats and dogs. Everything—work or play—seems to involve travel and that uses fuel and pollutes the air, and furthermore, the attempt to escape from the destruction of the natural environment through recreation is in turn destroying more of the natural environment.

Environmentalists advocate programs that vary in degree. For some, no price is too high for preserving the environment; to them no trade-off is possible. At the other extreme are those who believe in economic development at any cost; they see only the economic dimension of life and care not about its quality. The socially responsible landowner finds himself in the middle; he has to contend with people who would turn his land into a park and not pay for it, on the one hand, and those who would destroy the environmental value on the other.

Some compromise is necessary. The absorptive capacity of the air, the land, and the water impose some limitations on development. The costs and trade-offs are complex issues.

Fortunately, we have a legal system with a hierarchy of rights. Constitutional protections rank first. And the constitutional protections encompass due process. Under this system, no one can be deprived of his property without due process and just compensation.

Local regulation of land is way down in the hierarchy of rights. Local government, which derives its power from the state, may control land use through the police power, through eminent domain, and through taxation. This system also has constraints, and disputes about them are fought out in the courts.

The enemies of the landowner are not those who disagree with him politically but those who would undermine the institutions which give a free society its strength. That is why the no-growthers and environmentalists are not necessarily enemies of the land investor. They are just part of the contemporary forces with which the investor has to reckon. To ignore their impact would be folly. To take them into consideration as part of the total picture will help in making a profit.

THE ATTRACTION TO LAND

The attraction to land is emotional as well as economic. Environmentalists are not alone in wanting to preserve the status quo. Some people want to claim land as theirs no matter how undesirable it may seem to others. The street gangs that fight over "turf" are making claims of ownership that are essentially exclusionary. One of the rights in owning any property is the right to use it and exclude others from using it. That right may not be economic; in the case of the street gangs, it seems to be an emotional claim to possession.

The emotional claim may be even greater at the national level. Consider, for examples, Alsace-Lorraine, Jerusalem, or Pakistan-Bangladesh. The attachment to land on a national scale may be as strong and violent as in the shootouts of the old West when the homestead or ranch was threatened.

The investor is concerned with property rights, but he may also be moved by emotion. The feeling may be one of attachment, or it may be pride of ownership. It may also be the desire to become a member of the landed gentry. Whatever the motive, an emotionally charged element is involved. That emotion extends to making money.

The landowner's adversary may be a local governmental authority that is regulating away some of the property rights, and hence the value of the land. Or it may be the federal or state government administering laws on land-use control. The government may be concerned not only with the land itself but with using the land to control other aspects of urban life. Or, at the local level, the purpose may be to exclude certain groups from the community.

For years, in the finest suburban communities, the device of large-lot zoning excluded persons of lesser economic means. It also excluded many blacks. Land-use control has been used to prevent construction of housing for persons of low and moderate incomes—including many blacks, Indians, or Mexican-Americans.

Land use may also be controlled for demographic purposes. Some local ordinances limit the percentage of apartment units with more than one bedroom, thus excluding families with children. The intention, of course, is to keep down the need for public schools, which are financed through property taxes. The support for such ordinances comes from property owners who are already resident there. Similar land-use controls may be employed to head off traffic congestion, water pollution, or the overloading of existing public facilities. Sometimes the state provides a "sewer moratorium" banning new construction tap-ins to existing public sewers, hence effectively preventing new construction.

The implications of land-use control are so widespread that one can hardly find a public issue in which some element of land-use control could not be directly or indirectly used for some nonland purpose. The result is endless conflict over the control of land.

Nevertheless, investment in land is still an excellent way of making money. Every public authority is limited in what it can do to regulate and limit land use. The population continues to grow, and the U.S. government is unlikely to require that prospective parents obtain a permit to bear children. Nor is it likely to restrict marriage as a method of reducing the demand for apartments. It is even less likely to forbid people to move to large cities.

The market system has a way of overcoming even the most formidable regulations, as the following story shows. The Soviet Union has sought to limit the influx of people to Moscow by requiring a person to have a job there before he can have living accommodations. But in order to get a job in Moscow one must first live in Moscow. One young man got around this restriction by employing a marriage broker. The broker arranged a marriage with a woman who had an apartment in Moscow. The groom gave the bride an expensive wedding present, but the marriage inevitably did not work out. After it had been annulled, the new Moscow resident remained in the apartment and went out looking for a job.

The most thoroughgoing regulations cannot stifle the demand of people for freedom, better housing, and the opportunity to better themselves. All that such regulations can do is to make the development of land more expensive. For example, if in order to control water pollution a government seeks to prevent the construction of more housing in areas close to a large city, it may only stimulate construction elsewhere. If the metropolitan area has economic opportunity, i.e., jobs, people are going to migrate to the area. If they cannot find housing close in, they will find housing far out. One must weigh the cost of added air pollution from the extra travel against the added water pollution from development close in. These actions and reactions may result in bringing more land into development patterns than is really necessary. The result is rising land prices.

Rising land prices mean investment opportunity. Land that would have taken decades to develop is now suddenly ready. One of the hazards of owning land, of course, is that it may lose its developability, but these same hazards also bring land investors high rates of return.

Nothing is wrong with taking risks. As Chapter 3 explains, there is no way an investor can escape from all risk. He must select the kind of risk that is acceptable to him. Moreover, the risks he seeks to take are really less than everyone else thinks they are. As in buying undervalued stocks, investing in land is not a question of buying below prevailing prices: it is a question of selecting a good investment at the right time.

In land, location and timing are crucial. The rewards are fantastic for investors who select locations that become more desirable. And if they select them at the right time they may come up with all the benefits of the several ways to great wealth we described above. They can corner the market at their location and be helped by the local government, which will fence out other developers. At the same time, the income-producing potential of their property keeps rising, and the market drives up the price that is paid for the expected rise in income.

The ensuing two chapters on rewards and risks provide, together with this chapter, an overview, "Land as an Investment." The group of chapters in the next part, "Changing Land Values," explain the forces that have been driving up land values. The third part, "Land Conversion," provides a perspective of what happens while the big increase in land value is taking place. For those who are ready to make an investment, the part on "Investing" explains how to get in.

The land-conversion process as a system among other urban systems is explained from the perspective of the land investor who is willing to take the inherent risks associated with land investment and wants to make the money that may reasonably be expected in such ventures. The purpose of this book is to help that investor improve the quality of the decision involved. The intent is to help him make more money.

Some readers of this book will doubtless be more interested in managing the urban development process than in making money. They will find insights to assist them in that endeavor. The result may be to reduce the profitability of some of the money-making land investors.

Land investment performs a useful social function. Its profits are inducements to get that function performed. The astute investor seeks out and gets paid for his work. If the managers of the urban development process are as astute, they will regulate the system so that the risks are less; then the rewards also will be less. A lot needs to be done to improve the system. In the meantime, a lot of money can be made because the problems also present opportunities.

2

Benefits from Land Investment

Benefits from real estate investment may be classified as cash flow, tax shelter, and proceeds of sale. The cash flow is the cash left over after receipts and disbursals have been made for the year. Tax shelter benefits are the savings from preferential income tax treatment of earnings from the property. Proceeds of sale is the money the investor receives when the property is sold and settled and income taxes paid.

Income-producing real estate thus provides a combination of benefits. The combination in a particular case depends in part on how much of the value of the property is in the land and how much is in the buildings erected on it. This is important because the higher the percentage of value in the buildings the higher the percentage of income that can be allocated for depreciation, and hence the more tax shelter the investor receives. The sharp rise in real estate values is related to the increase in land values rather than in building values. The greater the proportion of value in the land, therefore, the greater the proceeds of sale.

Other variables also influence the mix of benefits. For example, the amount of tax shelter depends in part on the remaining useful life of the building and on the depreciation method used. The amount of the mortgage loan, its interest rate, and the repayment period will influence cash flow, tax shelter, and proceeds of sale. All but the most heavily financed income-producing properties produce some cash flow as a part of the mix of benefits, and the tax shelter is also of substantial importance. The proceeds of sale are frequently considered relatively less important.

In the most profitable investments, the proceeds of sale will be the big benefit irrespective of whether the investment is in income-producing real estate or in vacant land. Benefits from vacant land, however, are generally limited to proceeds of sale.

The emphasis on proceeds of sale as *the* benefit from land investment arises because land is a special case of real estate investment. The land needs to be used in conjunction with buildings to produce income, or at least urban land does. Either the buildings are erected upon the land or the land has an accessory use such as a parking lot. The ability of the land to produce income depends on the kind and character of the buildings with which it is combined in use.

The benefit from land investment in the period prior to development is based upon an increase in value during the waiting time. When the waiting time is over, the land value significantly increases again by the transformation of the land into an income-producing asset.

The risk of having to wait a long time for land to be developed, and/or getting a less profitable use than might be hoped for, is recognized by investors so that they demand and get higher rates of return for investments in land alone than for investments in income-producing property. They also get the benefit of high rates of return because market preferences provide higher rates of return to those who will take most of their benefits in the form of proceeds of sale.

MARKET PREFERENCE

Each investor has his own preference as to the mix of cash flow, tax shelter, and proceeds of sale. The mix desired for a specific real estate investment will vary depending on individual investment portfolios, assessments of the future, and feelings about taking chances.

Most investors historically have had strong preferences for cash flow benefits. They reason, with substantial merit, that if the cash flows back to them quickly it won't take them long to get their money out. After that, it is all profit. The payout period for high risk ventures may be three to five years. Most of the time though, an investor will expect to get his money back in five to ten years.

This philosophy reflects an inability to adequately assess risk. Since the investor has difficulty determining the extent of risk, he tries to get in and out quickly so as to minimize the risk, taking whatever profit results. But, as will be seen later, an investor can lose more than his down payment. Moreover, it is difficult to acquire good investments in a competitive market without accurately assessing the benefits to be expected. Thus the approach of getting in and out quickly based on an expected short-term payout may not be realistic as a success formula.

In recent years investors have demonstrated a pronounced increase in preference for tax shelter among the several benefits. Cash flow becomes tax sheltered when the depreciation exceeds amortization (repayment of the loan). Even if no cash flow exists, the investment may produce tax shelter benefits under current law to the extent that depreciation exceeds amortization. And if the cash flow is negative (that is, if the investor keeps putting money in), additional write-offs may result.

Many investors are absolutely enchanted with the idea of making investments with "soft" money (i.e., pretax dollars). Under various schemes —in real estate, oil, cattle, vineyards, or even lease arrangements—the investor puts up a sum of money, say

$10,000, and has an immediate tax loss of $5,000, $10,000, or even $15,-000. If the investor is in the 50 percent tax bracket, he or she may reason that half of the tax loss is Uncle Sam's money. Thus, for the $10,000 investment with a $15,000 write-off, the tax savings amount to $7,500. Some investors figure that they only have $2,500 in it; others, who borrowed the $10,000 in the first place, figure that they not only have nothing in it, but have also saved $7,500 on taxes.

Such investors turn out to be right if they get the $10,000 investment back. If they do not, the tax loss becomes a real loss. What is often forgotten is that until the investor has sold his property there is no way of knowing how well he is doing. A great many of the tax shelter deals, in and out of real estate, either do not return the original capital or, if they do, involve taking inordinate risks in order to make the profit.

Popular as the tax shelter is, many investors have overpaid for this benefit. When the after-tax returns are considered, the investor gets a lower rate of return in shelter than he gets from proceeds of sale.

The third benefit, proceeds of sale, requires the most patience and is typically the most rewarding. We may consider tax-sheltered returns as variations of cash flow, since both involve getting one's capital out as soon as possible. On the other hand, the benefit of proceeds of sale takes time and involves greater uncertainty. Investors demand and get higher real rates of return from investing for this benefit.

Land investors get proceeds of sale as the major benefit because land ordinarily produces little if any cash flow, and when heavily leveraged—i.e., financed with borrowed money—will produce a large negative cash flow. The tax shelter is attractive on heavily leveraged land investments with little or no payment of principal. But the big benefit is proceeds of sale, which, for most investors, is a long-term capital gain.

This chapter is concerned with explaining the benefits of cash flow, tax shelter, and proceeds of sale as they apply to land investment. The sections which follow present the reasoning behind this introductory statement on rewards.

CASH FLOW

Cash flow is the difference between the sum of cash received in a period, usually a year, and the sum of cash disbursed. It is not income. It is not earnings. It is not profit. It is just the difference between what comes in, in cash, and what goes out, in cash.

The cash disbursed for mortgage payments is usually for both principal and interest, and is deductible in toto in calculating cash flow. The payments on principal (called amortization) are repayments of borrowed money and thus must be considered apart from interest when calculating income deductions for tax purposes, earnings on the investment, or profit. Interest is a deductible expense in calculating profit. It is also deducted in calculating cash flow. Repayment of borrowed money is not deducted in calculating profit, although it is deductible in calculating cash flow.

Depreciation is an accounting charge that allows for loss in value of property with use or the passage of time. Thus, depreciation is not considered in calculating cash flow; it is, however, when calculating tax liability or investment results.

Amortization and depreciation tend to be confusing when discussing the concept of cash flow. The income items are relatively straightforward. Income includes all income—even income from commercial signs on the property in the case of vacant land, or from vending machines in apartment buildings, or from resale or utility services in office buildings.

Figure 2–1 illustrates the format for an income-producing property with positive cash flow. The assumption is that the ten acres of industrial land are not yet ripe for development, but are being leased on an interim basis for yard storage. The rental payments do not reflect the full value of the land if it were improved with buildings that would make the most profitable current use of the land. The income reflects a lesser use of the land, but is enough to produce a positive cash flow.

FIGURE 2–1
Positive Cash Flow

Ten acres of land purchased for $50,000 with $12,000 down and $38,000 purchase money mortgage payable at $350 per month including interest at 8 percent until paid. The site has been used for a storage yard, is fenced and partially paved. The improvements are valued at $8,000 and the land at $42,000. The property is leased at $500 per month with the tenant paying all expenses except taxes.

Cash Flow

Income ($500 × 12)	$6,000
Expense of operation (property tax)	− 800
Income before mortgage payments	$5,200
Less mortgage payments (interest and principal—in early years approximately $3,000 interest and $1,200 principal)	−4,200
Cash flow	$1,000

In Figure 2–1 the cash flow is $1,000. If the monthly rent were $300, the calculations would be as follows:

Income	$3,600
Expense of operation (property tax)	−800
Income before mortgage payments	$2,800
Less mortgage payments	−4,200
Cash flow	−$1,400

The cash flow would be negative.

A more typical example would be vacant land without an income, as shown in Figure 2–2.

Most land investments will produce a negative cash flow. The negative cash flow is sometimes called "cost to carry."

Land which has been bought for all cash, or land on which all debt has been repaid, has quite a low cost to carry;

FIGURE 2–2
Negative Cash Flow

One hundred acres of land purchased for $200,000 with $20,000 down payment and the balance of $180,000 payable at 8 percent interest only for 5 years then 10 equal annual payments of principal plus 8 percent interest on the unpaid balance. Taxes are $3,500 per year.

Cash Flow

Income	-0-
Expense of operation (property tax)	−$ 3,500
Income before mortgage payment	−$ 3,500
Mortgage payment	− 14,400
Cash flow	−$17,900

its major expense is property tax. It is not unusual for property taxes on farm land to be as little as 1 percent of the market value. A ratio of property tax to market value of 2 percent is more typical for vacant land, and in high tax areas the ratio can be 3 percent or more. For discussion purposes, 2 percent is a reasonable average.

Land bought for speculative purposes is generally highly leveraged. That leverage, of course, drives up the carrying cost. For example, a down payment may be as little as 10 percent. For a property financed with a 90 percent loan, even with an 8 percent interest-only mortgage (involving no repayment of principle during the term of the loan), the carrying cost attributed to interest would be 7.2 percent of the purchase price (8 percent of 90 percent). Thus even interest-only purchases may well have carrying costs approaching 10 percent per annum.

Principal payments vary quite widely. On an amortized loan having level payments of principal and interest, the principal component may be as little as 1 or 2 percent in the early years. Thus the total ratio of mortgage payments (principal and interest) to original loan balance could be as little as 10 percent or less in some cases.

Principal payments on a land mortgage are frequently made in equal annual, semiannual, or quarterly payments in addition to interest. For example, an $80,000 loan might be payable at a rate of $8,000 per year for 10 years plus interest on the unpaid balance payable with each annual payment. The first year, for example, with an 8 percent loan, the payment would be $8,000 principal plus $6,400 interest (8 percent of $80,000) for a total of $14,400. The second year the payment would be $8,000 plus $5,760 (8 percent of $72,000, the unpaid balance) for a total of $13,760. The following table shows the payments as made quarterly, at the rate of $2,000 principal per quarter plus 2 percent interest on the unpaid balance (or one fourth of 8 percent on $80,000, the unpaid balance).

Payments of Interest and Principal with Level Repayment of Principal

Loan Balance	*Interest at 2 Percent*	*Principal Payment*	*Total Payment*
$80,000	$1,600	$2,000	$3,600
78,000	1,560	2,000	3,560
76,000	1,520	2,000	3,520
74,000	1,480	2,000	3,480
etc.			

For interest-only loans the principal payment is due in one lump sum. Hopefully the property will be sold before the payment comes due. Some loans are hybrid: they start off as interest-only loans, and after a period of time begin to be amortized with equal monthly payments of principal and interest, as in home mortgages, or equal periodic payments of principal plus accrued interest as in the schedule just described. A ten-year payout is not unusual. Sometimes the period is as short as five years. Another popular hybrid is an amortization-type loan for a period of time, say five or ten years, ending with a final lump-sum payment.

Since the terms of loans vary widely, the carrying costs also vary. They may be as little as 10 percent or less of the purchase price in highly leveraged property, or 20 percent or more if the principal is amortized. A very high negative cash flow (i.e., carrying cost) can be a significant disadvantage because it is a constant drain. But a modest negative cash flow may be advantageous in that it is paid with "soft" (pretax) dollars—that is, all or most of the carrying costs are deductible. This situation is explained in the discussion on tax shelter which follows.

TAX SHELTER

Tax shelter as a benefit of investment is most easily understood by first understanding the concepts of depreciation, amortization, and write-off. Depreciation and amortization have to be determined when income taxes must be paid on income-producing property. The write-off is a form of tax shelter, and is of concern when the expenses of an investment exceed income so that a tax loss results.

Depreciation. An investor who acquires an income-producing asset has the right to the stream of income from it for as long as that asset produces income. If the asset is sold for exactly the price paid, less depreciation, all the income after deducting depreciation will be earnings and taxable as income.

Deposits in savings and loan associations, purchases of bonds, and purchases of land leased out to users are investments in which the capital investment is expected to be recovered either by repayment of the debt or by sale of the asset to someone who then gets the right to the future income. The payments received during the term of the investment are returns *on* investment, with the return *of* investment coming when the debt is repaid or the asset is sold.

Investors who lend money to be repaid in installments—such as a mortgage on real estate or personal property—receive payments that include interest, which is taxable, and principal repayment, which is not. The mortgage or other loan loses value as the principal is repaid, and that reduction in value permits the investor to receive cash on which he does not have to pay taxes.

Investment in improved real estate is an investment in an income-producing asset. Although the services from it may be used directly rather than sold, that is another matter. The point is that real estate may produce income.

Although the income is produced by land and buildings together, the land is calculated to have a value separate from that of the buildings. Furthermore, the land can produce income under a lease for use, and such leasing will not use up the land. Thus the income from the lease is considered to be a return *on* the investment. The return *of* the investment comes when the land is sold. It could be sold for more or less than the investor paid, and the sale would accordingly produce a capital gain or a capital loss. But under ordinary circumstances the ability of the land to earn income is not expected to end as a consequence of the expiration of a lease. The investor expects to recover his investment in the land out of the sale of the property, not out of the rental income.

The investment in the building is a different story. The building is a wasting asset. Eventually it will wear out, or at least become so deteriorated that it must be virtually rebuilt to enable it to produce income. Thus the building is expected to decline in value while it is producing income. A method of dealing with this expectation is to allocate a portion of the income as the return *of* the investment in the building to reflect the decline in value.

Accountants deal in history, not valuation. And so does the Internal Revenue Service. No matter that construction costs may be rising so that replacement of the structure is becoming more costly. No matter that land values are rising so that total investment in land and buildings is gaining value. No matter that inflation is running rampant so that the price using the elastic measure of the dollar will be higher when the property is sold than when it was bought. What matters is that sooner or later the building will lose all or virtually all of its value. Thus, allowing the taxpayer to allocate a portion of the income to be counted as a return of capital investment seems only reasonable and prudent. This allowance is not only reasonable for tax purposes; accountants will insist upon it as good accounting practice. They will deal with the price the investor paid and take that historical price as a basis for calculating how much is to be recovered over the estimated remaining life of the asset.

The most generally accepted method for handling this loss of value expected to occur over the life of a wasting asset is to take the total amount of value to be lost and allocated it in equal amounts over the estimated number of years of remaining useful life. Accelerated methods of depreciation are allowed for residential properties and for new properties. The most accelerated methods are for new residential properties and for rehabilitation of residential property. The effects of acceleration is to take more depreciation in the earlier years, and less in the later years.

Because of the depreciation allowance, a substantial portion of the cash received is counted as return of capital and is not taxable as ordinary income when it is received. The amount so counted is, of course, greater in the earlier years of the investment when accelerated methods are used.

The normal accounting practice corresponds to the facts of life when land values are not changing and when building values are declining by an amount equal to the depreciation allowance. While the values of many properties approximate this, depreciation allowances on many more are too small because they are in rapidly deteriorating neighborhoods. Most cases do not conform to the normal assumptions. The buildings also may not lose value as fast as anticipated, and since land values are increasing, the increase in land value may offset some or all of the loss in value of the buildings. These calculations, however, are deferred until the time of sale.

Amortization. Amortization is simply a repayment of principal on a loan. The typical mortgage loan on a home calls for monthly payments which include principal and interest. The amount going to principal repayment is called amortization.

When an investor borrows money, he is not taxed on the amount of money he borrows. When he repays the money, it is not a tax deduction. So part of the mortgage payment, the amortization, is not deductible for tax purposes. Of course, the interest portion is deductible as is any interest payment.

Taxable Income. The relationship between cash flow and taxable income is simply one of starting with cash flow, adding amortization, and deducting depreciation to get taxable income, or, as has been so eloquently stated elsewhere:[1]

Cash flow plus amortization minus depreciation equals taxable income.

$$C_f + A - D = I_t$$

Clearly, if the value of the land has not changed and if depreciation has in fact occurred as implied by the depreciation schedule, the taxable income is what has really been earned. Inflation together with real increases in value may provide additional returns greater than cash flow and tax shelter. These factors are covered below, in the discussion of proceeds of sale.

Tax Write-Off. A tax write-off is a loss for tax purposes which may or may not involve a comparable cash expenditure. For example, take the case of a purchase of land which produces no income yet requires $3,500 in annual property taxes and $14,400 annual interest payments on the mortgage. That $17,900 is all deductible expense.

[1] See Maury Seldin and Richard Swesnik, *Real Estate Investment Strategy* (New York: John Wiley and Sons, 1970) for a more detailed discussion.

In the earlier case (Figure 2–2) the assumption was that the property was purchased for $200,000 with a $20,000 down payment and an interest-only loan for five years. Another reasonable assumption is that the land values increased 10 to 15 percent per year so that in 4 years the property was sold for a net price of, say, $300,000. During the 4 years the interest and taxes were deductible. So the cash flow was negative, but all of the cash expenditure counted for tax purposes as a write-off.

Tax write-offs are possible even without a negative cash flow. Recall that cash flow plus amortization minus depreciation equals taxable income:

$$C_f + A - D = I_t$$

It can be seen from this that to the extent that depreciation exceeds amortization, some of the taxable income is sheltered:

$$D > A = I_s$$

Thus, in the example of Figure 2–1 with $8,000 of depreciable improvements having an assumed life of 5 years, the annual depreciation would be $1,600. The taxable income would be as follows:

Income	$6,000
Less expenses (property tax)	− 800
	$5,200
Less mortgage payments ($3,000 interest plus $1,200 principal)	−4,200
Cash flow	$1,000
Amortization	1,200
Depreciation	−1,600
Taxable income	$ 600

Since depreciation ($1,600) exceeds amortization ($1,200) by $400, $400 of the cash flow is tax sheltered. Thus cash received is $1,000, but only $600 is taxable in the current year.

If the income were $5,000 instead of $6,000, the cash flow would be zero.

Income	$5,000
Expenses (property tax)	– 800
	$4,200
Less mortgage payment	–4,200
Cash flow	$ 0

But the depreciation would still exceed the amortization by $400 so that the investor would still have a tax loss or write-off of $400.

Cash flow	0
Amortization	$1,200
Depreciation	–1,600
Taxable income	$–400

Alternative:

Depreciation	$1,600
Amortization	–1,200
Tax-sheltered income*	$ 400

* Note that the $400 is the sheltered income, not the cash flow. Cash flow is zero. There is a write-off of $400 with no cash flow.

Rather than tax-sheltered income which is misleading when there is no cash flow, the investor may use the tax write-off formula that deals with cash outlay instead of cash flow.

Taking a variation of the problem outlined above and using a rental income of $4,000, the cash flow would be a –$1,000, the same as a cash outlay of $1,000.

Under the formula $C_f + A - D = I_t$ the calculation is as follows:

Cash flow	$1,000
Amortization	$1,200
Depreciation	–1,600
Taxable income	–$1,400

Using the new formula,

Cash outlay plus depreciation minus amortization equals tax write-off

$$C_o + D - A = T_w$$

Cash outlay	$1,000
Depreciation	1,600
Amortization	–1,200
Tax write-off	$1,400

While the tax write-off formula is usable in income-producing cases, it works best if used for investments which produce a negative cash flow. For example, from the same case used in Figure 2–2:

Cash outlay	
Taxes	$ 3,500
Mortgage payment	14,400
Cash outlay	$17,900
Depreciation	0
Amortization	– 0
Tax write-off	$17,900

Obviously, the greater the principal payments (amortization) due on the mortgage, the greater the cash outlay. But the increased outlay for principal repayments does not increase the tax write-off.

Leverage. Leverage is the use of borrowed money to magnify gains and losses. In the preceding illustration, substantial leverage was used. The interest payments were deductible from ordinary income. When they were recovered by the sale of the property, they were capital gains and taxed at a rate lower than ordinary income. The taxpayer thus saves on taxes. He not only pays less taxes, he defers the payment. It is a free use of tax money.

The wise use of the money occurs if the value of the property increases by at least enough to cover the interest costs. The interest is deductible and is thus part of the write-off. When it is recovered by sale of the property at a price large enough to cover the interest costs, that recovery is considered under tax rules as a gain and that gain may be taxed as a long-term capital gain. Furthermore, if the value of the property increases by more than the interest costs, the additional gain also goes to the investor as a profit from a capital gain and his rate of return is increased. That rate of return will depend, of course, not only on how much money is borrowed but also on the price received when the property is sold.

PROCEEDS OF SALE

Proceeds of sale is the reason for land investment. No investor buys land without expecting it to increase in value (except for some questionable "buy back" arrangements designed to convert ordinary income into capital gains).

Some investors attempt to buy relatively low-priced land for cash and hold it for long-run appreciation. The carrying cost will be minimal, and the land is considered a good place to store wealth. The results may also be quite attractive. But the number of people having that much wealth and patience would make a relatively small audience for any book. We assume that most of the readers of this book are investment swingers, or would-be investment swingers. They are looking for ways to make a lot of money, and see land as the best way—or at least as a pretty good possibility. These investors will do best to leverage their purchases so as to get as much profit as possible with as little cash as possible.

The approach, then, is to buy with a low down payment, say 10 percent or even less, and with low carrying costs, say 10 percent per year or less, and sell without having held on too long, in perhaps three, four, or even five years.

The way the numbers work may be illustrated using a previous example. Assume the 100 acres bought at $200,000 in Figure 2–2 were sold in four years at a net price of $300,000. In addition to the $20,000 down payment, four annual payments were made on the mortgage, and the taxes were paid.

Under the tax laws, the sale would push the investor into a higher tax bracket. The example shows a federal tax cost of $25,000. (See Figure 2–3.) If we assume that the investor was in the 50 percent bracket when he was making the interest payments, then the $71,600 carrying cost would have been an after-tax carrying cost of $35,800 so that his total after-tax investment (because of tax savings) would have been:

Down payment	$20,000
After-tax carrying cost	35,800
Total investment (after tax)	$55,800

His average investment would have been $20,000 plus, say, one-half (because of the time factor) of the $35,800 or $17,900 for a total of $37,900. Thus, with an increase in value of 50 percent in four years (about 12.6 percent average per year, simple, or 10.5 percent compound rate) the investor would have doubled his money in four years.

Net sale price	$300,000	
Less mortgage	−180,000	
Pretax proceeds	$120,000	
Less taxes	25,000	
After-tax proceeds		$95,000
Less		
Total *after-tax* investment		
Down payment	$ 20,000	
After-tax carrying cost	35,800	
		$55,800
After-tax profit		$39,200
Average investment	$ 37,900	
After-tax profit	39,200	

That doubling represents about 25 percent per year average profit, or a compound rate of about 20 percent per year, after taxes.

In order to earn 20 percent after taxes in the assumed tax bracket of 50 percent, the investor without any shelter would have to earn 40 percent before taxes. Most investments capable of producing 40 percent returns before taxes are somewhat riskier than land selected on the basis of a minimum increase in value of 10 percent per year.

The return on investment may be analyzed in various ways. Only the simplest ways have been used in the illustration. With the kind of returns that are contemplated, elaborate mathematical analyses are likely to be more precise than accurate. The crucial factors are the price at which the land is sold, and the time the investor has to wait to get it.

The difficulty is in the waiting. Buying land means buying an investment

FIGURE 2–3
Taxable Profit

Down payment		−$ 20,000	
Carrying cost			
Taxes	−$ 3,500		
Interest	− 14,400		
	−$17,900/year		
	times 4 years =	− 71,600	
Total investment		−$ 91,600	
Proceeds of sale			
Net sale price		$300,000	
Mortgage		− 180,000	
Pretax proceeds		$120,000	
Income tax			
Net sale price		$300,000	
Cost basis		− 200,000	
Taxable profit		$100,000	$100,000
Taxes assuming long-term capital gain rate (say 25 percent)		− 25,000	−25,000

program. The buyer must have the ability to stay with the investment, and the strength of conviction to keep on investing. If he can do that, and if he is right, the rewards will be exceptional. The main difficulty lies not in the calculations but in the choice of land.

CONCLUSION

The selection of the type of investment with which the investor can live is the first and foremost consideration in any investment strategy. If the kinds of rewards that appeal to the investor include proceeds of sale, and if really big returns are sought, land investments are worth examining because they offer a lot of potential. They can provide some tax shelter, particularly in the form of substantial tax write-offs, and are especially suited to high leverage short-term investing. Land investments are not suitable if one seeks the benefit of cash flow. Indeed, land investors must have sufficient cash to enable them to keep investing in the same parcel of land. An ability to stay with it and the willingness to do so are required for success.

The benefits are great because of the risks. But these risks may be assessed and taken in doses that are reasonable for the individual investor. The next chapter discusses the various risks.

3

Risks in Land Investment

Investors who cannot stand to lose are in a hopeless situation because there is nothing one can do with money that is completely without risk. Investors who keep their money in cash will lose some of it as inflation erodes away its purchasing power. That loss is as real as if the money had been stolen.

This chapter discusses the risk of inflation, which leads investors to land. It also discusses the lack of liquidity that should be considered in all land investment decisions. It explains these risks so that investors may assess the kind, character, and extent of exposure that is bearable for them. One should take only the chances one can afford to take. Within those constraints, however, investors may accept some very big risks.

Prudent investors try to determine a strategy that suits their own purposes and temperaments. The word "strategy," here as elsewhere, refers to policies and plans for taking chances in order to achieve objectives—in this case, making a profit.

The major risks in land investment are those associated with giving up liquidity and evaluating the potential income-producing ability of the land. Thus, land investments are for those who are looking for substantial gain with reasonable risks of the type they are prepared to accept. The strategy involves taking a particular set of risks in order to achieve a rather large profit. The rewards may be well worth the risks.

PURCHASING POWER—THE PRICE-LEVEL RISK

Price-level risk is the chance of loss from an erosion of purchasing power through inflation.

Inflation eats away gradually, almost imperceptibly, except for those spurts that lead one to believe that some great rip-off is taking place. Well, it is! Between 1967 and 1973 the value of the dollar declined so that in 1973 it took $1.32 to buy what one dollar bought in 1967. Over the six years, inflation averaged more than 5 percent per year.

Changes in consumer purchasing power are measured by the Consumer Price Index of the Bureau of Labor Statistics. Figure 3–1 shows how the prices of goods consumers buy changed in the years from 1965 to 1974. It shows the costs of food, rent, and medical care separately, as well as a composite of all items (food, apparel, transportation, health, recreation, and housing).

A supposedly prudent investor who put away $887 in 1960 for retirement in 1967 lost almost 13 percent in purchasing power between those two dates, or less than 2 percent a year. But as noted before, in the six years after 1967 the index moved up to 132.4—a 32.4 percent increase or an average of 5.5 percent per year.

Investors who kept their money in cash because they did not want to take any chances therefore suffered a real loss. What were the alternatives? One alternative was to invest in a savings account, which paid about 5 percent in the 1960s. For an investor in a 40 percent marginal tax bracket, that meant a 3 percent return after taxes. In a period of low inflation such an investor would get a real return of 1 percent (3 percent after taxes less a 2 percent loss from inflation). In a period of high inflation, such as the last few years, the investor could suffer a real loss of 2 percent (3 percent after taxes less an average loss from inflation of say 5 percent per year).

Some "safe" investments pay rates of interest high enough to more than compensate for a 5 percent inflation. High-grade corporate bonds, for example, can produce rates of interest several percentage points above the expected level of inflation. The bonds, however, entail certain other risks. The point here is that holding presumably riskless assets does not provide 100 percent protection from loss.

Note that in Figure 3–1 food prices went up sharply after 1967, and medical care outrageously. Rent was among the components with more modest increases. But these are only averages in a set of expenditure patterns for urban wage earners and clerical workers. Inflation has been higher for certain

FIGURE 3–1
Consumer Price Index
(1967 = 100)

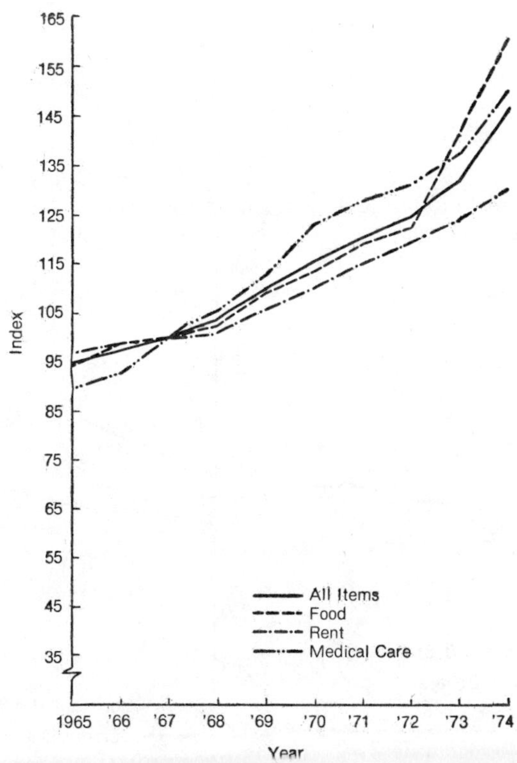

Source: U.S. Department of Commerce, *Statistical Abstract of the United States: 1973,* 94th ed. (Washington, D.C.: U.S. Government Printing Office, 1973), and *Federal Reserve Bulletin,* vol. 61, no. 2, February 1975.

other sectors of the economy, and particularly so for land.

For the economy in general, the best comprehensive indicator is the so-called implicit price deflator of the gross national product. It is the index used to adjust the money value of all goods and services produced in the national economy to the values of a base date. For example, the implicit deflator based on 1958 had the following values in other years:

Year	*Implicit Price Deflator (1958 = 100)*
1950	80.2
1955	80.9
1960	103.3
1965	110.0
1970	135.2
1973	154.3
1974	170.2

Three charts showing the effect of changes are presented in Figure 3–2. These are changes in the value of gross national product and personal consumption expenditures, and gross private domestic investment. The data indicate broad and substantial inflation.

To land investors, the implications of inflation are quite favorable. Table 3–1 shows the extent to which farmland prices have risen since 1950. The gains in finished lot prices, of which raw land is a significant component, are even higher. (See the appendix for a list of prices in selected cities.)

All the prices shown are average prices. In some cases land has risen much more in price than is indicated by the average. Changes in average land

FIGURE 3–2

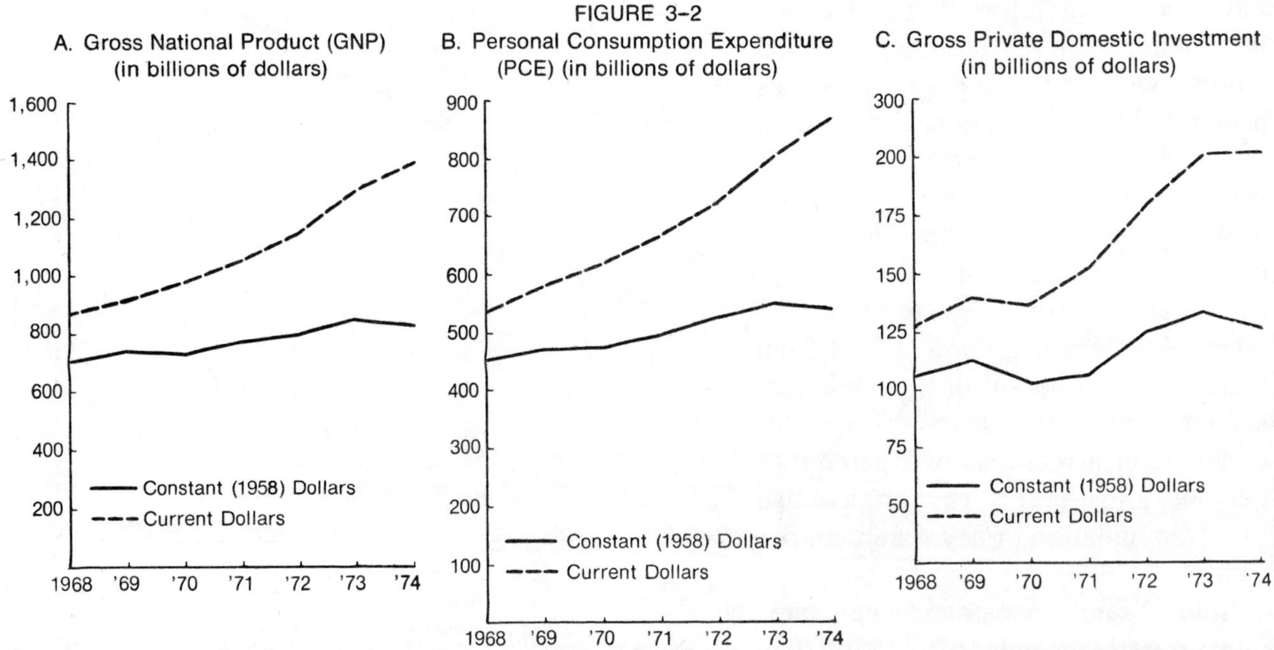

Source: 1968–1971 data from U.S. Department of Commerce, *Survey of Current Business*, July 1972, pp. 7 and 16. 1972–1973 data from *Survey of Current Business*, July 1974, p. 7. 1974 data from U.S. Department of Commerce, *Survey of Current Business*, February 1975, p. 4.

TABLE 3–1
Farm Real Estate Values

Year	Index of Average Value (1967 = 100) of Farm Real Estate Per Acre
1950	40
1960	68
1965	86
1969	113
1970	117
1971	122
1972	132
1973	150
1974	187

Source: U.S. Department of Agriculture. Economic Research Service, as stated in U.S. Department of Commerce, Bureau of Census, Social Science Research Council, *The Statistical History of the United States from Colonial Times to the Present Historical Statistics of the United States, Colonial Times to 1957, and Continuation to 1962, and Revisions* (Stamford, Conn.: Fairfield Publishers, Inc., 1965, and the U.S. Department of Commerce, *Statistical Abstract of the United States: 1974*, 95th ed. (Washington, D.C.: U.S. Government Printing Office, 1974).

prices above the general changes accounted for by the implicit price deflator are changes in the relative values. One can see from the tables in this chapter that investment in land and other real and nonmonetary assets offers significant protection against inflation risk. The investor who puts money in the bank, on the other hand, or in any monetary asset, takes a substantial price-level risk.

FINANCIAL AND MARKET RISKS

Financial Risk. Financial risk is the chance of losing the money invested because the borrower fails to repay. Even banks sometimes fail, although the risk to depositors is quite small in insured institutions because agencies of the federal government insure deposits up to $40,000. Almost no financial risk is involved in lending money directly to the federal government through savings bonds and a whole range of other interest-bearing securities. Some of them have paid higher interest rates than that obtained in savings accounts in recent years.

Higher rates of interest may be obtained by accepting an increased financial risk. Good grade corporate bonds will yield several percentage points more interest than savings accounts. Mortgages are available at comparable or better yields. Table 3–2 shows yields on a variety of investments (see also Figure 3–3).

A premium is earned for additional financial risk. But the premium may not be enough. If an investor has a large or complete loss of capital, many winners will be needed to make up for that loss. The important factor then becomes not the earnings but whether the capital is repaid. Usually the interest payment and capital repayment go hand in hand; if an investor can get one he can probably get the other. That is, a borrower who pays the interest will probably repay the debt.

Land investors, however, do not receive payment of their invested capital as though it were a debt, because no debt exists. The investor buys the rights to the land and may get his money back by selling the owned rights to someone else. After the sale, the investor can calculate his profit based upon the price received in the market. Thus financial risk to the land investor is really a market risk, since the market determines what an investor can get for a parcel of land at the time of sale.

Market Risk. The functioning of a market system entails wide swings in

TABLE 3-2
Percentage Yields on Some Selected Investments, 1963–1974

	Government Bonds		Corporate Bonds			Stocks		
	United States	State and	Indus-	Rail-	Public	Dividend/ Price Ratio		Earnings/ Price Ratio
Year	(long term)	Local AAA	trial	road	Utility	Pre-ferred	Com-mon	Common
1963	4.00	3.06	4.42	4.65	4.41	4.30	3.17	5.68
1964	4.15	3.09	4.52	4.67	4.53	4.32	3.01	5.54
1965	4.21	3.16	4.61	4.72	4.60	4.33	3.00	5.87
1966	4.66	3.67	5.30	5.37	5.36	4.97	3.40	6.72
1967	4.85	3.74	5.74	5.89	5.81	5.34	3.20	5.71
1968	5.25	4.20	6.41	6.77	6.49	5.78	3.07	5.64
1969	6.10	5.45	7.22	7.46	7.49	6.41	3.24	6.08
1970	6.59	6.12	8.26	8.77	8.68	7.22	3.83	6.51
1971	5.74	5.22	7.57	8.38	8.13	6.75	3.14	5.40
1972	5.63	5.04	7.35	7.99	7.74	7.27	2.84	—
1973	6.30	4.99	7.60	8.12	7.83	7.23	3.06	5.50
1974	6.99	5.89	8.78	8.98	9.27	8.23	4.47	7.12

Source: *Federal Reserve Bulletin,* vol. 59, no. 6, June 1973, and vol. 61, no. 3, March 1975.

prevailing prices. These swings result from changes in the numbers of buyers and sellers, or from changes in their expectations. Whatever the cause, anyone entering the market pretty well has to accept the price which prevails at that time.

What the seller sells is the right to future benefits, discussed in some detail in Chapter 2. The buyer pays a price

FIGURE 3-3
Yields on Some Selected Investments, 1963–1974

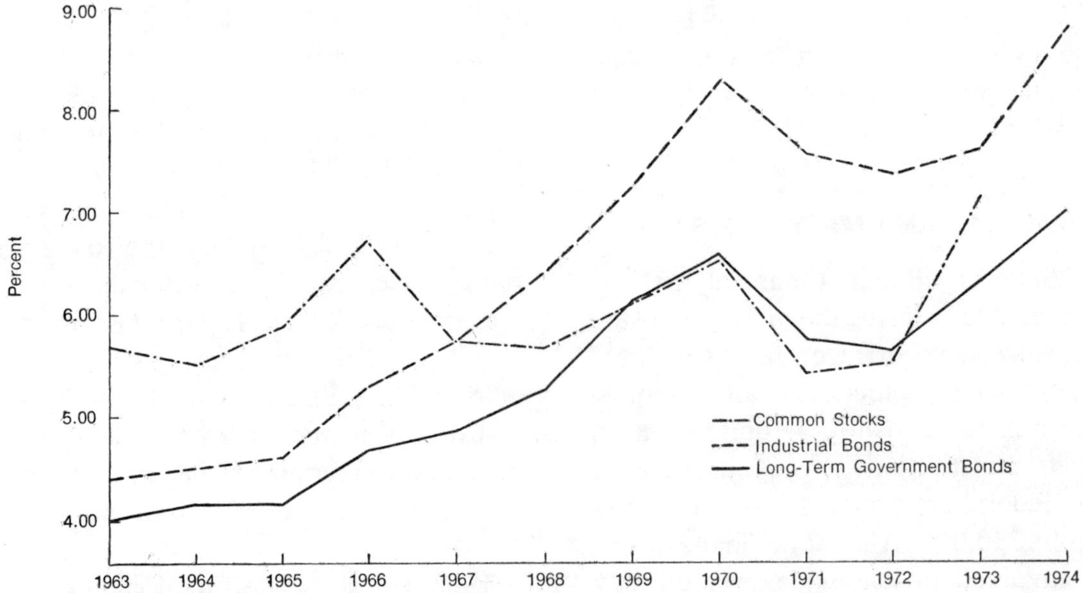

Source: *Federal Reserve Bulletin,* June 1973 and March 1975.

based on personal expectations in competition with others who also have expectations as to future benefits. Since the only way to get out is to sell to someone else, who in turn has to look to the future for benefits, the market is one of expectations.

The critical difference between markets for nonmonetary assets such as land and markets for monetary assets such as bonds and mortgages is that the latter markets are based on instruments with due dates. The investor can wait, albeit sometimes a long time, and be paid on the specified date. The investor can also get out before the due date by selling the debt instrument in the market. The investor then takes a market risk which obviously includes the chances associated with general expectations as to the ability of the debtor to repay. This "market" risk aspect is aside from, but related to, changes in inflationary expectations and such other risks as may affect the price. The point for the real estate and stock investor is that elements of market risk are present in all investments that do not have a provision for getting back the capital on demand. Investors who require that protection can do best with savings bonds and bank deposits which can be withdrawn virtually on demand.

INTEREST RATE AND CAPITALIZATION RATE RISKS

Interest Rate Risk. The rate of return expected in the market place is based upon more than the financial risk. For bonds and other monetary assets it is also based on the expected rate of inflation and the general cost and availability of money.

The interest rate may be thought of as having components which reflect different kinds of risk. One component is financial risk, that of not getting the money back. A second component is price-level risk, that of reduced purchasing power of the money when it is repaid. A third component is what may be considered a pure interest rate, the price paid for foregoing the use of the money.

That pure rate depends on how much money is available for loan and how much is demanded, at various prices, in the market place. It changes depending upon changes in savings rates, monetary and fiscal policy, and the market's assessment of the profitability of the use of borrowed money.

Investors in monetary assets take an interest-rate risk, which in part is simply being committed to a rate of interest which may turn out to be lower (or higher) than a later prevailing rate. So, for example, investors may contract for a six percent return, and if the rate rises to seven percent they lose by foregoing the one percent. Right? Not necessarily.

If the investors have their money in savings accounts from which they can withdraw and reinvest without penalty, the rate change is no problem. There is no loss or foregoing of interest. But if they have made loans with due dates far in the future, they can either wait, taking the lower rate interest, or they can sell at a discount.

The sale at a discount serves to ad just a buyer's yield to the prevailing rate. Thus if the loan is due in a year, a

$1,000 bond paying 6 percent will have to sell for about $990 in order to yield 7 percent. If the due date is ten years away the price will be around $900. In the case of a 30- or 40-year bond, the price will be close to $860. If it is a loan or bond with no due date, simply paying interest forever, the price will be $857.

If prevailing interest rates drop, rather than increase, the values of monetary assets will rise instead of fall. For example, if the prevailing rate drops from 6 percent to 5 percent, the $60 per year fixed interest—in the case of the $1,000 interest-forever bond—will make the bond worth $1,200. (The value is equal to the income divided by the interest rate when the income is perpetual.)

While investors in bonds, mortgages, and other monetary assets run into substantial interest-rate risks, investors in land have a counterpart risk—the capitalization rate.

Capitalization-Rate Risk. A capitalization rate is used to convert future income to present value. Thus, $60 per year forever, when capitalized at 6 percent, is worth $1,000. When it is capitalized at 5 percent, it is worth $1,200. When it is capitalized at 7 percent, it is worth $857. The formula is: value times rate equals income, or value equals income divided by rate.

$$V \times R = I \quad \text{or} \quad V = \frac{I}{R}$$

Other formulas are used to calculate nonperpetual income. Tables are available that show the present worth of single payments or series of payments. Such tables indicate the values based upon rate and time, as does Table 3–3.

If land is leased for a long period of time, e.g., 99 years, the extent of the capitalization-rate risk obviously becomes almost equivalent to the extent of the interest-rate risk. The present value of income after 99 years does not amount to much.

Income-producing real estate may or may not be leased for long periods of time. Without a lease the rent is free to vary with prevailing conditions. Thus the capitalization rate for real estate, instead of having to contain a premium to protect the investor from inflation, can in fact be low relative to other interest rates in a highly inflationary period. When interest rates move from 6 percent to 9 percent because of inflation, capitalization rates for real estate, say at 7 percent, do not necessarily rise by 3 percentage points. They change their relative positions depending upon a variety of expectations, including the assessment of the ability of real estate to get increase rentals because of inflation.

What happens to the capitalization rate will depend in part upon the expected extent and character of inflation. In the stock market, a severe inflation increases the capitalization rates to unusually high figures, depressing prices because the inflation becomes mixed with fears for future profitability. (The price/earnings ratio becomes low. It is the inverse of the capitalization rate.) A little inflation, on the other hand, permits stocks to sell at low capitalization rates (high prices) because stocks may provide a hedge against inflation. In the real

TABLE 3–3
Patterns of Values of a Level Annuity

A. $4,329	is the present worth of $1,000 per year for 5 years at	5 percent
$4,212		6 percent
$4,100		7 percent
$3,993		8 percent
$3,791		10 percent
$3,605		12 percent
$3,433		14 percent
B. $7,772	is the present worth of $1,000 per year for 10 years at	5 percent
$7,360		6 percent
$7,024		7 percent
$6,710		8 percent
$6,145		10 percent
$5,650		12 percent
$5,216		14 percent
C. $12,462	is the present worth of $1,000 per year for 20 years at	5 percent
$11,470		6 percent
$10,594		7 percent
$ 9,818		8 percent
$ 8,514		10 percent
$ 7,469		12 percent
$ 6,623		14 percent
D. $18,256	is the present worth of $1,000 per year for 50 years at	5 percent
$15,762		6 percent
$13,801		7 percent
$12,233		8 percent
$ 9,915		10 percent
$ 8,304		12 percent
$ 7,133		14 percent
E. $20,000	is the present worth of $1,000 per year forever at	5 percent
$16,667		6 percent
$14,286		7 percent
$12,500		8 percent
$10,000		10 percent
$ 8,333		12 percent
$ 7,143		14 percent

estate market inflation may also exert upward pressure on capitalization rates, largely because of the profitable alternatives. But the increase in rates is generally not as great as that of interest rates. For real estate, however, the increase in capitalization rates may not mean a decline in value because the same forces which push up the rates may also push up income and income potential. Thus the capitalization rate contains components of financial risk (income-producing ability), price-level risk (inflation) and the pure rate (the price based upon basic demand/supply conditions for money).

Of all the risks discussed, the capitalization risk is the most difficult to understand, analyze, and explain. But the sum and substance of it is that inflation affects capitalization rates, and in an inflation real estate has less risk from changing rates than do other long-term investments.

All of the risks—price level financial/market, and interest rate/capitalization rate—are interrelated. Obviously an investor has no way to get reasonable returns on invested money without undergoing some risk or combination of risks. The easiest way to look at the combination of capitalization/interest rate and market/financial risk is to consider them as a liquidity risk.

LIQUIDITY RISK

Liquidity risk is the chance the investor takes of losing some of his investment when converting an asset into cash. For investors in land, the liquidity risk is high. Investors in monetary assets may wait until maturity and get all of their money back, assuming they paid the face amounts. The maturity dates may be 10, 20, 30 years or longer from issuance.

If an investor purchases at par a bond which pays 6 percent and resells it to someone who also is satisfied to earn 6 percent, the investor does not suffer a capital loss. If, however, the interest rate has risen so that the purchaser expects to earn 7 percent, the bond will have to sell at a discount. The bigger the increase in interest rates or yields, the bigger the discount. The longer the time to maturity, the larger the discount.

For example, a 6 percent $1,000 bond issued in 1960 and due in 1980 would in 1967 have sold at $915.50 to yield 7 percent or at $840.00 to yield 8 percent. In 1973 that bond would have sold at $945.00 to yield 7 percent and at $894.40 to yield 8 percent. Of course, the investor could have waited to maturity. But liquidity is being able to get the money without waiting and without loss.

In the aforementioned cases, the liquidity risk really stems from an interest rate risk. That, as will be recalled, is the chance of loss because of a change in interest rates. Table 3–4 shows some historical interest rates and bond prices.

Investments in land, on the other

TABLE 3–4
Some Historical Interest Rates and Bond Prices

		Bond prices (percent of par)		
Year	*Price Rate (percent per annum)*	*U.S. Government*	*State and Local*	*Corporate AAA*
1963	$4\frac{1}{2}$	86.31	111.3	96.8
1964	$4\frac{1}{2}$	84.46	111.5	95.1
1965	$4\frac{1}{2}$–5	83.76	110.6	93.9
1966	5–6	78.63	102.6	86.1
1967	$5\frac{1}{2}$–6	76.55	100.5	81.8
1968	6–$6\frac{3}{4}$	72.33	93.5	76.4
1969	$6\frac{3}{4}$–$8\frac{1}{2}$	64.49	79.0	68.5
1970	$6\frac{3}{4}$–8	60.52	72.3	61.6
1971	$5\frac{1}{4}$–$6\frac{3}{4}$	67.73	80.0	65.0
1972	$4\frac{1}{2}$–6	68.71	84.4	65.9
1973	6–10	62.80	85.4	63.7
1974	$8\frac{1}{2}$–$12\frac{1}{4}$	57.45	76.3	58.8

Source: *Federal Reserve Bulletin,* vol. 59, no. 6, June 1973; vol. 60, no. 1, January 1974; and vol. 61, no. 3, March 1975.

hand, are really quite illiquid. Attempts to convert them to cash at short notice are generally costly. The best prices are obtained when it is possible to choose the right time to sell, and when the timing is right. Having adequate time to expose the property to the market for sale also helps in getting the best price.

Bonds may be sold in minutes, with settlement in days. Land may take months to sell, and then months to settle. Land investors give up liquidity, but they get paid for it.

The rising interest rates which hurt the bondholder may help the landholder. A rising interest rate is in part a reflection of increased inflationary expectations. Since the land is a hedge against inflation, and the rising interest rates are brought about by the same forces that tend to help land values, the successful land investor seeks to buy land in anticipation of these changes. Hopefully, the investment is heavily financed by borrowed money at low rates of interest.

LEVERAGE

Frequently a land purchase is financed by the seller, who carries the mortgage. Thus, the purchaser need put up only a small portion of the purchase price. Inflation enables the investor to pay in cheaper dollars for the purchase of land of rising value, while at the same time paying only a modest interest rate on the mortgage.

If deflation should occur, the land purchaser would be paying back more expensive dollars. The risk, of course, is that the land value would not keep pace with the rising value of money. But deflation does not seem to happen much.

Very little land is purchased for all cash. When it is, or when all the mortgages have been paid, it requires very little in the way of carrying costs. Taxes can be 1 or 2 percent of value and may well be offset by income from farm rentals or other modest sources. Leveraged land, however, requires interest payments and, at some point, principal payments. On an annual basis, principal and interest together with taxes can easily add up to 10 percent of the value of the property, and even twice that or more. The big risk is in not being able to hold onto the land and choose the right time to sell.

OTHER RISKS

A variety of other risks needs to be considered in land investment. These include legal risks, natural hazards, and developability.

Legal Risk. Ownership of real estate is ownership of a bundle of rights: the right to use and to exclude others from use, the right to build or to pass over as in an easement, and the right to encumber as with borrowing or with any lien.

When investors purchase property, they expect to get clear title. The legal risk is that of getting something less than they bargain for. The title may be "cloudy," meaning that some other claim of ownership exists. This can be determined through a careful title examination, since those who have such claims protect them by recording their interest in public records at the county court house.

Legal risks in the ownership of real estate may be insured against by title insurance. The investor should know what his policy specifies. In some cases the seller provides a warranty deed in which he warrants that the title is clear, but that is not always enough. In these matters, legal counsel is generally advisable.

Natural Hazards. Natural hazards pose a risk in that while the overall legal description of the surface of the land may not change, land surface has been known to slip into the sea. Or land may become innundated with water and rendered unusable. Fire may reduce the land to a charred desolation, which is not attractive on the market. Slides and slipping also affect the usability of land; for such problems, geological expertise is in order.

Developability. The risks of developability have been discussed in the first chapter and will be discussed again and again. Any factor which affects the ability to put the land to an intended use affects value, particularly the availability of necessary utilities. Developability is a matter for professional analysis. However, not all land investors hold land right up to the time of developability; they may seek to acquire it early and hold it long enough for a sharp rise from low values.

SUMMARY AND CONCLUSION

Land investment is both a risky and a rewarding business.

Accepting the risks is a question of knowing what they are and choosing those which are suitable in the light of potential rewards. Land investors are prepared to take the risk of an illiquid investment. They put their money in and keep putting it in because they have confidence that the value is rising. They do not need, or at least they do not get, the reassurance of daily price quotations in the newspapers. They do not get a steady flow of cash, but rather they wait until the sale. The sale is the big benefit. It is achievable by ordinary investors if they understand what is happening.

Intelligent investors can learn to understand what is going on and how the system operates. They can learn the difference between management and mismanagement, so that they can make investments which will provide exceptional returns.

Investors should not put money into anything they do not understand. Investors who go after a big profit without knowing what they are doing will have an experience that will be of great value in years to come and never grow dim or doubtful which is what Mark Twain said about carrying a cat home by the tail.

Investors who are not ready to learn the business should consider the alternative of professional management for their investment funds. But people who are intelligent enough to have earned and saved money are intelligent enough to put it to use if they will only try to understand how the system works.

Chapter 2 explained the benefits involved in land investment. This chapter has explained the risks. It concludes the first section of this book. The second section deals with the changing land values that produce the benefits of high proceeds of sale. It is followed by additional explanations of how the system works, and the process through which the investor may reach an intelligent decision. The intent is not to develop appraisers or land economists but rather to bring to bear a point of view through which investors can make profitable investment decisions for themselves. They can appraise daily events in the context of land decisions and thus evaluate the available opportunities.

The ensuing four chapters, which make up Part Two of this book, are for investors who want to understand changing land values. The analysis will also be useful to those in the business of selling land or developing it, as well as to government policy makers and administrators who need to know how the system works.

Part Two is not meant to be a cookbook for evaluating property. It is a presentation of knowledge useful to investors and others concerned with land. It aims to provide the underlying basis of judgment necessary to reward the investor with profits from a location of rising value.

Part two
Changing Land Values

4

Changes in Land Value

Investors seeking land with the potential for appreciation logically ask what makes the value of land go up. Having received an answer to that question, they will have a basis for investing.

There are many popular misconceptions of the concepts of land and value and of why land rises in value. The concepts need to be clearly understood as does the operation of the market system as it is heavily regulated by local government.

CONCEPTS OF LAND

Physical Characteristics of Land. Land as a physical good includes the surface of the earth, all above it, and all below. This is illustrated in Figure 4–1.

As a practical matter, however, most people look at land as the surface of the earth together with such improvements as are built below ground level or constructed above ground. For some segments of the population, land is a resource used in agricultural production or in extractive industries such as coal mining.

The extractive industries provide good illustrations of the many dimensions of land as a physical good. Gravel pits and stone quarries are readily visible. In addition, subsurface minerals may be extracted and used for economic purposes. The extractive process may ravage the surface, as with strip mining. Or it may undermine the load-bearing strength of the surface so as to impair the use of the surface for support of structures.

The extraction of oil may also deplete the resources and even cause land to subside to the extent that in some locations the ground becomes inundated with water. Even without oil wells, land in many localities such as Venice, Italy, and Long Beach, California, is slowly sinking.

Obviously, the use of the physical good affects the land's value. In agriculture this is illustrated by cultivation. Something is done to the natural resource land, making it yield agricultural produce. The productivity of land affects its value; so do its physical characteristics: Both may be altered by the way it is used.

Land used for human habitation is valued according to other characteristics, such as its load-bearing qualities or the quantity of water available, or its ability to absorb waste water.

The importance of various physical characteristics of the land is different for land in an urban environment than it is for land in a rural environment. A potable water supply from the ground is not a necessary condition for the use of urban land, since water is generally provided from a distant source through a network of pipes. The same is true for the disposition of waste water. The waste water in urban areas is usually piped out to a treatment plant before it is returned to the environment.

FIGURE 4–1
Land as a Physical Good

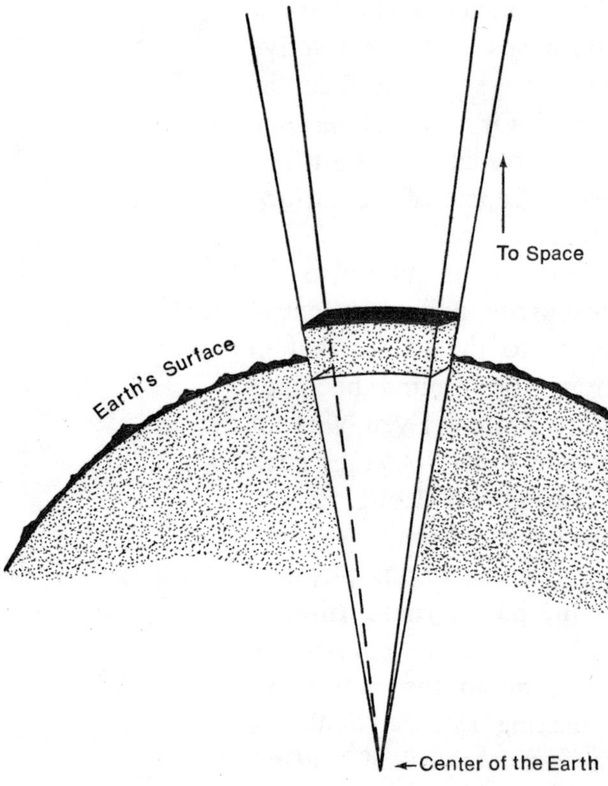

The value of urban land is most significantly affected by its location in respect to other land which in turn may depend on a public road network, railroad, or other transportation media.

Location and accessibility are the linkages of human activity. To survive, a civilization must produce at least a subsistence amount of food. To prosper it must organize for specialization of agricultural and industrial production. The productivity of agriculture and industry enable a part of society to establish a claim on the broad range of resources by other than basic productive efforts. Education, the arts, and recreational industries are supportable in urban areas as long as they are linked to production elsewhere in the economy.

Out of this arises a whole set of spatial relationships, which include accessibility to locations for spending money. Within certain limits, the more accessible the location the more productive it is, because less travel time and other resources are used in getting to it. Access to places where the money is spent is also important; a complex pattern of expenditures links the firms that employ the local population and their suppliers.

Economic Characteristics of Land. The link between land as a physical good and as an economic good is to be found in the elements of cost and productivity. An economic good differs from a free good in that it has both scarcity and utility. A free good may be quite useful—for example, air or water. But if it is freely available, no one will pay for it.

The free good becomes an economic good when something must be given up to obtain the product. The cost of piping in water changes it from a free good to an economic good.

Prices paid for land that is traded in a market reflect both the anticipation of the costs of putting it to use and an assessment of the productivity of that use. That productivity is ordinarily the result of combining land with improvements including structures.

The improved real estate may be an income-producing property that is managed as though it were a business. It produces rent in the same way as a business produces income from sales. It has expenses of operation. The remainder, adjusted for change in the value of the asset, is earnings. The flow of earnings and the right to sell the flow of earnings are determinants of the value of the real estate as an economic good. Its value is not changed if the owner chooses to use the property rather than sell the property services.

Legal Characteristics of Land. Land in the legal sense is the right to the physical good rather than the physical good itself. Thus, real estate is land and everything permanently attached thereto, including buildings. Real property is the ownership of the rights to real estate.

The owner has rights that are created under the system of law and are enforced by law. They are also limited by law. This means that landowners do not have absolute control over the use of their land. They may use it and permit others to use it. They may exclude others from using it, give or deny limited rights to others to cross over it, pledge it as security for a loan, or sell it or leave it by will. They may do all these things by virtue of the bundle of rights that they have.

But the use to which the land may be put may be regulated under the police powers of the state. The state also has the right to take private property for public use provided this is done under due process of law and that just compensation is given. For example, the government may force the sale of land to acquire a right of way for a highway or a site for some public purpose. But a continuing battle rages as to what extent the government should use its legal powers.

Part of the battle is over what property rights will be preserved and what will yield to public purposes ranging from freeways to preservation of open space. Part of the battle is over the restricting of development rights in order to limit the growth of the community.

In addition to police power and eminent domain, the right of the state to exact taxes is a limitation on ownership. If the taxes are not paid the state may force the sale of the property to satisfy the taxes.

The three concepts of land—the physical, the economic, and the legal—often become so intertwined that the term "land" is not sufficiently specific for many purposes.

CONCEPTS OF VALUE

Increasingly, the concept of land as an economic good is being confused with the concept of land in a legal sense by those who say that "land is not a commodity to be exploited and traded." They argue that since land is a resource, not a commodity, a different set of rules should apply.

Exploitation is a strong word and the connotations are negative. It is a use for profit with the connotation of selfishness. One can argue that any commerce has possibility for exploitation even though exploitation is not inherent in commerce.

Economic persons seek to make the most effective use of their resources and so does an economic society. The concept of value in an exchange economy inherently deals with getting the greatest utility out of the available resources. Recognizing that uses have bounds is merely recognizing that society imposes rules of conduct and thus limits the rights of private ownership. These limitations on rights are more severe for land than for virtually all other economic goods in our society.

FIGURE 4–2

Amendment V

No person shall be held to answer for a capital, or otherwise infamous crime, unless on a presentment or indictment of a Grand Jury, except in cases arising in the land or naval forces, or in the Militia, when in actual service in time of War or public danger; nor shall any person be subject for the same offence to be twice put in jeopardy of life or limb; nor shall be compelled in any criminal case to be a witness against himself, nor be deprived of life, liberty, or property, without due process of law; nor shall private property be taken for public use, without just compensation.

Source: Article V, Amendments to Constitution of the United States.

The legal battles over property rights turn upon the phrase from the Fifth Amendment to the Constitution, "nor shall private property be taken for public use, without just compensation." (See Figure 4–2.) The issues are whether property owners desiring to make some particular use of their property should be denied that right because others want to enjoy certain rights which they believe would be abridged if the property were developed for that use.

The purpose in owning land is to use it for something. It can be used for agricultural production, for recreation, or for some urban purpose, which implies development. The current owner need not be the person who transforms the land into an income-producing asset, but unless the chain of ownership permits that possibility the land does not have any value.

Of course, there are people who buy one square foot of land in Alaska for $10 just so they can say that they own land in Alaska. But this may not really be an exception to the rule. The land provides them with an income of sorts, though it is only a psychic income—pride of ownership. Others have bought larger parcels of land in New Mexico deserts and similar areas of minimal potential development. Many such "investments" presumably have a high prestige of ownership, because the values cannot be explained by reasonable expectations of future income.

Market. On Wall Street they used to say "do not argue with the ticker tape." In other words, stock is worth whatever it is selling for. If investors want to buy, that is what they have to pay; if they want to sell, that is what they can get. The price is the value of the stock.

In a sense that statement is correct. It is the same as saying that a share of General Motors stock at $90 is worth three pairs of shoes selling at $30. It is also worth ten steak dinners selling for $9 each.

Now the purchaser of a steak dinner uses up the good over a relatively short period of time. It would have to be an exceptional dinner for the memories to go on providing services after the next memorable dinner.

The shoes may also be a good value in terms of the current ratio of exchange. With rising prices, however, the shoes may increase in value as defined by the current ratio of exchange —i.e., they may sell for $35 or $40. The shoes still provide essentially the same services, so why should they increase in relative value? What has changed is the cost of getting the services, so that not only has the ratio of exchange changed, but the present value of future services has also changed. The services as used become more valuable.

The case for the General Motors stock is a little different. If the price drops from $90 to $60 without a corresponding change in the ability of General Motors to produce income, it was either overvalued at $90 or is undervalued at $60. That means implicitly that the ratio of exchange does not provide a correct assessment of the worth of the future benefits of the stock. The benefits did not change, only the assessment.

Income. In security analysis the concept of value based on future benefits is sometimes called "inherent" value to denote the assessment of the long-run benefits. These benefits may be presented in dollar terms. Then a calculation may be made of the present value of the future income. That conversion of future income to present value is called capitalization.

Obviously, value in this sense depends on the cash flow and the future sales price. Changes in the cash flow or the future sales price will change the long-run benefits. This in turn will change the present value. Consider a parcel of land valued at $100,000 and leased for 99 years to produce a 7 percent return. The net annual income would be $7,000. If the prevailing rate of return changed to 8 percent and the owner of the land wanted to sell the land subject to a lease that would still give him $7,000 a year, the buyer would have to pay only $87,500. On the other hand, if the rate of return fell to 6 percent, the $7,000 a year stream of income would be worth $116,667. The formula again is value times rate equals income:

$$V \times R = I \quad \text{or} \quad V = \frac{I}{R}$$

$$100{,}000 = \frac{7{,}000}{.07}$$

$$\$87{,}500 = \frac{7{,}000}{.08}$$

$$\$116{,}667 = \frac{7{,}000}{.06}$$

The changes in rates of return (capitalization rates) reflect changes in general economic conditions—especially in the general price level—as well as changes in the cost and availability of money.

Cost. A third concept of value, especially used by appraisers, deals with the value of the resources used in making the economic good. Thus in valuing real estate an appraiser will take current construction costs, financing cost, overhead, profit, and of course land cost to get the total value of the property. If the property has depreciated, the appraiser will estimate how much it has depreciated—based upon today's replacement cost—and deduct this amount to get the current value. The difficulty with this method of valuing real estate is that sooner or later the investor has to get back to raw land, which must be valued either at what it will sell for or for its productive potential.

Value still rests on expectation. The buyer buys for future benefit, and while the land may sell at the prevailing price or close to it, the ultimate question is what it can eventually be used for.

CHANGES THAT AFFECT VALUE

Changes in Rights. One of the most profitable changes affecting the value of land is a change in its permitted use, such as a change in zoning. Suppose a tract of agricultural land happens to be in the path of urbanization. Economic forces work toward conversion of the land to an urban use. Improved road networks bring the land closer to the activities of the city. Indeed, the city itself expands to the periphery of the land. Water and sewer lines are built near enough to permit development. But there is a catch: the land has previously been zoned for low density use, so that developers are limited to one-acre sites, or perhaps two- or five-acre sites.

The productivity of the land has been limited by law. It can accommodate physically and economically 4, 10, or even 20 housing units to the acre. But because of the way in which the urban development process is being managed, or not managed, an artificial constraint has been imposed. The land is available only for relatively expensive single-family residential development.

The rationale for this may rest on the feeling that good planning principles require holding land back from development until the time is ready, or on the feeling that it is a great way to exclude poor people and especially poor black people. Whatever the rationale, the fact is that most of the rapidly growing metropolitan areas tend to expand laterally and engulf a great deal of land. Many people argue that more land than necessary is being brought into development, and that the resulting pattern is horrible. The argument has substantial merit.

The pattern is horrible from an economic point of view because it is inefficient; from an aesthetic point of view because the result is ugly; from a social point of view because it is inequitable; and from an administrative point of view because the roads, the utilities, and the school capacity are not all built in the same location.

The public authorities who are responsible for the pattern may mean well; however, some are not so much public spirited as private spirited. This does not mean that they are incompetent, despite the problems of attracting qualified people to such public service. But they have far too much discretion as to which land is to be rezoned.

Unfettered rezoning puts little premium on the higher density (i.e., more productive) land uses because ample land is available for that use. The land most economically suited to development tends to be developed, except for that which is held off the development market for some reason. The result is scattered development, limited to the permitted land use.

At the other extreme from unfettered rezoning—very strict limitations and rigid enforcement of a predetermined long-range plan—some land use categories do not receive a high enough allocation (generally the higher density uses), so land zoned for those uses sells at exceptional premiums. Land that is rezoned under these circumstances is the most valuable. Prices paid for it, however, necessarily reflect its potential use so that the actual rezoning does not produce a great windfall unless the rezoning was not generally anticipated.

Most cases of rezoning are somewhere between the extremes just described. Usually the land has been overzoned for low density and underzoned for high density and nonresidential uses. The rezoning makes it more valuable. The more restrictive the zoning the more valuable the land becomes upon rezoning. The less certainty as to which land will get the desired rezoning (as in the absence of a master plan) the greater the risk on any parcel. The big rewards go to those parcels with a high risk of not being rezoned but which in fact are rezoned.

Many investors cover their bets by hiring the "right" zoning attorneys and paying fees contingent on the results they get. Some of this activity is quite legitimate. Some of it, however, turns out to be—in one way or another, with or without the right attorneys—a corruption of the system.

We are not concerned at this point with how to reform the system, but we may note that essential elements of an improved system would include open hearings and deliberations, the disclosure of personal investments by public officials, and improved public administration processes. The investor functioning *within* a system, however, has to deal with as it is. If the system is corrupt, there is little he can do about it except to get out. If it is not corrupt but simply ineffective, then the mismanagement is going to create legitimate opportunities for profit when the time comes for rezoning.

The secret is to anticipate rezoning. This means owning land that by all reasonable standards should be rezoned, with two provisos: first, that the market forces and societal forces will continue to build while the land is speculatively held, thus maintaining its value; and second, that the regulatory authority, either in its present officials or in their successors, can reasonably be expected to see the merits of a community-interest point of view.

The risk involved in this type of approach can be quite high in some localities because of the attitude toward growth that prevails there. On the other hand, the risk can be relatively low in areas in which no-growth pressures have not pushed too far and where there is political and administrative competence. In these areas the authorities usually want to rezone in accordance with the economic and social needs of the community. The investor's analysis must go beyond the economic arena into the political arena. Such analyses are sometimes made for developers in selecting locations for geographic expansion. Consider the following quotation taken from a consulting group's study of Frederick County, Maryland:

> Currently a building boom is in the making (by County standards) but there is a limit to the extent of this activity. Our assessment of the County's attitude and policy toward facilitating growth has concluded that they are just beginning to come to grips with growth problems. We expect that they will develop environmental problems, and, as of now, they do not have the tools with which to pursue solutions. This will cut back on housing production but there undoubtedly will be a period with an overbuilt condition.
>
> Based on the facts concerning development committed and very sketchy sales rate data as well as the limited ability of the County to facilitate development, there is a reasonable expectation that there will be a feasible market.[1]

Rezoning is not the only change in rights that can affect the permitted use of land. Deed restrictions or other private covenants may be used to limit the use of land. These function, in effect, as a kind of private zoning limitation.

The private limitations arise as a matter of private contract, usually placed upon the land by the subdivider with restrictions that run with the land. Thus when the subdivided land is first sold by the developer to the user it may prohibit all but single-family dwelling uses of one unit to the acre, or some such maximum density. That restriction will run with the land so that it binds successive owners for some limited period of time. Other landowners will have a right against any owner who might attempt to develop a higher density.

Under certain conditions such a covenant may be broken. If it is found to be against public policy, or if all parties to it agree that it should be broken, the land restriction may be unenforceable. Usually, however, it is merely a matter of waiting until the covenant runs out. If, when it runs out, economic justification will support a more intense land use the value of land will rise in anticipation of that change. The price paid based upon the anticipated change will reflect in part the risk of getting the change, and in part the time that must elapse before the change can take place. The effect of a covenant is thus similar to zoning; the investor's decisions keep coming back to risk and time.

Changes in Environment. The value of land is also affected by any change in environment that affects the desirability of the location.

Negative changes include increased

[1] Metro Metrics, Inc. (Washington, D.C., 1972).

traffic, congestion, smog, or a social and economic decline of the location. These changes, which reduce the demand for land and hence its value, are most frequently associated with older neighborhoods in urban or close-in locations. But outlying communities with employment problems often suffer the same deterioration.

Environmental changes do not necessarily have to be negative. They can be positive. A nuisance may be removed. Additional amenities may be provided. The classic case of removing a nuisance is the famous deal that William B. Zeckendorf made with the United Nations site in New York. The neighborhood around the site—on the east side of Manhattan—contained slaughterhouses, which gave the area a distinctly undesirable odor. Land had reportedly been selling for $2.50 per square foot. Zeckendorf paid up $17 per square foot, and bought not only enough for the UN buildings but also the land containing the slaughterhouses, to get rid of them. The result, no more smell. He made only a modest profit on the resale because it was for the UN site, but the price could have been higher.

Similar possibilities for positive change exist elsewhere. One way to find them is by seeking out the nuisances (for example, airports of declining use, or noisy manufacturing facilities). Ways of improving the environment also include providing such amenities as golf courses, man-made lakes, and other aesthetic and recreational facilities. The provision of commercial facilities also changes the environment. There are many examples of such environmental improvements.

A major department store (reportedly the May Company) is said to have bought up much land near the site of a new store in what is now Leimert Park in Los Angeles, in the immediate post–World War II days when some strip developments were being made. The store was the catalyst for development of the neighborhood. The company had to sell a lot of dry goods before it made as much money as it had earned on the nearby land.

Astute shopping center developers now make a practice of buying nearby land because they are changing the character of the area. After the shopping center is built, apartments or lesser commercial facilities nearby become feasible. This process is the reverse of that followed by the large-scale residential developer who holds back land for shopping center development.

Another classic case is that of Disney Enterprises. The developers of Disneyland in California found that in creating the park they changed the surrounding neighborhood in terms of its potential commercial use. Accordingly, when they came to build Disney World in Florida, they carefully bought up much of the surrounding land.

A developer can choose either to pick locations in which the environment will change, or to initiate the change himself. Initiating the change requires a great deal of capital. Picking a location that is going to change requires only a little. Many areas are passing through an upsurge of development. Thus in Washington, D.C., the

Georgetown area went through a private redevelopment in the 60s. Capitol Hill is now on the move and the West End appears to be next. The point is that purchases need not be limited to vacant land; they can be made wherever the land potential is great, and that is where the environment is going to change. The elements of change include many things—from changes in fashion among the well-to-do to changes in the supply of public facilities such as police protection and street safety.

Physical and Other Changes. Of course, physical changes in the property may also affect value. For example, land slides, erosion, and the like will affect the usability of a site. Stretching the concept of physical change, one could also include a decline in the quality of the water piped to the location.

Current and Anticipated Uses. Some changes in value are related to the way the property is used. For example, if the land is used for farming and the productivity of farming increases, then the land becomes more valuable. Or if it is used for housing and the neighborhood gets better (or worse), the value rises (or falls).

The biggest and most profitable changes in value generally come from anticipated uses rather than current uses—for example, when land that for years was thought to be usable only for farming is bisected by an interstate highway and an interchange, with the result that gas stations and restaurants can be built on it; the anticipation of that change in use will give rise to an increase in value.

The previous examples of land near shopping centers, or residential land that is rezoned for shopping centers, are also cases of anticipation. The expected demolition of garden apartments to make way for high-rise apartments will give rise to an increase in land value long before the apartments are in fact demolished.

In urbanized areas many such changes, even when only anticipated, will bring profit to someone who has bought the land at the right time. The time to buy such urban land is before the potential use becomes obvious to everyone.

Rural land at the urban fringe tends to rise in value in anticipation of urban development. In the few decades since World War II the suburban land boom has made fortunes for people who happened to own land which was drawn into development by the extension of highway networks and public facilities, such as water and sewer lines, which make the land developable. Land which was once far out has become close in.

Some writers claim that all the really big opportunities are gone. Don't believe it. Development is being pushed out to unprecedented distances. Employment locations are shifting. The pattern of land uses is changing, and plenty of land is going to become more valuable. Some of it is located close in, and will be subject to new uses because of the energy situation.

Much of the pattern of urban development is unwise and there is cause to seek reform in the system. But appealing to the consciences of landowners, developers, or lenders is not going to change anything. Perhaps appealing to the conscience of the local and national political leadership may help somewhat. Reformers who want to change the pattern of urban development should start with the politicians. Interfering with the market will only get rid of some of the less efficient operators while rewarding those who know how to make the system work for them.

For those who accept the system as it is, profitable land investment is really a question of seeking out land which will undergo some change in use. But the rules for doing this are no longer the same because the forces behind urbanization are changing them. The next chapter examines these forces and how they work.

5

Forces for Change

The biggest changes in land value arise out of the expectation of a change in land use. One needs to understand the pattern within which land use changes take place in order to forecast them. But patterns do not endure forever. Old patterns give way to new patterns. While investors can make money by following historical trends of land development, they can make more money by anticipating new trends. Land use patterns do not change rapidly. But they change, and the pace of change has been accelerating.

The largest profits accrue to landowners who have land in the path of development based on the emerging patterns rather than the old patterns. Land for such developments as new communities, theme parks, and outlying industrial parks shows a much greater annual percentage increase in value than land used for garden apartments and neighborhood shopping centers.

Before discussing the specific pattern of development for a local community (Chapter 8) and the character and rates of growth for various communities (Chapter 7), one should consider the forces underlying the old patterns and the new ones that are emerging. By understanding the forces, the investor can anticipate the changes and buy in advance of the general expectation which pushes the prices up.

URBANIZATION

Agricultural Productivity and Industrialization. The two great forces for urbanization were a growth in agricultural productivity accompanied by industrialization. They enabled the cities to support an increasing population.

Consider that at the turn of the century the United States was still an agrarian community. Figure 5–1 shows the shift from a rural to an urban society.

The urbanization of the early part of the century was not simply a movement of rural population to urban centers; it was also an inmigration of urban population. An average of 880,-000 people immigrated to the U.S. each year in the early part of the century, and most of them settled in the cities.

Transportation. The level of income rose rapidly in the first few decades of the century (see Figure 5–2). But until the transportation system improved and a large segment of the population was affluent enough to afford substantial daily transportation, the community development pattern was compact.

Land use patterns at the turn of the century featured row houses (old-style versions of townhouses) on lots as narrow as 20 and 30 feet, or even less. The premium was on frontage, with the objective of making as many units as possible accessible to places where money was made and spent. The two primary modes of transportation were public (e.g., the trolley car) and private (i.e., on foot).

The best commercial locations, called 100 percent locations, were where the most used public transportation lines converged. That is where land values were highest. The values fell as one went farther away from those locations. Values were related to accessibility, and when far-out locations gained access to the center by rapid rail transport their land values skyrocketed.

SUBURBANIZATION

Affluence. Despite all that can be said for living in town, a great deal can be said for getting out. Urban problems were not invented in the 1960s. They

FIGURE 5–1
Shifts in Population: 1880–1970

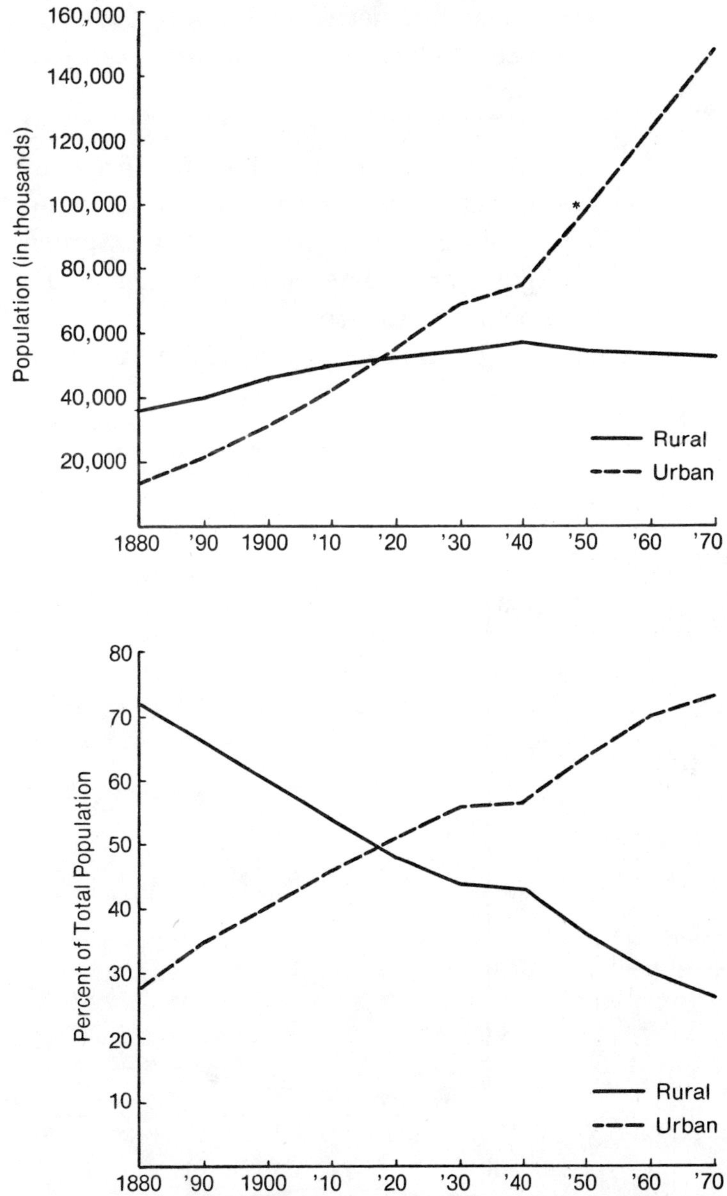

* In 1950 the Bureau of the Census adopted the concept of the urbanized area and delineated boundaries for unincorporated areas. All the population residing in urban-fringe areas of 2,500 or more are classified as urban according to the "current" definition.

Source: U.S. Department of Commerce, *Statistical Abstract of the United States: 1973*, 94th ed. (Washington, D.C.: U.S. Government Printing Office, 1973).

existed a half century earlier, only most people were too poor to know it. Everybody, or almost everybody, lived in crowded housing amid the noise and dirt of the city, except, of course, for those who lived in the country. The country people did not have indoor plumbing and worked longer than city people—twelve hours a day, six days a week.

Those city people who could afford to work less, who had the price of travel by commuter railroad, and who could afford the house with its green grass and white picket fence, had the option of suburbia.

Suburbia was the site of the American dream. A private house away from the dirt of the city, and a place for the children to play, were part of an idealized life-style. The breadwinner would commute, and thus give up some of the gains of the shorter workweek. Many of the values of small-town America now seemed accessible, at least as indicated by the scale of urban development.

The forces creating suburbia began to develop before the Great Depression. Incomes had risen (see Figure 5–2), and transportation networks were developing. Not only were the commuter lines having a strong effect, but mass production was bringing the

FIGURE 5–2
Natural and Disposable Income, 1900–1970
(in billions of dollars)

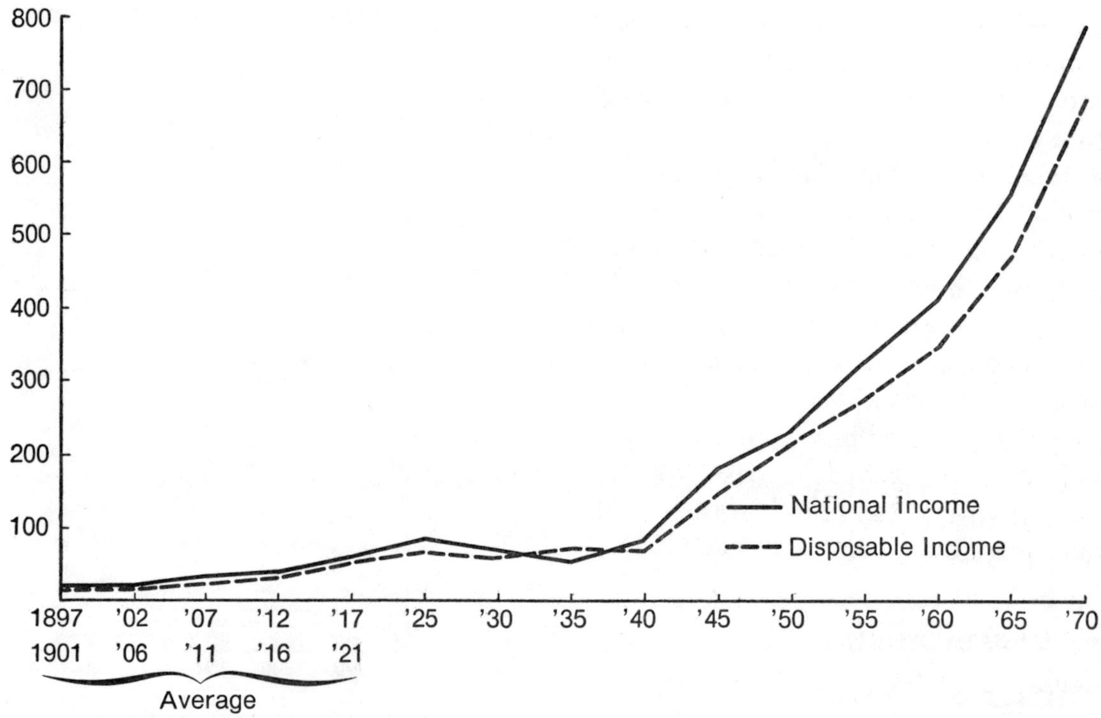

* Averages for the years indicated.
Source: U.S. Department of Commerce, *The Statistical History of the United States from Colonial Times to the Present (Historical Statistics of the United States, Colonial Times to 1957, and Continuation to 1962, and Revisions)*, Stamford, Conn.: Fairfield Publishers, Inc., 1965; and U.S. Department of Commerce, *Statistical Abstract of the United States: 1973*, 94 ed. Washington, D.C.: U.S. Government Printing Office, 1973.

automobile within the reach of increasing proportions of the population. More and more people could escape from the city.

But then came the Great Depression. Instead of moving to suburbia many families went back to the farm where starving cost less than it did in the city. Housing values declined (see Figure 5-3). The situation got so bad that some families even sold their cars.

Not much suburbanization occurred during the decade of the thirties, but at the end of the decade urbanization started again. Jobs were available in the city because the country was at war. The war effort called for a giant increase in production, and this resulted in tremendous population shifts during the first half of the forties.

Economic Opportunity. War production was concentrated in places where industry already existed, and especially on the coasts. People moved to those locations, at first absorbing vacant housing and later causing the conversion of nonresidential space to living quarters and of single family to multi-family units. New construction was severely limited because resources had to be used for war production. The result was that urban growth took place mainly in cities where there was war production and associated activities such as military installations. Within a city, the places that grew were those where industrial facilities already existed. Housing and commercial patterns were therefore intensifications of those of the two previous decades.

But in the decade following the end of World War II, the lid blew off the housing market.

For one thing, the population had become more mobile. Over sixteen million men had gone into the armed forces. Six million people had moved to the cities. The interpersonal lines of communication had been stretched over great distances. And perhaps the system had begun a fundamental change—at least, one trend reversed itself.

That trend was the birthrate. The birthrate had dropped precipitously during the depression. Demographers then were projecting that population would stabilize at 155 million by 1950. But after the war it surged upward. The returning war veteran got down to the serious business of finding a wife, getting an education and a job, and starting to raise a family.

Availability of Housing. He was apt to find a house in suburbia. No matter

FIGURE 5-3
Prices of New Single-Family
Detached Homes for Selected Years

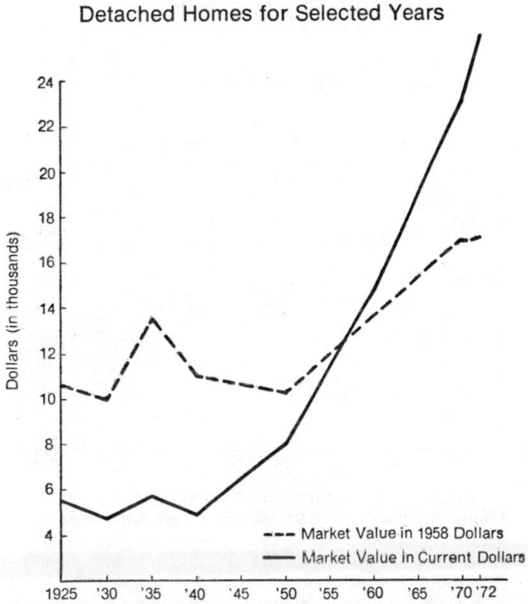

Source: National Association of Home Builders of the United States, *Economic News Notes*, January 1973.

FIGURE 5–4
Goods Output in Relation to
Gross National Product (1930–1970)

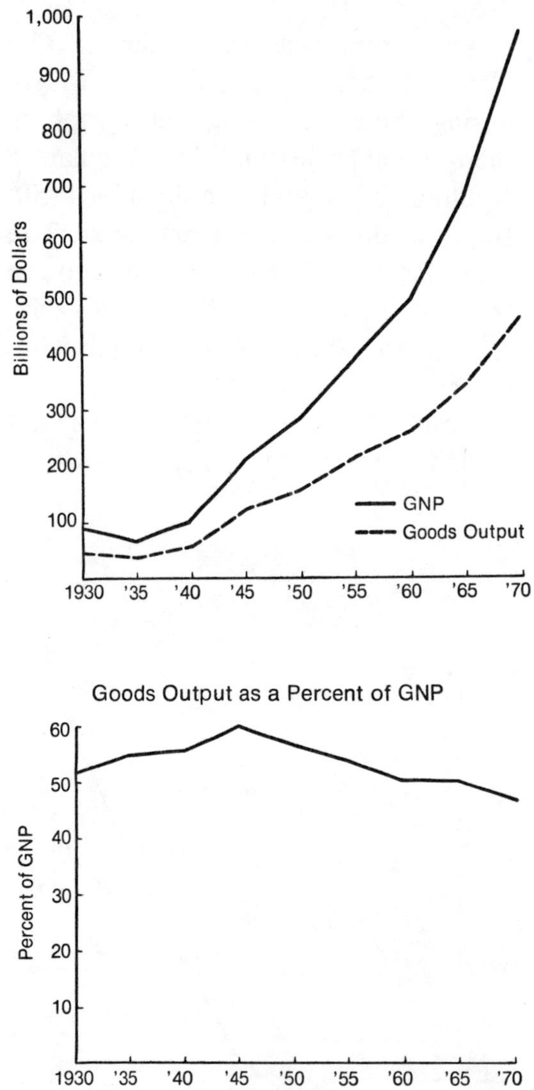

Source: U.S. Department of Commerce, *The Statistical History of the United States from Colonial Times to the Present, Historical Statistics of the United States Colonial Time to 1957, and Continuation to 1962, and Revisions* (Stamford, Conn.: Fairfield Publishers, Inc., 1965); and U.S. Department of Commerce, *Statistical Abstract of the United States: 1973,* 94th ed. (Washington, D.C.: U.S. Government Printing Office, 1973).

whether all that suburban development made sense in the larger view. No one thought of social costs in those days. Pollution had scarcely been heard of (except as dirt in the air of the city). There was no talk of quality of life. Veterans were accustomed to living in barracks, and were delighted to get their own homes even if they also were like barracks.

Under the G.I. Bill of Rights, returning veterans were able to obtain home loans with little or no down payment. The payments were comparable to rent, and many bought homes because they couldn't find anything to rent. The Federal Housing Administration—created in the thirties to help restore lender confidence in badly battered institutions—also was pressed into service, facilitating the conversion of the would-be renter to a buyer.

Building new neighborhoods on the periphery of the urbanized area was easier than filling in vacant land. In large measure it was easier because financing made it easier. The federal government, which guaranteed loans under Veterans Administration programs, or insured them under FHA programs, facilitated the suburbanization pattern. Rating and approving the neighborhood was easier when it was new, and who was thinking about other problems?

Land available for housing was also increasing. While the supply of land is limited, the supply of *urban land* is not limited. It increases when undeveloped land is drawn into development by extension of road and utility networks.

Thus urban land increased, and

values soared. The supply of accessible land increased along with the road network and the use of the automobile (Figure 5–5). As the freeways and other highway networks emerged over the decade following World War II, so the outlying areas gained in accessibility. The premium on accessibility of the close-in areas was destroyed by the innovations in autos and roads that made previously outlying areas now competitive.

Increasing affluence fed the fire. The generation that entered the housing market in the 50s was a work-ethic generation. Its members were believers in the dream of the 30s. And they were making it. Not only were their incomes going up but their investments were also making them rich. Even if they did not have a business or profession that enabled them to make substantial investments in stock and real estate, their jobs and houses were enriching them.

The house they bought in the late 40s for $8,000, no money down and $60 a month, was great for a family with one child and an income of a few hundred dollars a month. It was a two-bedroom, one-bath house on a 50-by-120-foot lot. In five years perhaps $1,000 of the mortgage was paid off, but inflation and rising values had already pushed the price to $11,000. It was no trick to sell the house and use the extra cash for a down payment on a three-bedroom one-bath house selling for $13,500. The mortgage payments were higher, but so was the owner's income. That house in turn was resold in a few years for $16,000, $17,000, or even $18,000, and the proceeds took care of the down payment on one priced in the mid-20s. Within a decade, the homeowner could be in a house costing three or four times the price of the one he had originally purchased (which by this time had doubled in price from inflation), and the dollar equity might approach five figures. The next decade brought equities in the tens of thousands of dollars. And people today are living in houses worth 50, 60, and 70 thousand dollars whose total cash investment, not counting, of course, the monthly payments and upkeep, goes back to a few hundred dollars down for the first house with no added capital investment.

FIGURE 5–5
Road Mileage and Motor-Vehicle Travel in the United States

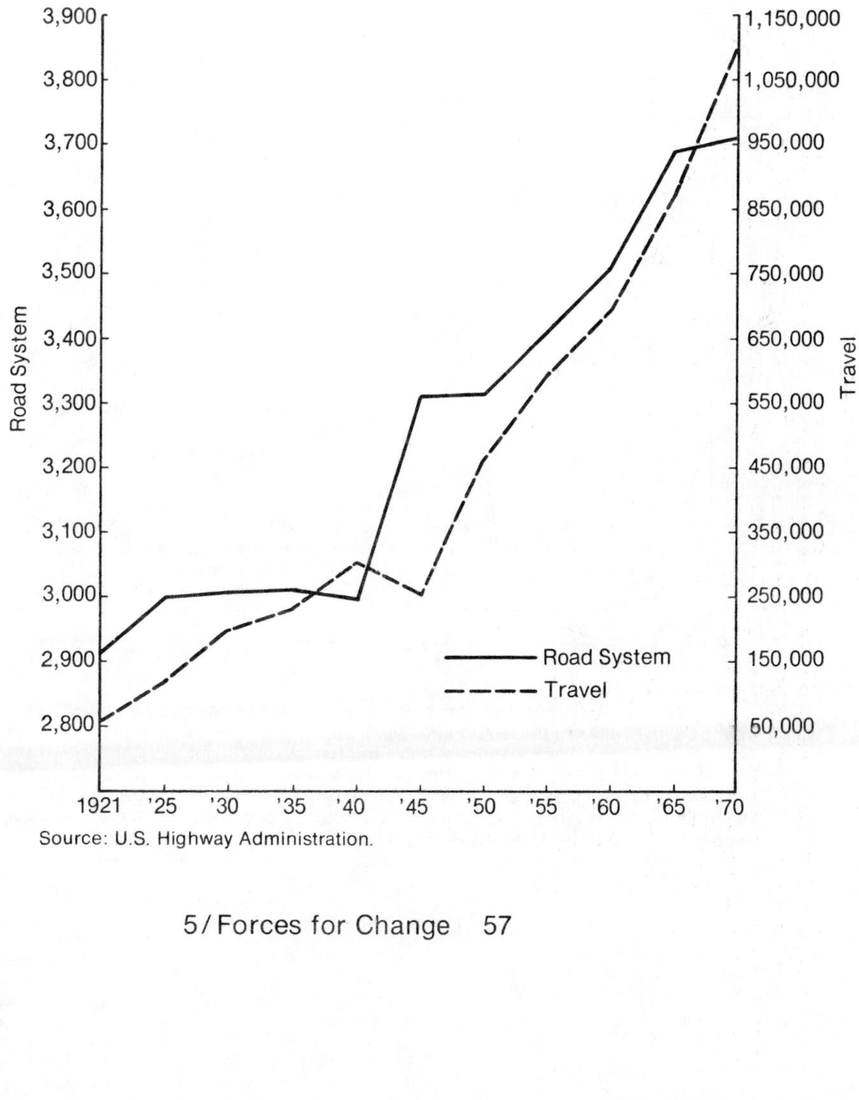

Source: U.S. Highway Administration.

That first wave of post–World War II suburbanites was followed by a second wave, some of whom moved up through the same houses. But in the next decade, starting in the early 60s, a wave of apartment construction (Figure 5–6) brought renters to suburbia.

The level of affluence kept rising, and so did the use of cars. Small shopping centers sprang up near the new neighborhoods. Then bigger shopping centers came that provided more than convenience goods; they could save a trip downtown. Regional shopping centers followed, rivaling the downtown areas and dealing some of them a mortal blow even before the subsequent era of the covered mall.

FIGURE 5–6
Total Housing Starts, 1925–1974
(thousands of units)

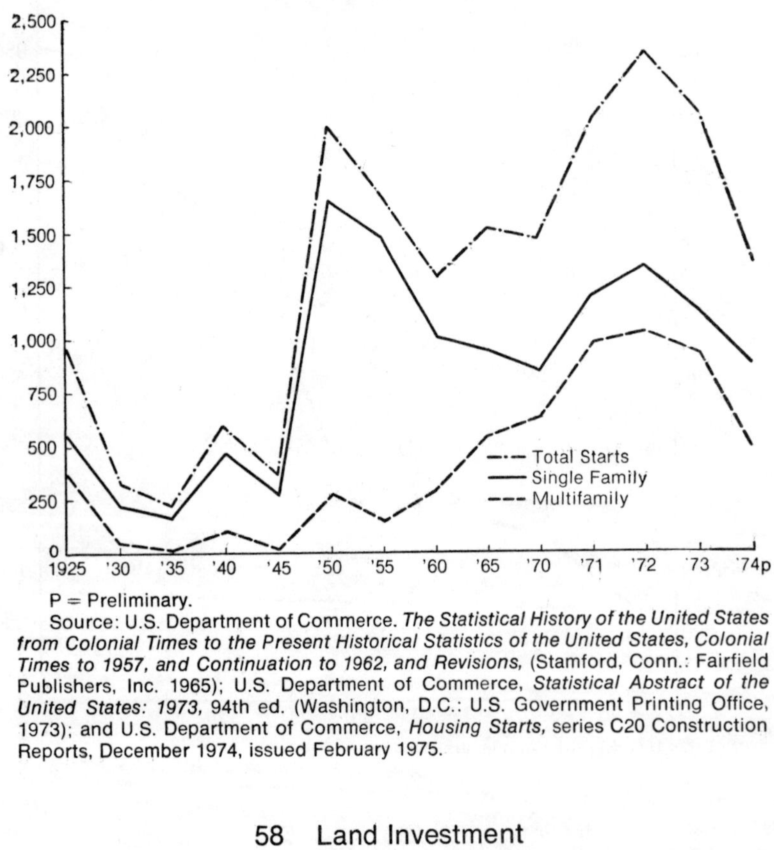

P = Preliminary.
Source: U.S. Department of Commerce. *The Statistical History of the United States from Colonial Times to the Present Historical Statistics of the United States, Colonial Times to 1957, and Continuation to 1962, and Revisions,* (Stamford, Conn.: Fairfield Publishers, Inc. 1965); U.S. Department of Commerce, *Statistical Abstract of the United States: 1973,* 94th ed. (Washington, D.C.: U.S. Government Printing Office, 1973); and U.S. Department of Commerce, *Housing Starts,* series C20 Construction Reports, December 1974, issued February 1975.

INTERURBANIZATION

Growing Together. The current pattern in city growth is interurbanization. It started first in such places as Los Angeles, which engulfed surrounding communities that were also going through suburbanization. The growing together is facilitated by the interstate highway system, which carries an enormous amount of commuter traffic. Cities closely linked by high-speed traffic arteries thus produce a corridor of development, assuming of course that the necessary zoning permits and public utilities are available.

The corridor is really an extension of a previous pattern of growth along main traffic arteries. It simply pulls the development farther out, and in the case of a beltway wraps it around the center city.

What makes interurbanization a new pattern is that not only are the regional shopping centers (now generally covered malls) located on these beltways and leg routes, but that employment opportunities have also shifted to outlying locations.

Some of the forces of the previous era are still at work, some have reversed direction, and some new forces are appearing on the scene.

The agricultural revolution has continued, bringing sharp gains in farm output per man-hour. One farm worker produced enough food for 10 people in 1930, 16 in 1950, and 47 in 1970. (See Figure 5–7.) Employment in agriculture during that same period went from 10.3 million in 1930 to 7.2 million in 1950 and only 3.5 million in 1970 (Figure 5–7). Meanwhile, nonagricultural employment more than doubled, from 35.1 million in 1930 to 75.2 million in 1970.

Employment Shifts. The jobs, however, were not all located in the central city. More and more the increase in employment went to the outlying jurisdictions of metropolitan areas.

Part of the shift is explainable because the nature of the jobs changed. A technological and demographic revolution took place during the postwar years, and it included the following developments:

1. An enormous growth of consumer credit. The charge accounts once used primarily for consumer durables are now widely used as a substitute for money in payment for services as well as for goods. This shift, together with the expansion of the service industries, has brought new styles of spending money and accounting for the transactions.

2. An innovation in communication that has reduced the need for face-to-face relationships so much as to change the character of some jobs and their location requirements.

3. A technology of intercity air travel that permits commuters to travel

FIGURE 5-7
Agricultural Employment and Productivity, 1930–1970

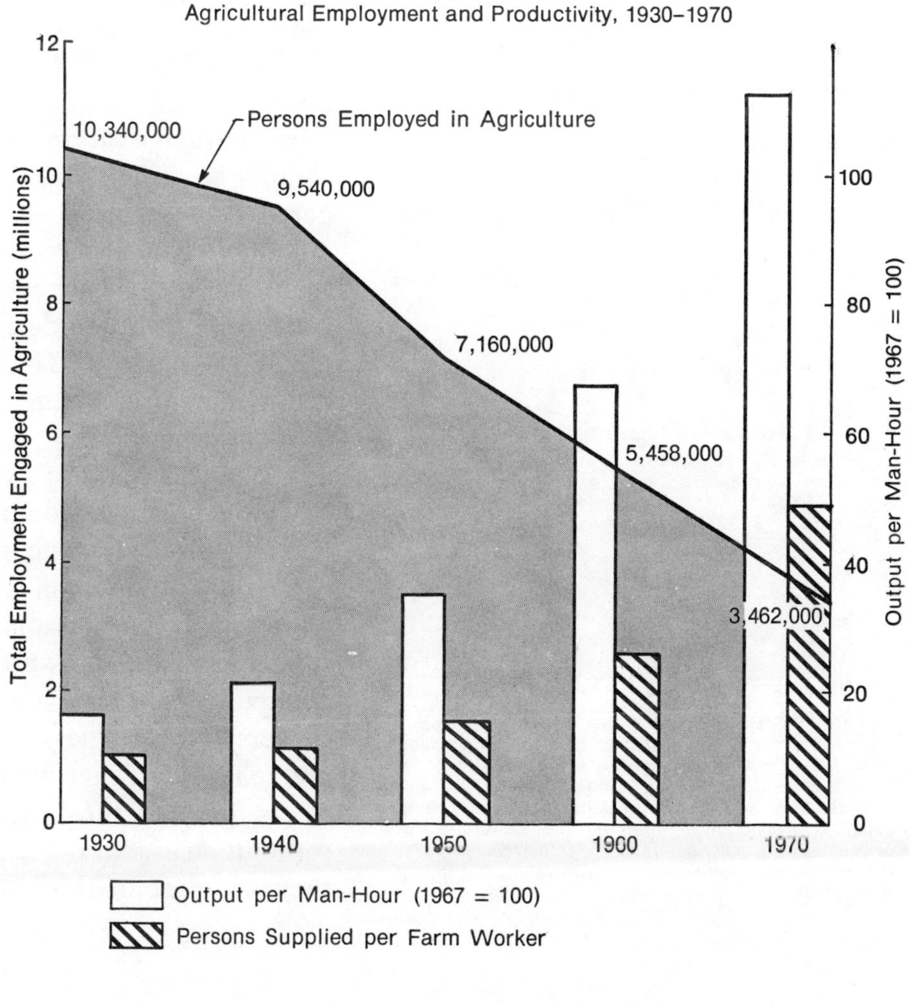

a third of the distance up and down each coast, and to make same-day round trips a third of the way across the country. As a consequence, job activity is increasingly concentrated around airports.

4. A shift to government-provided services in contrast to market-purchased services, resulting in increased employment in government, especially in local governments scattered about the interurban cityscape.

5. A reduction in the birth rate, accelerated by the pill, and a corresponding reduction of household size. At first this provided a strong element of demand for center-city housing accommodations. Now, however, living complexes designed for small households have sprung up in suburbia near the new job opportunities.

FIGURE 5–8
Civilian Labor Force, 1930–1970
(in thousands, except percent)

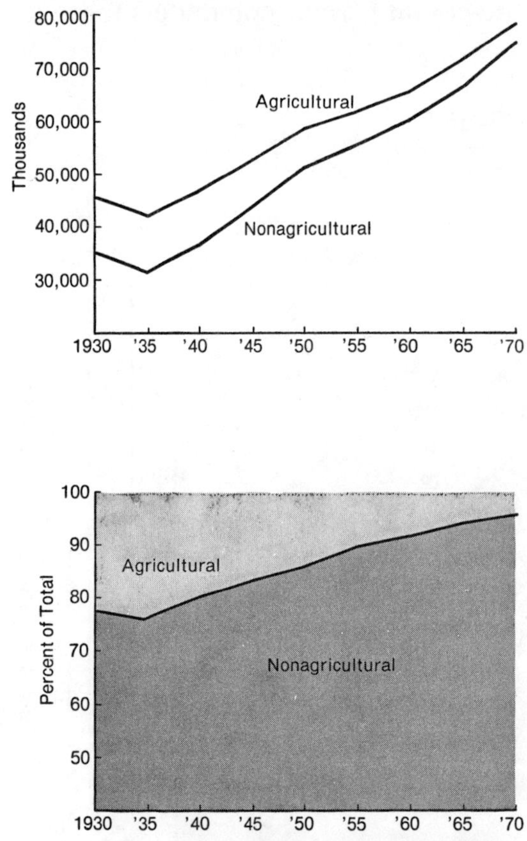

Source: U.S. Bureau of Labor Statistics in U.S. Department of Commerce, *The Statistical History of the United States from Colonial Times to the Present, Historical Statistics of the United States, Colonial Times to 1957, and Continuation to 1962, and Revisions* (Stamford, Conn.: Fairfield Publishers, Inc., 1965); and U.S. Department of Commerce, *Statistical Abstract of the United States: 1973*, 94th ed. (Washington, D.C.: U.S. Government Printing Office, 1973).

Changing Life Styles. The demographics have changed. There are more old people and more young people. Families are smaller. The youngsters who rebelled in the 60s against the values of their parents (who were happily living the dream of the 30s, the economic dream) have now entered the work force. The youngsters have not necessarily copped out. They have jobs, but their expectation of what work should be differs from that of their parents. They elect to spend larger amounts of time in recreation than did their parents. Their view of what is acceptable in urban design and amenities is different, too. They represent the economic mainstream. They expect more of society, they are searching for new patterns.

The new towns offer no panacea. They have their drug problems, and the would-be solution of jobs for the people who live there is less apparent than the solution of express buses, with cocktails, to and from employment centers. Nevertheless, the new towns are being built. They have to be thought of as part of the interurban pattern rather than as separate cities. In a sense they are part of the interurbanization process—and, one might be tempted to say, of the interurbanization problem.

THE PROBLEM

The problem depends on one's vantage point. Interurbia is a problem because its transportation network is depleting fossil fuels and polluting the air. The waste of fossil fuels can be lamented from several points of view: because the long chain molecules can be used for other production, or because some greedy oil company executive will press for an inane foreign policy, or because commuters will balk at the outrageous fuel costs necessary to feed the gas-eating monsters.

Interurbia can be a problem because its massive scale tends to isolate its inhabitants from the rest of the world. Those who have it made and get there first will keep the others out, and may see nothing wrong in this. The genteel way of price 'em out of the market has worked really well in the past. But some people regard these exclusive enclaves as dangerous to society, quite aside from the simple matter of equity. There is also much to be said for bringing up children in a world with some diversity, so that they do not need a public school excursion to show them how others live. "This is where the rich people live; this is where the poor people live. See the black children at play. See the pretty park."

Values are changing, in ways which significantly affect land use. If one could control land use one could influence the fulfillment of those values. Some control is economic. Some is political. Some is social. In all, it is institutional.

There is a pattern in all this. The threads are thin and the cloth is being pulled, but the pattern is visible. It is being patched and changed and different hands are working on it. The next two chapters describe, from one vantage point, how economics and urban development are affecting the emerging patterns.

This understanding can be used by investors to make a profit. They can see which land is worthy of an investment position. The understanding may also be used by those who are managing the environment.

6

National Patterns of Monetary and Fiscal Policy

This chapter deals with monetary and fiscal policy as it affects national patterns of development. The intent is to assist the investor in gaining an insight into how the interaction of national forces gives rise to trends affecting local investment. The investor will want to identify these trends in order to (a) determine the timing of investments, and (b) evaluate the potential of the metropolitan area in which he is interested.

TRENDS IN MONETARY POLICY

Monetary policy refers to the activities of the Federal Reserve Board in expanding and contracting the supply of credit. It does this by (*a*) changing the rate of interest the Federal Reserve Banks charge member banks for borrowing funds, (*b*) changing the reserve requirements of member banks, and (*c*) buying and selling government securities, which has the net effect of increasing or decreasing the amount of money available for reserves. (See also Chapter 13.)

In this way the Federal Reserve Board influences the cost and availability of money for all borrowers. It may seek to stimulate economic activity (by creating conditions that will make money available at relatively low cost) or to dampen excessive expansion (by creating conditions that make money expensive and hard to get). Thus monetary policy is a tool for managing the national economy.

The effectiveness and appropriateness of monetary policy depends somewhat on the school of economic thought to which one subscribes. Some investors feel that monetary policy tools are appropriate and effective, when properly used in conjunction with fiscal policy (federal taxing and spending). Others, however, believe that the political and administrative leadership ought not to use such tools, holding that experience with them has not been good. Better, they assert, to use a fixed or automatic method of increasing the availability of money and credit for a growing national economy and not have it discretionary.

Both positions have merit. Fiscal and monetary policy offer certain benefits in stabilizing the economy, but substantial oversteering has occurred from time to time. Attempts to use these tools for more than can realistically be expected from them have led the financial system to the brink of disaster.

Consider the following editorial from the October 6, 1973, issue of *Business Week:*

WHY THE FED WENT WRONG – If the U.S. goes into a recession next year, the Federal Reserve will get the blame. Its power to manipulate the nation's money stock may very well be abridged by legislation, and its discretion may be limited by instructions from Congress forbidding any attempt at countercyclical monetary policies (page 100).

There might be a certain grim justice in such an outcome. Monetary policy in the past eight years has been uniformly bad. The money managers have missed the turns both going up and coming down. They have overreacted to small fluctuations in the economy and sat on their hands while major trends were developing. On the record, monetary policy has been counterproductive rather than countercyclical.

But the real blame for the dismal record of the years since 1966 does not lie at the Fed's door. It lies in the White House, where first President Johnson and then President Nixon forced the money managers to try to shelter the economy from the consequences of irresponsible taxing and spending policies.

The trouble began when Lyndon Johnson demanded that the Fed control an economy violently stimulated by his Vietnam War spending. The trouble continued when Richard Nixon left the Fed with the main burden of slowing down the inflationary economy in 1969. And the trouble came to a head when the Nixon Administration poured huge surges of deficit spending into the system in 1971 and 1972. The real sin of the money managers was in pretending that monetary policy could offset bad fiscal policy.

The lesson to learn from the unhappy record is that effective economic policy begins with the federal budget. Monetary policy can reinforce good fiscal policy, either restrictive or expansive. It cannot pick up the pieces when the budget makers go wrong.*

The Uses of Inflation. The purpose of this chapter is not to attempt to resolve the controversy on how monetary policy should be managed but rather to explain what has happened and how it has generated the inflation of recent years. An understanding of changing inflationary rates will assist in making judgments about forecasted economic conditions as well as about timing of investments.

The place to begin the analysis of trends is with the period of World War II. It provides us with a high water mark for the use of inflation to finance government expenditure.

Governments often go to printing presses to finance wars. On the simplest level, they literally print up more money. Before they are through the currency may be so cheapened that new currency has to be issued with extra zeros, or purchasers have to carry wads of bills of large denominations. When the public starts fleeing

* Reprinted from the October 6, 1973 issue of *Business Week* by special permission. ©1973 by McGraw-Hill, Inc.

FIGURE 6-1

A Politician's Dictionary on Inflation

Inflation—A mechanism which transfers wealth from creditors (lenders) to debtors. It enables those who have borrowed large amounts of good dollars to pay back debts with much less valuable dollars. Since the owners of real estate, for example, usually have large debts, one can regard inflation as a siphon for transferring wealth from owners of savings accounts (loan investors) to owners of real estate (equity investors).

Inflation Game—It is currently in vogue as a ploy with which to increase Uncle Sam's income and thereby decrease the budget deficit. This noble result is achieved since a higher percentage of tax has to be paid on inflated salaries and on larger incomes. This sneaky budget balancing game of boosting prices and salaries, rather than taxes, is in reality an efficient means of collecting additional taxes.

Printing Press—A potential engine of inflation—it is the traditional tool for accelerating monetary growth.

Deficit Budget—A more sophisticated method of accelerating monetary growth than the printing press. The government merely creates the paper and the credit dollars through the banking system to cover the deficit. It is one of the finest tools the politicians have invented for decreasing the value of the dollar. With this outstanding device at their disposal, the politicians can keep spending more and more without raising taxes. They merely raise the price of everything we buy by periodically raising the debt ceiling and spending about $20 billion/year more than the government collects in taxes.

Primary Cause of Inflation—Expanding the supply of money and credit much faster than goods and services are produced. Acceleration of monetary growth usually leads, after a time lag, to acceleration of inflation.

Trade Deficit—A clever method of using up the excess dollars which were printed above and beyond the goods and services produced in this country. The buying of oil and Volkswagens with the printing press would be outstanding examples of this technique. It can be regarded as a convenient means of exporting our inflation. This is a fine game as long as the prodigal dollars do not return to America.

Devaluation—A decrease in the worth of the dollar. This is caused by the ever growing flood of about $100 billion which are sloshing around the world's money markets while looking for some place to go. As a result of the last two devaluations, we have to pay more for what we buy and get less for what we sell.

Secondary Cause of Inflation—Demand Pull—A devalued (weak) currency makes our goods look like real bargains to foreigners. In the process of gobbling up our commodities (wheat, soybeans, lumber, etc.) with their prodigal supply of dollars, they cause a domestic shortage of these items and drive up our prices.

Source: Allan Kukk, "Dictionary of Economics for Politicians," (unpublished manuscript).

from currency to real goods as a way of storing wealth, it is a sign that the monetary system is failing. Most governments would rather face that than risk disaster on the war front. Not all governments push it to the extreme, but many use it as a way of financing the war effort.

Inflation enables a government to pay its debts in cheaper money. It is also a way of taxing the population without telling it that it is being taxed. In addition, when the government prints money it is obtaining funds for little more than the expense of printing the additional currency. Figure 6–1 gives one author's view of how it works.

The United States government does it in a more sophisticated way. The U.S. Treasury taxes and spends (fiscal policy) and, of course, borrows (part of fiscal policy is debt management). And, like other economic units, if it is spending more than is coming in, it must borrow or steal.

The agency that authorizes the printing of the currency is the U.S. Treasury Department. The currency is distributed through the Federal Reserve System. The Federal Reserve also determines the monetary policy, which affects how much money can be created in the monetary system. As part of that process it buys and sells U.S. government securities. It may pay for those securities by, in effect, giving the seller a check. As a practical matter, the payment is the same as a Federal Reserve check made out on the seller's bank, because the bank's deposits at the Federal Reserve Bank are increased by the amount of the "check" for the bonds.

Thus, the process of financing World War II was in some measure through the purchase by the central bank (Federal Reserve Bank) of whatever bonds were necessary to make loans available to the U.S. government. This process, of course, increases reserves of member banks and permits a substantial expansion of bank credit.

As a practical matter the system operated with the commercial banks holding much of the federal bonds and the central bank standing ready to buy whatever it needed to provide the commercial bank with liquidity necessary for its lending and reserve requirements. The process was carried out by the Federal Reserve supporting U.S. government bond prices. That is, it bought whatever was necessary to stabilize the bond prices.

The "Accord." This went on until the early 1950s when the U.S. Treasury and the Federal Reserve reached an "accord." They agreed that the Federal Reserve would only prevent disorderly markets and not continue to support the U.S. government bond market. (These are not Series E Bonds. Rather, they are very large denomination bonds paying prevailing interest. They are held by major financial and other institutions as a source of liquidity second to cash and short term obligations. They entail no financial risk, only some liquidity risk arising out of changes in the prevailing interest rate.)

That accord was chronologically the third major event in the history of monetary policy since World War II. The first was the wartime financing itself. The second was the Employment Act of 1946.

The Employment Act of 1946. At the end of World War II it was feared that there would be another depression or at least a recession that would arise from the structural adjustment necessary to move from a wartime economy to a peacetime economy. The idea was that the return to civilian life and the general changes in jobs in industries which themselves were to undergo drastic change would, in the process, provide an instability in which gross national product would decline for a time.

The Employment Act of 1946 legislated against any depression. It said that as a matter of national policy the U.S. government would pursue policies leading to high levels of income, output, and employment and presumably with reasonable price stability.

That legislation set up the Council of Economic Advisors and popularized the national income accounts. These accounts show gross national product according to investment/expenditure accounts and according to income accounts. (See Figure 6–2.) The council

FIGURE 6–2
Gross National Product, 1974
(billions of current dollars)

Expenditures				*Income**
Personal consumption expenditures 876.7	Durable goods	127.5	1,397.4	GNP
	Nondurable goods	380.2	119.5	Less: Capital consumption allowances
	Services	369.0		
Gross private domestic investment 209.4	Fixed investment	195.6	1,278.0	Equals: Net National Product
	Nonresidential 149.2		126.9	Less: Indirect business tax
	Residential 46.0		5.2	Business transfer payments
			−.1	Statistical discrepancy
	Change in business inventories	14.2	−2.9	Plus: Subsidies less current governmental enterprises surplus
			1,143.0	Equals: National Income
			106.2	Less: Corporate profits and inventory valuation adjustment
Net exports of goods and services 2.1	Exports 140.2			
	Imports 138.1	2.1		
			101.5	Contributions for social Insurance
Government purchases of goods and services 309.2	Federal	116.9	−.5	Wage accruals less disbursements
	National defense 78.7		134.6	Plus: Government transfer payments
	Other 38.2			
	State & Local	192.3	42.3	Interest paid (net) by government and consumer
			32.7	Dividends
			5.2	Business transfer payments
Total GNP		1,397.4	1,150.5	Total Personal Income

* Includes preliminary 4th quarter figures.
Source: U.S. Department of Commerce, *Survey of Current Business*, vol. 55, no. 3, March 1975, pp. 7–8.

advises the president on pursuit of policies that would provide high levels of income, output, and employment, presumably with some element of price stability.

The Council of Economic Advisors is a powerful force in the administration of the executive branch of the government. However, authority in the executive branch is somewhat diffused in that the Federal Reserve System with its Board of Governors is an independent agency. There is much to be said for agency independence in the pursuit of monetary stability. But when conflicts occur among the multiple goals of national government, not all agencies necessarily subordinate their own objectives to those of others. Indeed, many agencies generate problems for other agencies. Difficulties in reconciling differences, and the lack of balance of the entire system, show up in inconsistent policies.

Interest Rates and Inflationary Change. With that as a backdrop, the periodic changes in interest rates and inflation are somewhat more understandable. The accompanying charts (see Figure 6–3) indicate interest rate changes and inflationary change.

The rise in interest rates over the last quarter century is more a reflection of the rise in inflation than in the real cost of money. Thus the monetary policy trend has been inflationary. This has caused some severe problems within the last decade.

The money crunch of 1966 was the first of the recent series. That situation arose from expansionary demands for borrowed funds from the private sector coupled with increased public sector financing. The crunch came when the monetary authorities excessively tightened monetary policy.

Inflation then subsided for a very short period of time. The tight money situation came back in 1969. The rate of growth of bank credit (one of the measures of the money supply) was sharply contracted once again. In the 1966 crunch, after bank credit had grown for the first half of the decade at a rate of 7.7 percent per annum, it declined in the third quarter of the year. In the 1969 crunch, bank credit also declined after having grown during 1967 and 1968 at rates of about 9.7 percent. From 1970 to early 1974, bank credit grew at an annual rate of 12.5 percent.

The 1974 situation had large elements of inflation, but this time other

FIGURE 6–3
Inflation and Interest Rates

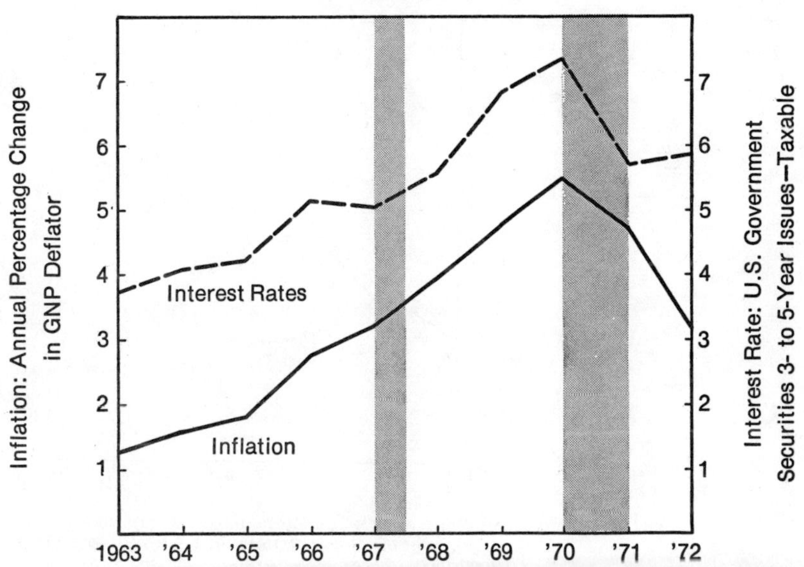

Recession shown by shaded areas.
Source: First National City Bank, *Monthly Economic Newsletter*, New York, August 1973. pp. 8–9.

factors were at work. Not only did bank credit increase, but there were shortages of physical goods. Much of the price rise was attributable to rising energy costs related to fuel scarcity, rising raw material costs related to scarcity in that area, and rising food costs. The public's attempts to protect its savings from inflation brought a tendency to shift out of money to commodities and real goods, a change which seems to have accentuated the price rise. The recession that is in the making at this writing may temporarily ease the inflation and the tightening of money that has developed. The ball game is changing again. But until both monetary policy and fiscal policy are used to restrain excess demand, inflation will continue to be a chronic problem.

FIGURE 6–4
Mortgage Rates and Residential Construction

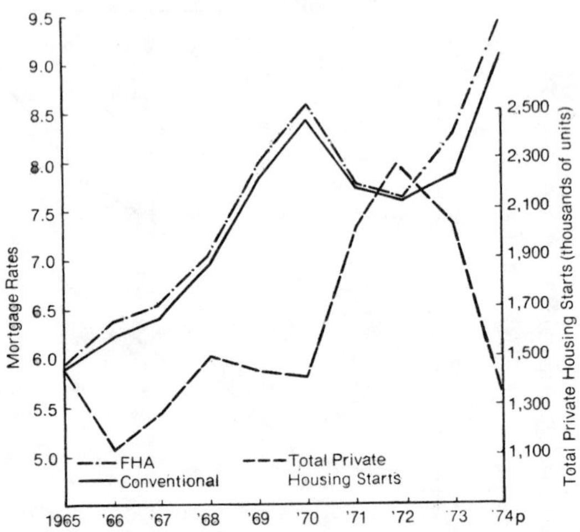

P = Preliminary.
Source: U.S. Department of Commerce, *Statistical Abstract of the United States: 1973,* 94th ed. (Washington, D.C.: U.S. Government Printing Office, 1973); *Federal Reserve Bulletin,* vol. 61, no. 2, February 1975, and U.S. Department of Commerce, *Housing Grants,* Series C20 Construction Reports, December 1974, issued February 1975.

The impact of these conditions can be seen by looking at residential construction. Figure 6–4 shows mortgage rates on one scale and the volume of residential construction on the other. Obviously the tightening of money adversely affects the volume of construction.

The volume of construction naturally affects the demand for developable land. The best land prices are obtained when rising demand sends the developer scurrying for more land in order to capture the market while it's hot. An easing in money supply facilitates the demand.

Note that the time to buy land is just before an inflation causes prices to rise, and that the time to sell is when interest rates (which rose with the inflation) have eased and buying becomes easier. This rule may be altered by special local conditions affecting land values. But as long as inflation is a recurring condition, it must be reckoned with as a force for making money in land.

FISCAL POLICY

Fiscal policy is of consequence to the economy in various ways. Beyond its effect on the economy in general, it has different impacts in different localities.

Implications of Sources of Funds. Federal tax revenues come from a multiplicity of sources (see Figure 6–5), but rely heavily on income taxes, both corporation and personal. The income tax treatment accorded various classes of investor/taxpayers influences their decisions, especially those of real estate investors.

Just as the use of investment credits spurs business investment, and the use of depletion allowances and associated drilling write-off provisions spurs oil exploration, so do depreciation and other write-off provisions affect real estate investment.

A set of rules governs the relationship between government and taxpayers. That set of rules influences investors in their decisions. From time to time the rules are changed and the flow of investment funds is altered. For example, in the tax reforms of 1969, the use of the most accelerated forms of depreciation was limited to residential properties and denied to commercial and industrial properties. The effect was to make existing residential properties, which could be depreciated at 125 percent of straight-line depreciation rates, more attractive than existing commercial and industrial improvements, which were limited to straight-line depreciation rates. The existing inventory of residential properties gained relative to commercial and industrial property. Also, the more accelerated forms of depreciation for new construction were permitted for residential properties (200 percent declining balance, and sum of the digits) but not for new nonresidential properties (150 percent declining balance). The effect of that change was to favor new residential construction, which was the intent. Another result was that the price of residential land tended to rise relative to that of other land.

From time to time new tax reforms are discussed. At about the time of this writing some authorities in Washington were talking of doing away with much of the tax benefit allowed during construction. Under current law investors may buy land, hold it, and deduct the taxes and interest they pay. The fact that the value may rise sufficiently to permit them to recover their investment does not affect their ability to deduct property taxes and interest—which are deductible in their own right—and then when they sell pay taxes on the recovery as a capital gain. They pay at a long-term capital gain rate which is generally lower than the ordinary income rate used for writing off interest and taxes.

Now, suppose an investor bought land five years ago at a fraction of

FIGURE 6–5
Federal Government Tax Receipts, 1974 (est.)
(billions of dollars)

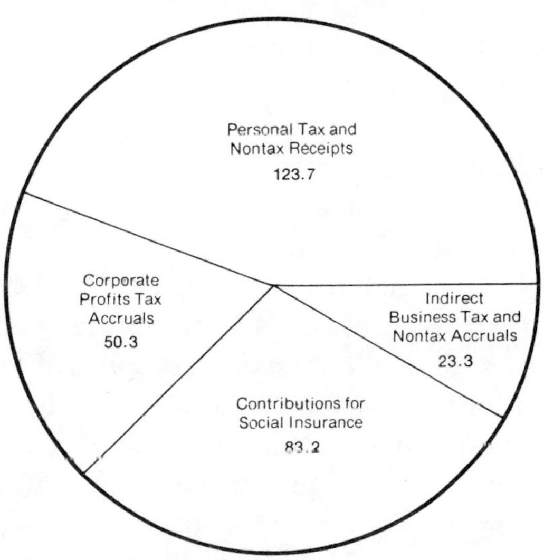

Total Receipts: 280.5

Source: U.S. Department of Commerce, *Statistical Abstract of the United States: 1974*, 95th ed. (Washington, D.C.: U.S. Government Printing Office, 1974).

today's value, and decides to build on it now. The tax basis on the land does not change. He may start development and construction on it and develop a cost basis for the improvements, which he will then be able to depreciate.

Note that, according to tax regulations, while the investor holds the land as an investment he is not required to capitalize the carrying costs when computing income taxes. When he starts building on the land, the situation does not really change. During construction he may continue to deduct the property taxes and interest for income tax purposes. Mortgage lenders, however, will capitalize these costs when calculating value being added by the land development and building construction process. This increases the value of the land and also the amount of money the developer can borrow. Lenders will not only capitalize interest and property taxes but, in all probability, a whole host of other costs. Some of those costs, especially fees, may at the same time be written off as an expense for income tax purposes. This expense procedure, with very heavy borrowing, permits substantial tax loss during construction.

The result is that the equity required for new investors is in part pretax dollars or "soft money" as opposed to after-tax dollars. Naturally, if one already owns the land and is building, the same advantages occur. Thus the construction process may not only require no additional equity money but may even put tax dollars in the investor's pocket.

Thus far talk of changing the tax rules has remained only talk. But even if investment rules for the construction process are changed, land investors will probably still be able to deduct interest and property taxes while holding for appreciation.

Rising income tax rates together with inflation, which covertly increases income tax rates, keep pushing investors toward tax shelter. The push gets stronger as the investor earns more income. From time to time loopholes are discovered by the tax authorities and plugged, but some deductions seem pretty secure. And the capital gains tax has to be paid only after the sale.

With that in mind, investors can not only build on their land and hold for income, they can trade and transfer the tax basis from old to new investments. Any of these transactions requires good tax counsel. But it should be obvious that land investment is well protected from so-called tax reform.

The state and local levels present tax situations analogous to those of the federal level. While most of the revenue for local government comes from property taxes which are levied according to value, increasingly more funds are drawn from state and federal sources—both of which rely heavily on income taxes. In some cases the local government also has an income tax. Rising property tax rates, of course, are adverse for investors unless the money is being spent to make their land more valuable. The impact of local property taxes is softened by state and local income taxes, which are deductible expenses.

But tax reforms will come and go.

On balance, long-term investments in land fare comparatively well.

Implications of Spending Patterns. The implications of government spending patterns are of a different breed than those of sources of funds. In spending, the impact depends upon which segments of the economy are involved and which communities are affected. In those directly affected, the increased employment requires more construction and more land.

Thus spending on space exploration will create a boom in the engineering segment of the economy and in communities where the production takes place. National defense spending has a similar impact, depending upon which weapons are produced and where the production facilities are located.

Up until the early 60s the Los Angeles metropolitan area did well in getting government contracts. But then California began to fall behind in the relative amount of government spending, while New England forged ahead. Los Angeles lost relative to the San Francisco Bay area. This lagging behind, together with a variety of other problems such as the change from easy money in the early 60s to tight money in the late 60s and environmental changes, put Los Angeles construction into a tailspin. Those land speculators who had the wrong kind of land in the wrong location were badly hurt.

Government spending has additional effects when it becomes quite specific as to type of facilities. For example, the Federal Housing Administration's FHA 235 and FHA 236 programs spent money on housing for low- and moderate-income families through a subsidy route. The impact of that spending was to spur new construction. That new construction required more land, and generally at low-priced locations.

The termination of these programs also affects the communities concerned, and so does the initiation of housing allowance experiments in their place. The precise impact varies with the nature of each program and city, but a look at several instances of federal spending will suggest the magnitude of the effects.

In Washington, D.C., the office space market is at times absolutely wild (see Figure 6–6). While numerous forces draw land into office building construction in Washington, the biggest is federal spending, especially for employment. The impact of federal spending varies by location in the Washing-

FIGURE 6–6
Total Gross Floor Areas above Grade of New Privately Owned Office Buildings, Washington, D.C.
(in thousands of square feet)

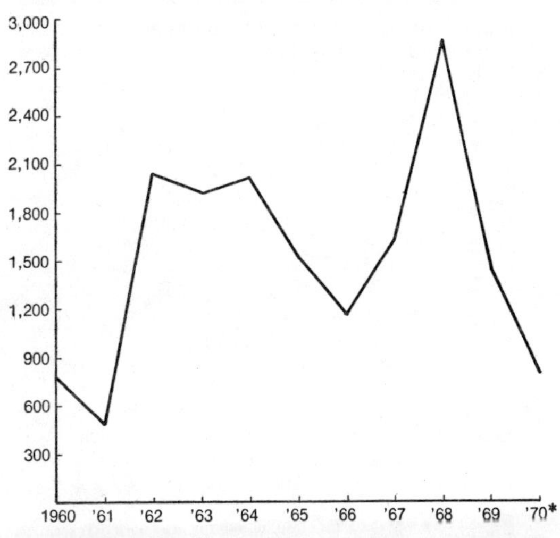

* Estimate.
Source: National Capital Planning Commission, Washington, D.C., April 1971. GPO Document no. 911.640, p. 1.

ton area. Figure 6–7 shows the variation in housing starts in Washington and three other metropolitan areas in the period of the 60s.

Local Fiscal Policy. State and local spending can generate similar effects through their influence on employment, as shown in Figure 6–8. Note that

FIGURE 6–7
Total Housing Starts
(in thousands)

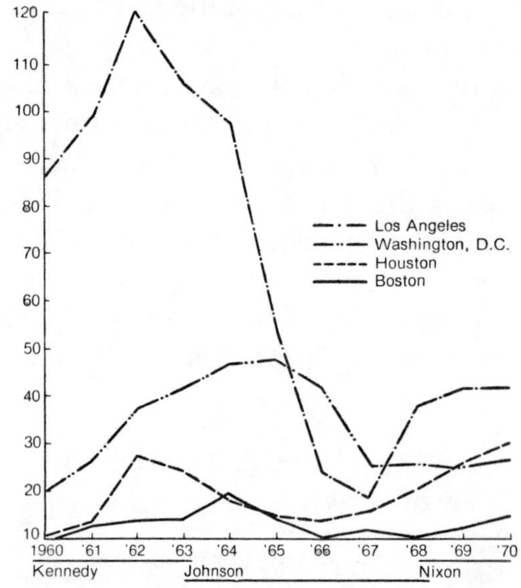

Source: Housing start data from National Association of Home Builders of the United States, *Economic News Notes,* October 1972.

federal employment is a big source of demand for space, and that state and local government are increasingly important.

Spending on facilities is also important because it influences the location of development. This is particularly true of highway construction and the building of sewerage treatment plant and pipelines. National trends have recently made these facilities more difficult to come by, resulting in developability problems.

In general, whether the spending is federal, state, or local, taking a look at the trends makes sense. If a shift is in the wind or if the demand for facilities seems to be outstripping the supply, then a problem in economic environment may be brewing.

Shifts in the spending of governments as they affect land development are best considered in their impact on local development. The next chapter examines the way national trends influence local development. It also includes a discussion of local economic and other conditions affecting community growth and development.

FIGURE 6–8
Employment Statistics—Four Metropolitan Areas
(in thousands)

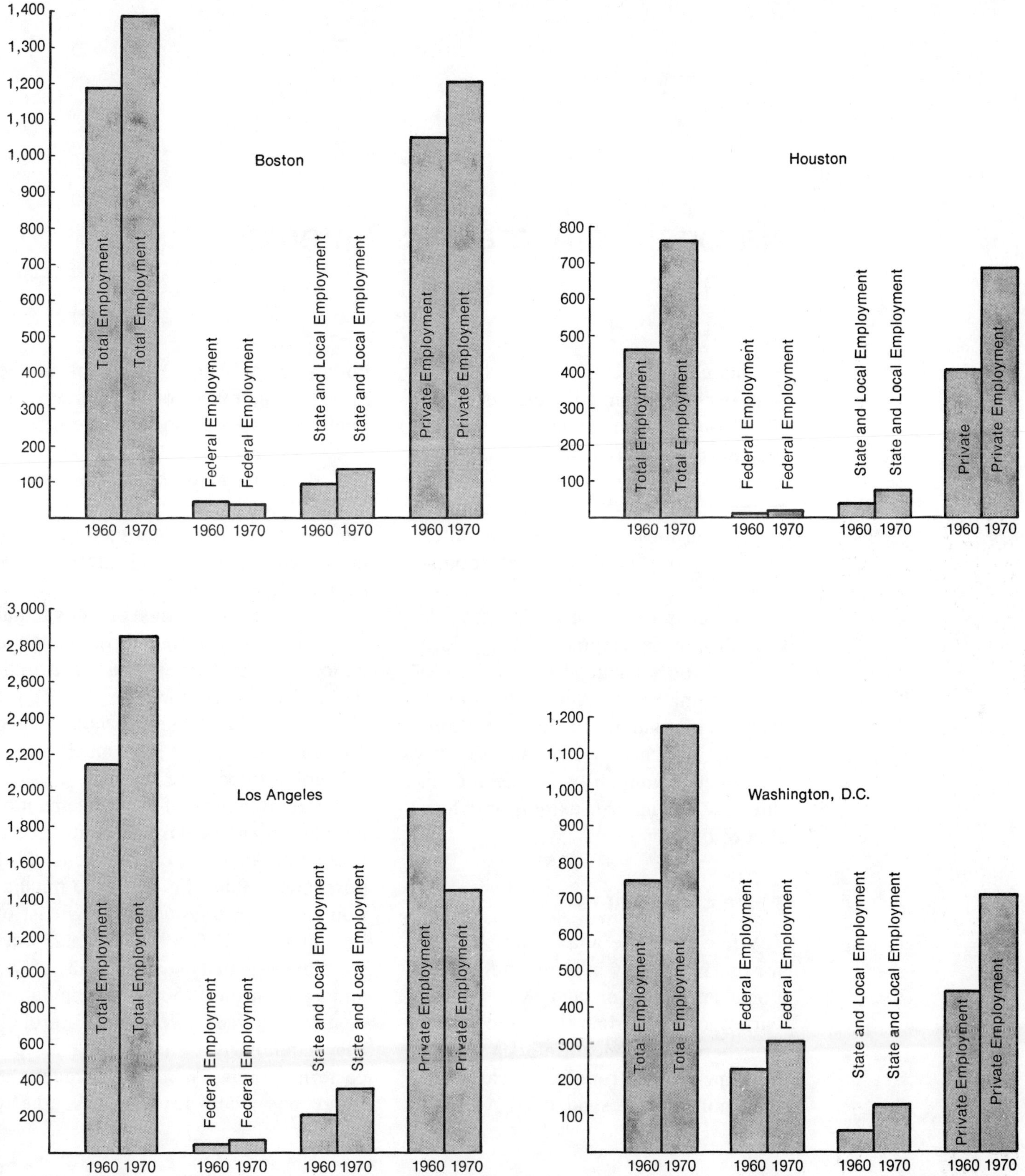

Sources: U.S. Bureau of Labor Statistics; Massachusetts State Employment Service; and Texas Employment Commission.

7

National Demographic Patterns

This chapter deals with the national patterns of economic development and population movement as they indicate locations of increasing demand and hence rising values. The investor needs to be familiar with these trends in population location as background for evaluating any particular metropolitan area.

This chapter also explains how the growth and development of any local area will be influenced by the base of its economic activity, as well as by its location in relation to national patterns. Further, the chapter examines the way in which community leadership influences the nature, extent, and location of development.

POPULATION SHIFTS

While there are ample opportunities for making money in farm land, recreational land, and in land devoted to a variety of new urban uses, the discussion here will concentrate on the development of metropolitan areas across the country. We shall begin with the country as a whole, then look at the areal configuration of the states, and finally turn to metropolitan areas.

The Country as a Whole. The general distribution of population in the United States is best described by a dot map (Figure 7–1). As can be seen, heavy concentrations of the dots appear in several metropolitan areas, but numerous communities of substantial size are also scattered throughout the nation. The best investment opportunities are not necessarily in the biggest cities. The crucial factor is not how big a community is, but how much bigger it is going to become.

To get a picture of the movement of population in the United States, consider the location of the centers of population. Back in 1790, the population center of the country was east of Washington, D.C. Movements west were made with a big surge in the 1870s and again in the 1950s. The population center moved westward through Maryland, Ohio, and Indiana into eastern Illinois. In recent decades the trend has been toward a southerly

FIGURE 7–1
Population Distribution: 1970

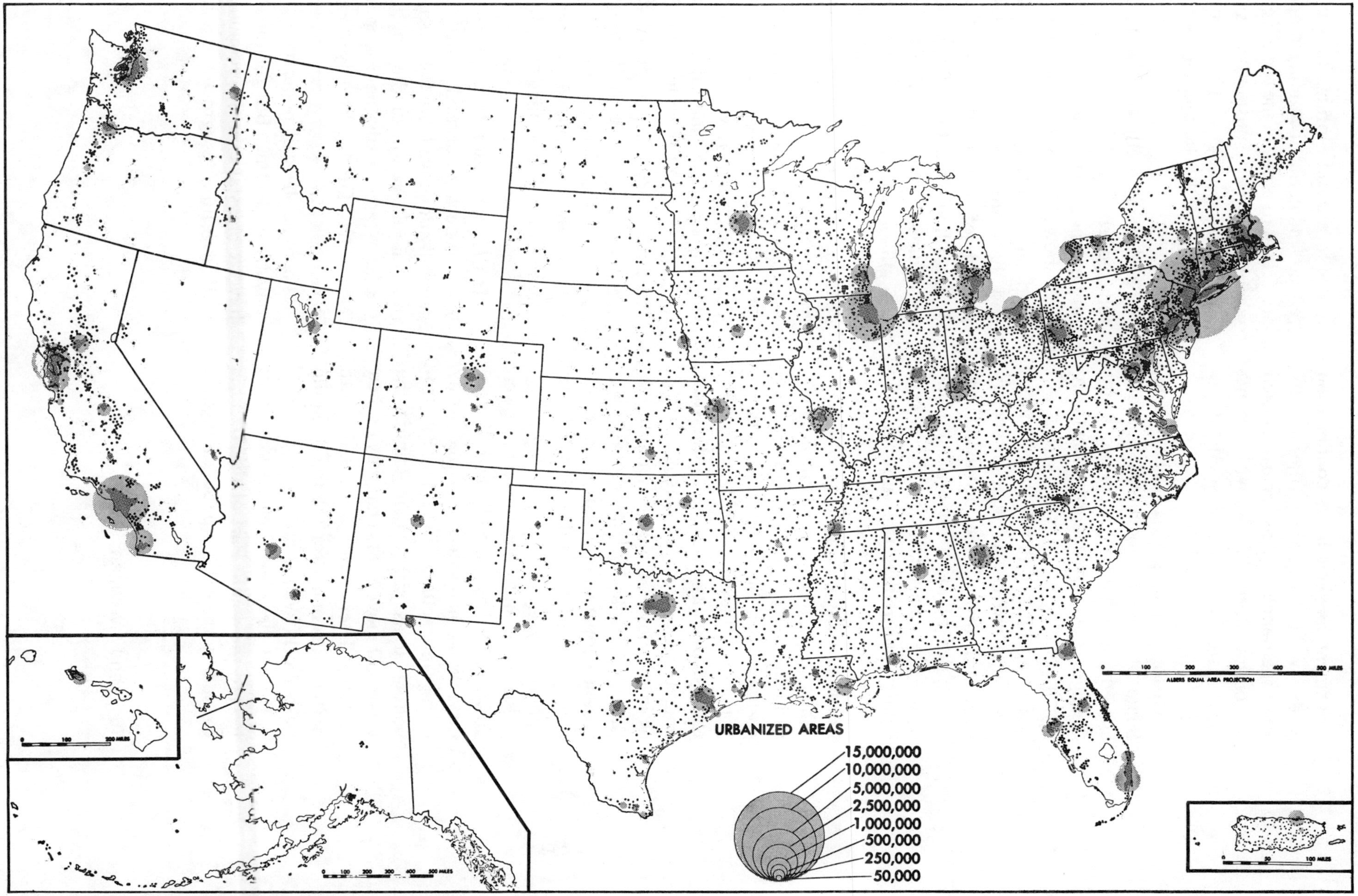

One dot equals 10,000 persons outside urbanized areas.
Source U.S. Bureau of the Census, U.S. Census of Population 1970, *Number of Inhabitants,* Final Report, United States Summary (Washington, D.C.: U.S. Government Printing Office, 1971).

movement as well as a continuation of the westward boom of the 50s. By 1970 the population center had shifted to southwestern Illinois, with the big growth to the west and south of the center.

History explains what has happened. Some of what has occurred was discussed in Chapter 5, "Forces for Change." A few more items are worthy of note.

The opening of the West a hundred years ago moved an agrarian society westward toward the economic opportunities of the 19th century. One of the great movers of people is economic opportunity. It is not the only mover by any means, and it requires freedom in order to get a natural flow. When that freedom is impaired by national policy, the flow toward opportunity can be significantly abated. Sometimes barbed wire and machine guns stop it, as with the Berlin Wall. Sometimes a head tax ransom is used, as in the Soviet Union emigration tax. But, if one looks for the forces that will attract people to opportunity, one will find growth at the location of that opportunity.

But the movement west slowed down in the last part of the 19th century. What happened was that many immigrants settled in the major metropolitan areas rather than joining the westward movement. That they or their children later went west and south partially accounts for the trends in the post–World War II era.

Recent decades show a movement toward the south. Part of this trend is caused by the elderly population going to California and Florida. But part of it reflects industrial location: companies are drawn to areas of inexpensive labor where there is a substantially smaller potential for strikes. The picture is made clearer by looking at particular areas.

The States. Getting a picture of the total population of each state is a useful beginning. The bar graph in Figure 7–2 shows that California and New York are in the 18–20 million range, and have respectively 9.8 and 9.0 percent of the total. Pennsylvania, Texas, Illinois, and Ohio cluster around 11 million. There are 22 states in the 2–5 million range. Thus, while population is somewhat substantially concentrated, opportunities for growth are spread fairly wide.

Figure 7–3 shows the diverse growth rates of different geographic locations. The states near New York show substantial percentage increases, although they have smaller population bases. The Appalachian area, especially West Virginia, lost population in the 1960s, as it had in the 1950s (see Figure 7–4). Whether this trend may be reversed by the energy crisis is uncertain, but not to be dismissed out of hand.

In the south, Florida has grown most. The eastern seaboard states have generally done well. On the other hand, the central section of the continental United States, with the exception of Texas, has fared relatively poorly in development.

To some, lack of population growth may be a blessing. But for those who have a big stake in the economy—as land investors do—growth is vital be-

FIGURE 7–2
States Ranked by Total Population: 1970

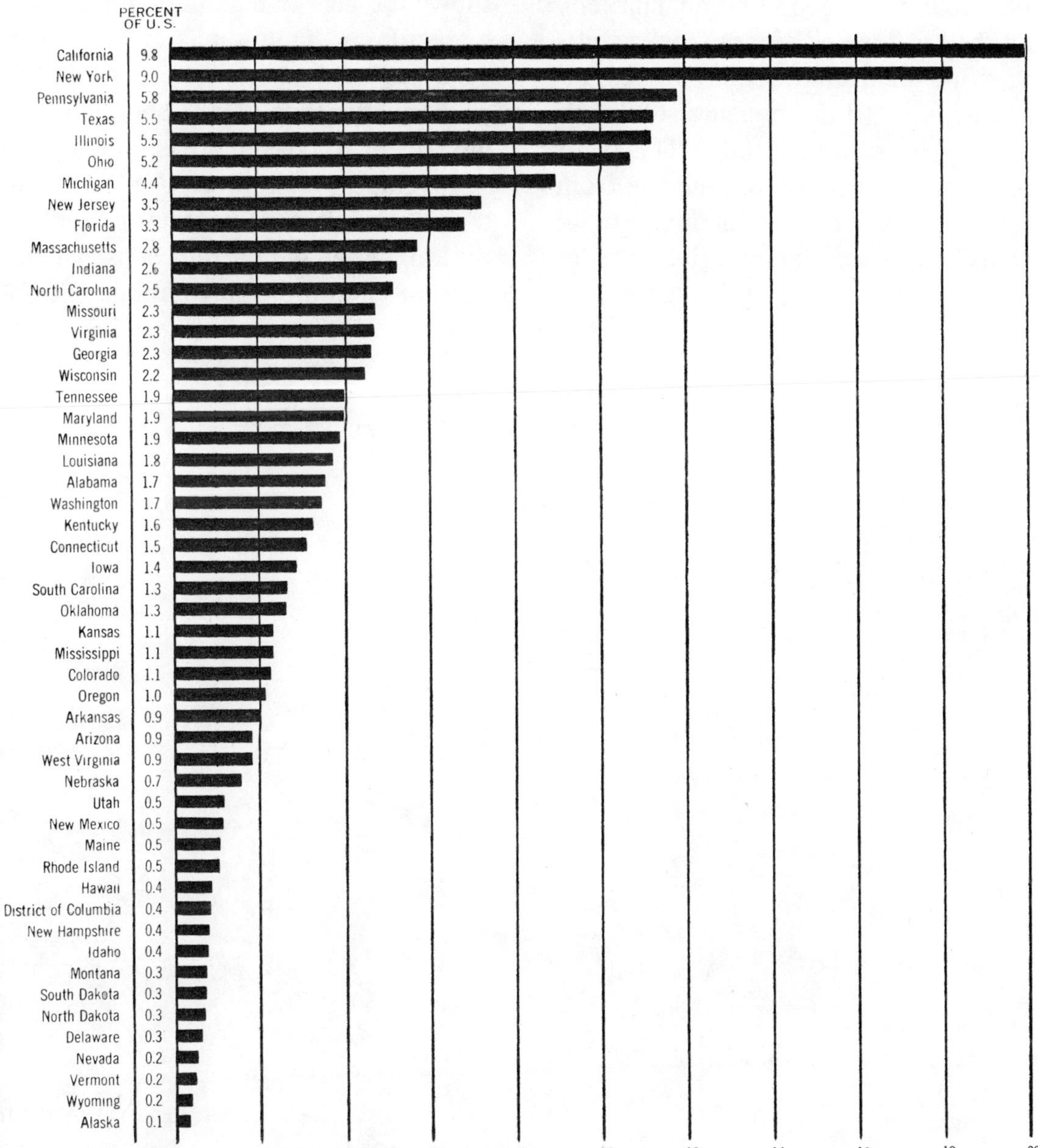

Source: U.S. Department of Commerce, Bureau of the Census, U.S. Census of Population, 1970, *Number of Inhabitants, Final Report, United States Summary* (Washington, D.C.: U.S. Government Printing Office, 1971).

cause prosperity is built on growth. However, the growth may take various forms.

In some industries, growth in income, even without population increases, will mean prosperity. To some degree this is true for real estate in the upgrading and second-home markets. But the big demand comes from a shifting population that requires substantial additions to the housing stock and other types of real estate. This shift calls for a conversion of land use from rural to urban and/or an increase in intensity of use. Comparative rates of urbanization are shown in figure 7–5, which gives percentages of change in urban population by states. Figure 7–6 shows the rate of change in rural population by states.

The Counties. The population growth is shown in more detail on a county-by-county basis. Figure 7–7 shows the year of maximum population by counties. One can almost see an emptying out of the center of the country over time. Also note the heavy movement to coastal areas.

Investors looking at the historical trend can get a contemporary picture by looking at the current density (Figure 7–8) and the change in population.

FIGURE 7–3
Percent of Change in Total Population by States: 1960 to 1970

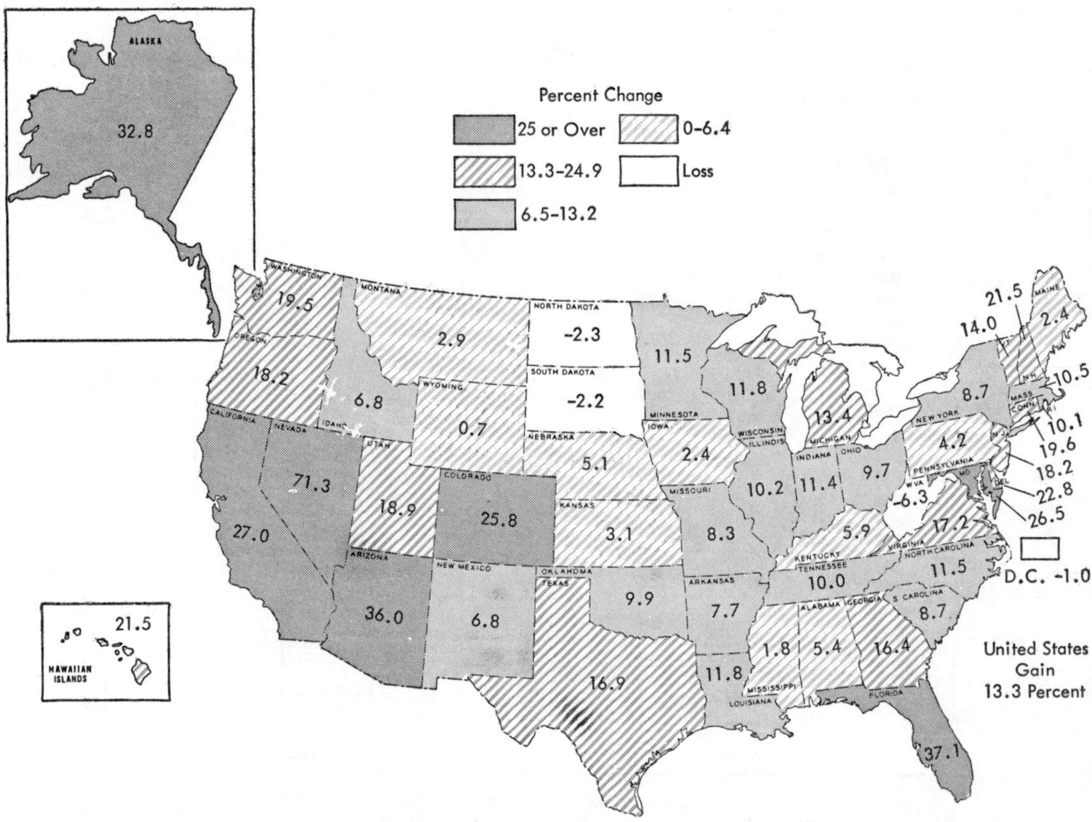

Source: U.S. Department of Commerce, Bureau of the Census, U.S. Census of Population, 1970. *Number of Inhabitants*, Final Report, United States Summary (Washington, D.C.: U.S. Government Printing Office, 1971).

These provide one with a feel for where the population has been moving. As to where it will be moving in the future, the best perspective is offered by examining metropolitan areas that are agglomerations of counties (based on Bureau of the Census tabulations and Office of Management and Budget definitions).

Metropolitan Areas. A metropolitan area, as defined by the Census Bureau, is a group of contiguous counties (or in some cases other jurisdictions) that have a city or cities of predetermined minimal size as a focal point about which a socially and economically integrated area has developed. The idea is that such an area, though having a number of different governments, really forms a socio-economic entity, ordinarily thought of as a city and its suburbs.

Since counties as wholes are included in the Census Bureau's standard metropolitan statistical area (SMSA) (of which the U.S. had 243 in 1970), and not all parts of a county are necessarily urbanized, the areas do not exactly correspond to the physical development. The urbanized area, as depicted in Figure 7–1, presents a better physical description. But for the

FIGURE 7–4
Percent of Change in Total Population by States: 1950 to 1960

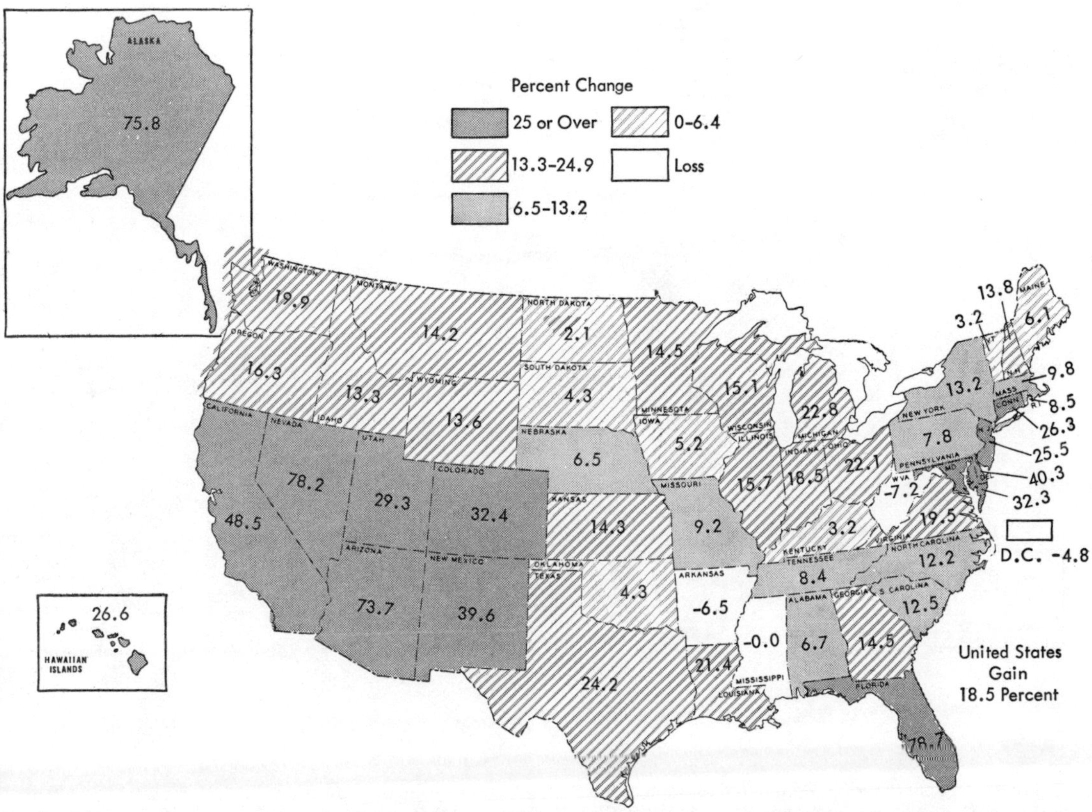

Source: U.S. Department of Commerce, Bureau of the Census, U.S. Census of Population, 1970, *Number of Inhabitants*, Final Report, United States Summary (Washington, D.C.: U.S. Government Printing Office, 1971).

purpose of studying urban growth the SMSA is useful.

The SMSAs are shown in Figure 7–9 and the urbanized areas in Figure 7–10. Obviously a lot of land within the political jurisdiction of the SMSAs is not urbanized. But much of that land, the reader will note, is a candidate for urbanization. Additionally, contiguous counties are drawn into the SMSA as they meet the definition standard. For example, during the 1960s the counties listed in Table 7–1 were added to the SMSA category.

The growth of a community is determined by its economic base—that is, the sources of its income. This fact is discussed in the next section of the chapter. By way of perspective, Figure 7–11 shows the percentage of population in each state living in standard metropolitan statistical areas. That percentage provides background for the specifics of an SMSA considered for investment.

Table 7–2 lists the 243 SMSAs together with their 1960 and 1970 populations and the percentage in-

FIGURE 7–5
Percent of Change in Urban Population by States: 1960 to 1970

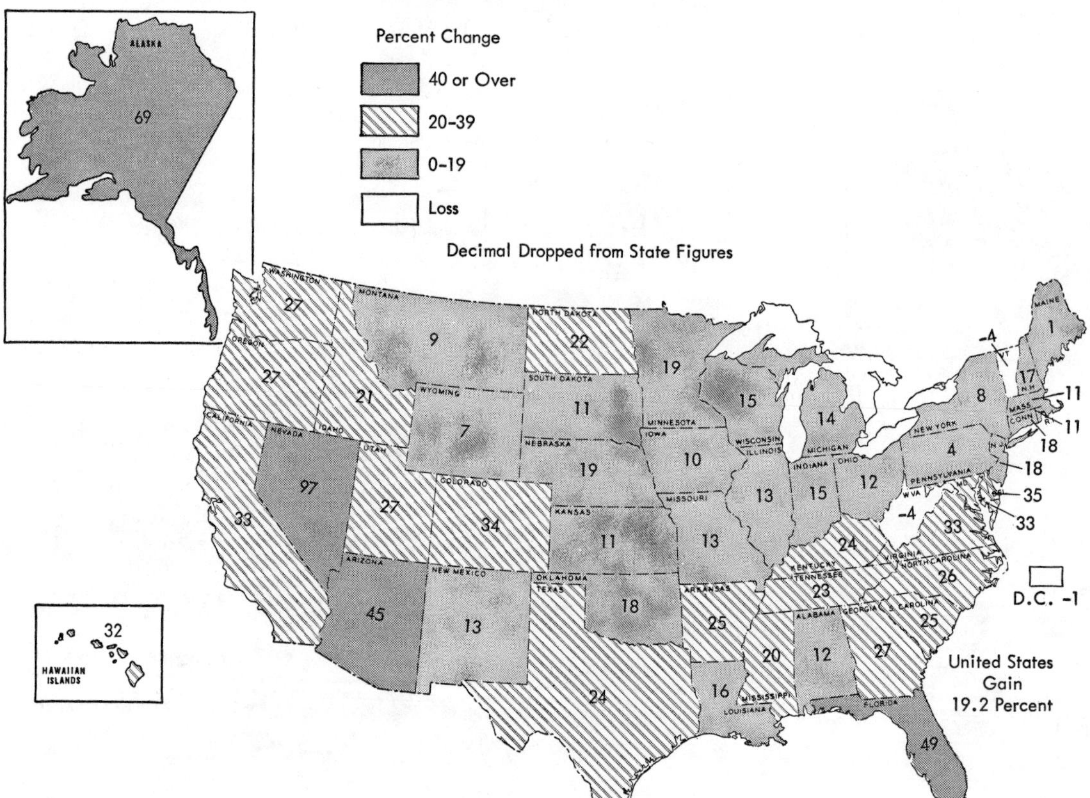

Source: U.S. Department of Commerce, Bureau of the Census, U.S. Census of Population, 1970. *Number of Inhabitants*, Final Report, United States Summary (Washington, D.C.: U.S. Government Printing Office, 1971).

creases or decreases. To get a view of the future, we have added some projections of population for 1980, made by the National Planning Association.

The reader should bear in mind that figures for past growth and projections for the future merely indicate the existence of opportunities. They do not show the structural aspects of growth or the components of it, both of which are discussed in later chapters. Neither do such figures explain the underlying forces which cause a community to grow, which is the next subject at hand.

LOCAL VITALITY

The traditional method of evaluating local vitality is to begin with the economic base. If a strong foundation for economic growth exists, then the community will grow and prosper—so the argument goes.

But the vitality of the community also depends on the ability of its political leadership to provide an environment conducive to economic prosperity. Political actions that needlessly frustrate economic development will hinder the community's growth. On

FIGURE 7–6
Percent of Change in Rural Population by States: 1960 to 1970

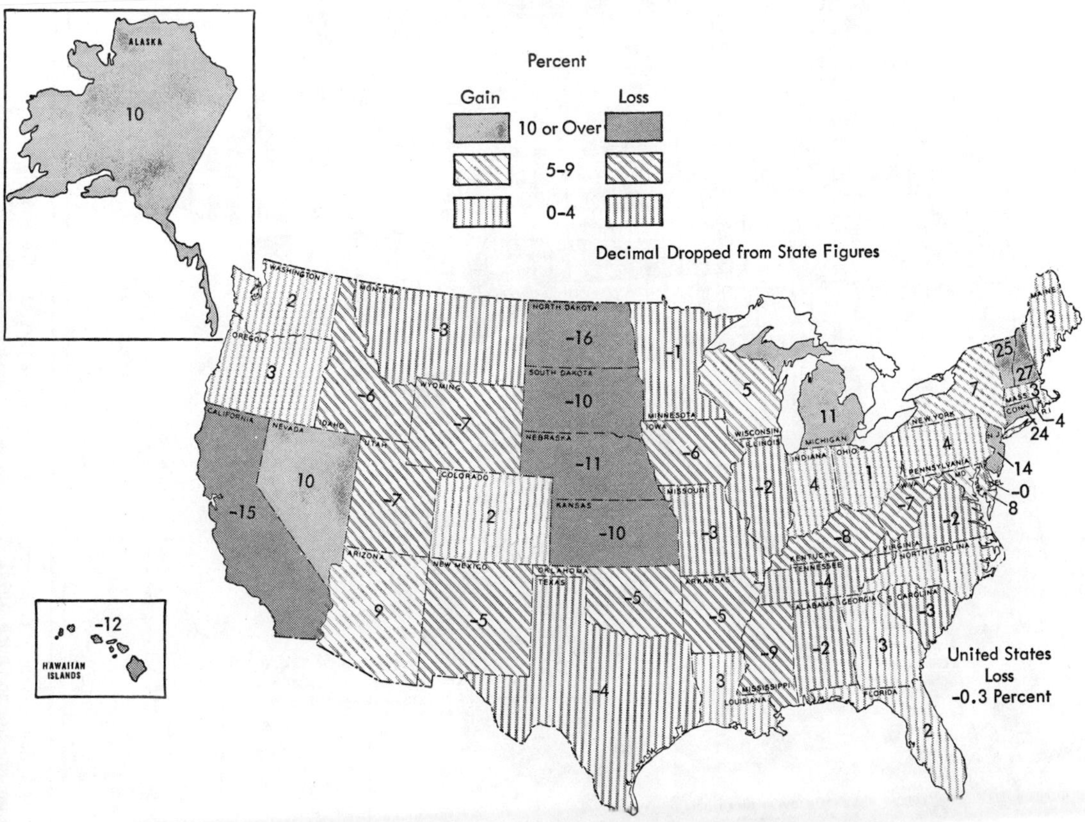

Source: U.S. Department of Commerce, Bureau of the Census, U.S. Census of Population, 1970, *Number of Inhabitants, Final Report, United States Summary* (Washington, D.C.: U.S. Government Printing Office, 1971).

FIGURE 7–7
Year of Maximum Population by Counties of the United States

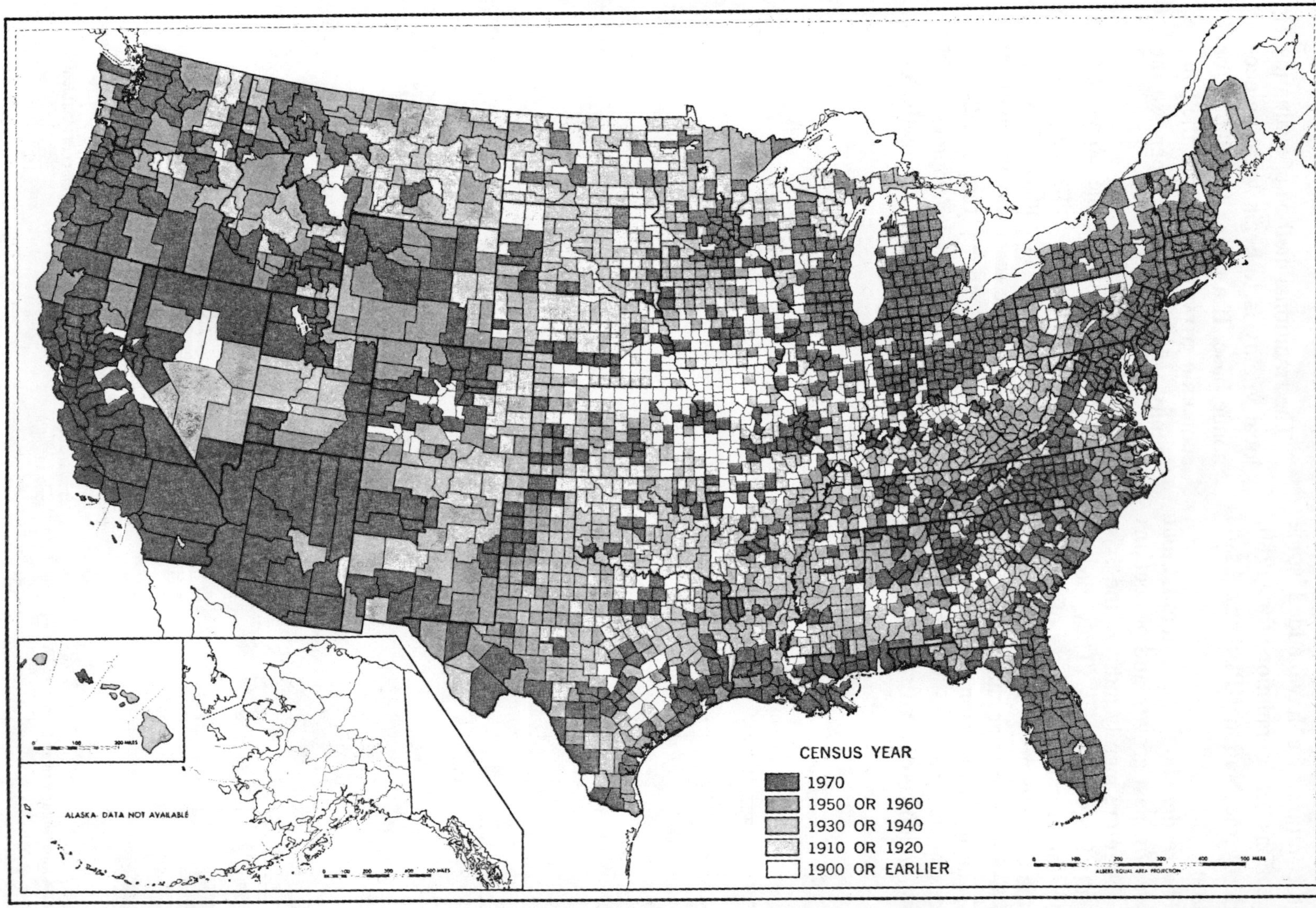

Source: U.S. Department of Commerce, Bureau of the Census, U.S. Census of Population, 1970, *Number of Inhabitants,* Final Report, United States Summary (Washington, D.C.: U.S. Government Printing Office, 1971).

FIGURE 7–8
Population Density by Counties: 1970

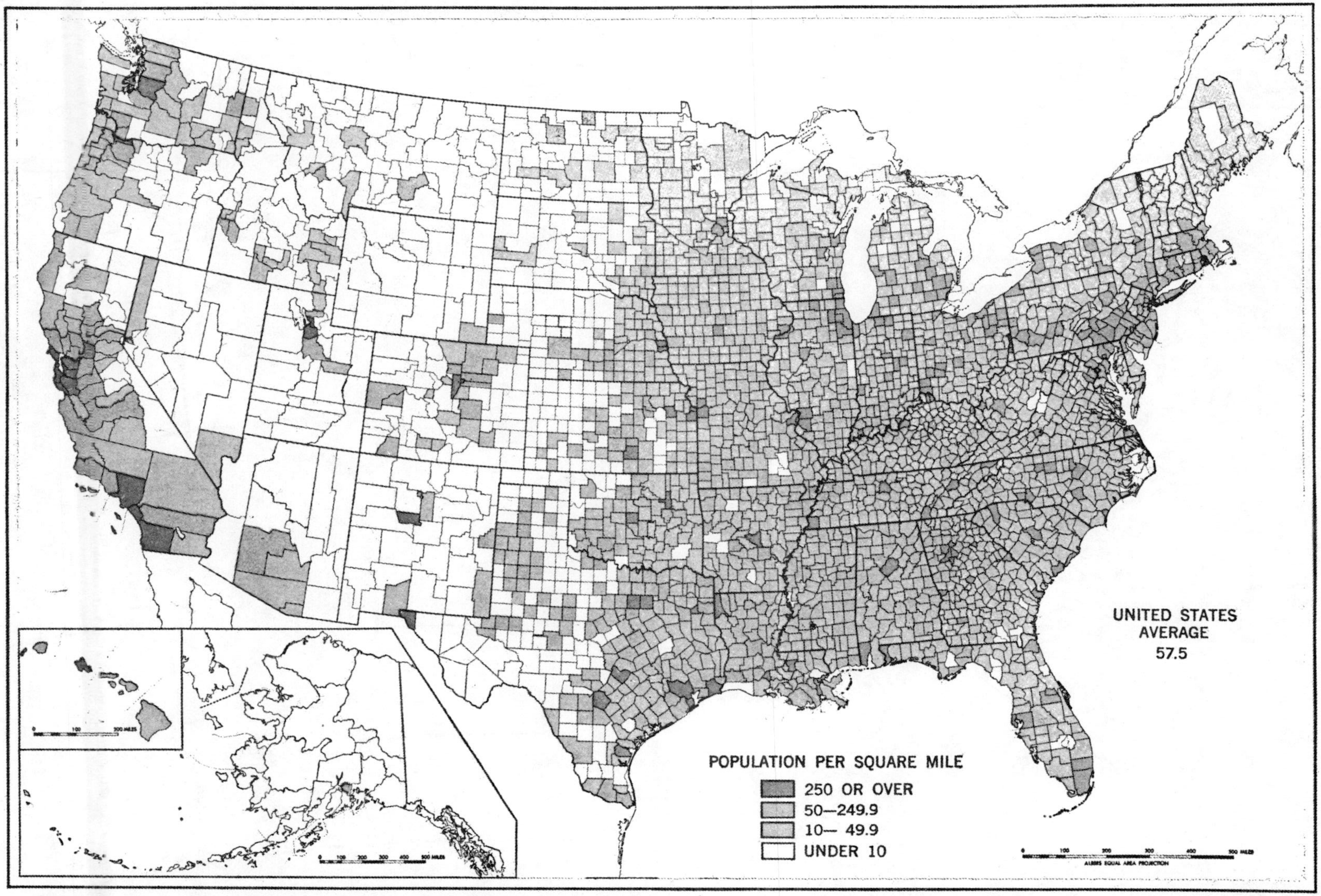

Source: U.S. Department of Commerce, Bureau of the Census, U.S. Census of Population, 1970, *Number of Inhabitants,* Final Report, United States Summary (Washington, D.C.: U.S. Government Printing Office, 1971).

FIGURE 7–9
Standard Metropolitan Statistical Areas of the United States and Puerto Rico: 1970

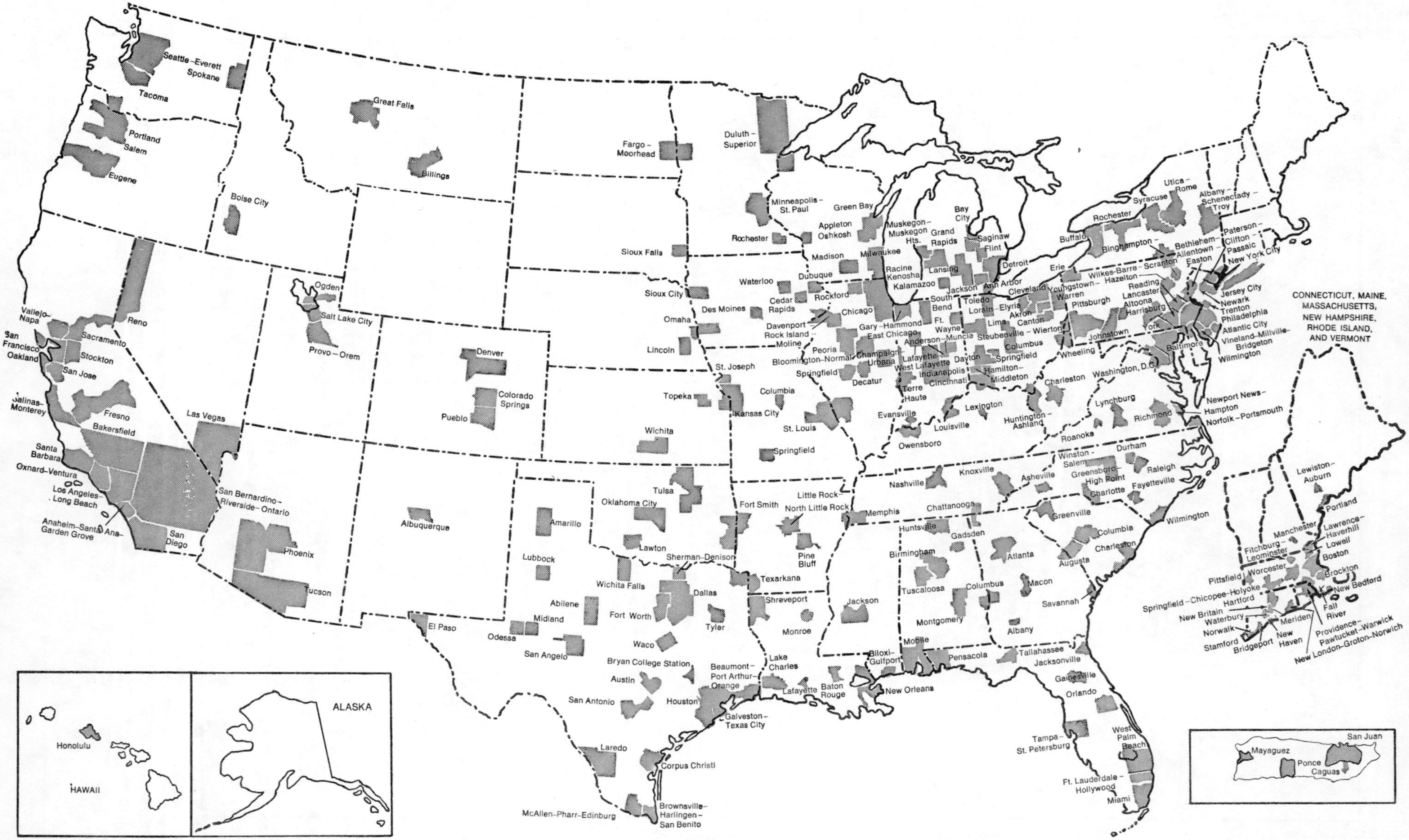

Source: U.S. Department of Commerce, Bureau of the Census, U.S. Census of Population, 1970, *Number of Inhabitants,* Final Report, United States Summary (Washington, D.C.: U.S. Government Printing Office, 1971).

FIGURE 7–10
Urbanized Areas: 1970

Source: U.S. Department of Commerce, Bureau of the Census, U.S. Census of Population, 1970, *Number of Inhabitants*, Final Report, United States Summary (Washington, D.C.: U.S. Government Printing Office, 1971).

the other hand, senseless accommodation to anything industry wants could be so destructive to other aspects of the environment that nobody would want to live there.

Vitality comes from the people and how they organize themselves. They organize themselves to achieve their economic goals, and also to achieve political goals. If their organization is not effective, little can be expected from the community. Effective community organization involves everything from safety in the streets to the provision of cultural services, and from a sense of community to the absence of such social disorder as riots.

The discussion that follows bears mainly on the economic requirement for local vitality, but this is seen in its relationship to political and social factors.

Economic Dimension. The local communities most likely to grow and prosper, and hence to have increasing land values, are those where employment opportunities are increasing. Communities, or really local economies, with declining employment opportunities will have falling real estate values and poor land investments.

A local economy is a specialized

FIGURE 7–11
Percent of Population in Standard Metropolitan Statistical Areas by States: 1970

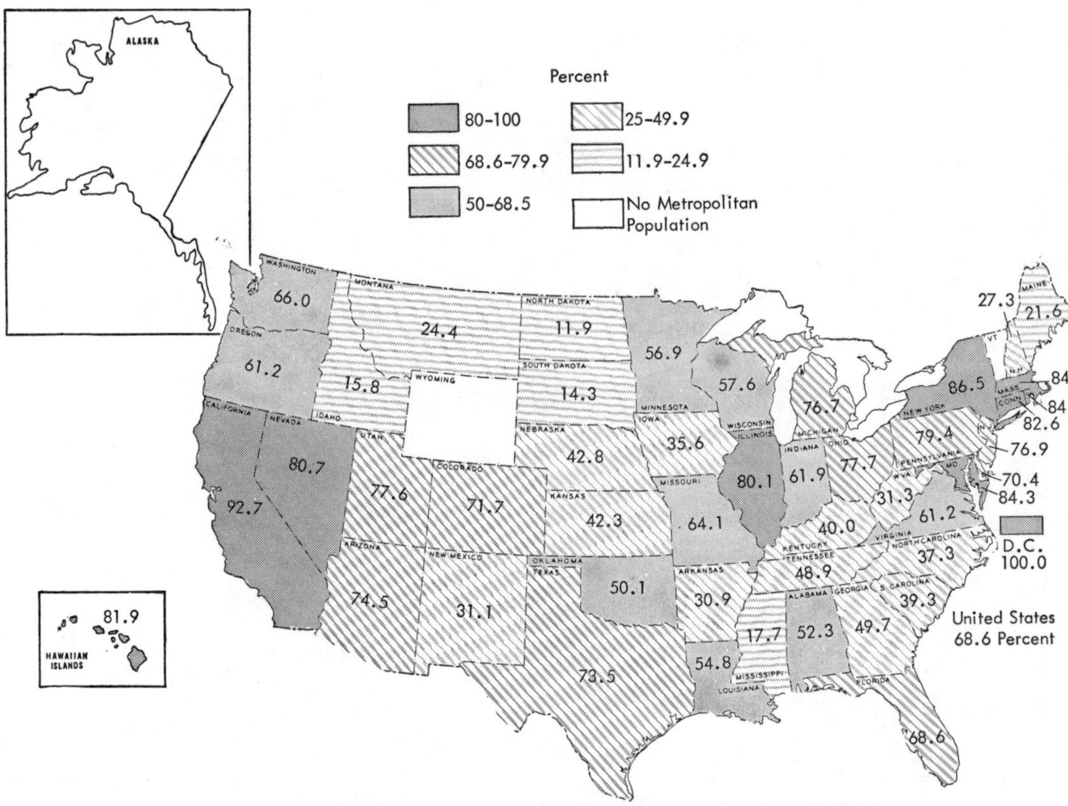

Source: U.S. Department of Commerce, Bureau of the Census, U.S. Census of Population, 1970, *Number of Inhabitants*, Final Report, United States Summary (Washington, D.C.: U.S. Government Printing Office, 1971).

TABLE 7–1
Counties Added to Existing SMSAs during the 1960s

SMSA	*County*	*Date*
Akron, Ohio	Portage	Oct. 1963
Baltimore, Md	Harford	March 1967
Binghamton, N.Y.–Pa.	Tioga, N.Y.	Oct. 1963
	Susquehanna, Pa.	Oct. 1963
Birmingham, Ala.	Shelby	March 1967
	Walker	March 1967
Charleston, S.C.	Berkeley	Oct. 1963
Charlotte, N.C.	Union	Oct. 1963
Cincinnati, Ohio-Ky.–Ind.	Clermont, Ohio	Oct. 1963
	Warren, Ohio	Oct. 1963
	Boone, Ky.	Oct. 1963
	Dearborn, Ind.	Oct. 1963
Cleveland, Ohio	Geauga	Oct. 1963
	Medina	Oct. 1963
Columbus, Ohio	Delaware	Oct. 1963
	Pickaway	Oct. 1963
Corpus Christi, Tex.	San Patricio	July 1965
Dallax, Tex.	Kaufman	March 1967
	Rockwall	April 1967
Davenport-Rock Island–Moline, Iowa-Ill.	Henry, Ill.	Oct. 1963
Dayton, Ohio	Preble	Oct. 1963
Durham, N.C.	Orange	March 1967
Evansville, Ind.–Ky.	Warrick	Oct. 1963
Flint, Mich.	Lapeer	Oct. 1963
Fort Smith, Ark.–Okla.	Crawford, Ark.	Oct. 1963
	Le Flore, Okla.	Oct. 1963
	Sequoyah, Okla.	Oct. 1963
Grand Rapids, Mich.	Ottawa, Mich.	Oct. 1963
Greenville, S.C.	Pickens	Oct. 1963
Greensboro-Winston-Salem-	Randolph	March 1967
High Point, N.C.	Vadkin	March 1967
Harrisburg, Pa.	Perry	Oct. 1963
Houston, Tex.	Brazoria	March 1965
	Fort Bend	March 1965
	Liberty	March 1965
	Montgomery	March 1965
Indianapolis, Ind.	Hamilton	Oct. 1963
	Hancock	Oct. 1963
	Hendricks	Oct. 1963
	Johnson	Oct. 1963
	Morgan	Oct. 1963
	Shelby	Oct. 1963
	Boone	March 1967
Jackson, Miss.	Rankin	Oct. 1963
Kansas City, Mo.-Kans.	Cass	Oct. 1963
	Platte	Oct. 1963
Lima, Ohio	Putnam	March 1967
	Van Wert	March 1967
Little Rock-North Little Rock, Ark.	Saline	March 1967
Memphis, Tenn.-Ark.	Crittenden	Oct. 1963
Milwaukee, Wis.	Ozaukee	Oct. 1963
	Washington	March 1967
Mobile, Ala.	Baldwin	Oct. 1963
Montgomery, Ala.	Elmore	Oct. 1963
Nashville, Tenn.	Sumner	Oct. 1963
	Wilson	Oct. 1963
New Orleans, La.	St. Tammany Parish	Oct. 1963
Oklahoma City, Okla.	Canadian	Aug. 1960
Peoria, Ill.	Woodford	Oct. 1963
Richmond, Va.	Hanover	Oct. 1963

TABLE 7–1 (*Continued*)

SMSA	*County*	*Date*
Rochester, N.Y.	Livingston	Oct. 1963
	Orleans	Oct. 1963
	Wayne	Oct. 1963
Rockford, Ill.	Boone	Oct. 1963
Sacramento, Calif.	Placer	Oct. 1963
	Volo	Oct. 1963
St. Louis, Mo.-Ill.	Franklin	Oct. 1963
Salt Lake City, Utah	Davis	Oct. 1963
San Antonio, Tex.	Guadalupe	Oct. 1963
Sioux City, Iowa-Nebr.	Dakota, Neb.	Oct. 1963
South Bend, Ind.	Marshall	Oct. 1963
Terre Haute, Ind.	Clay	Oct. 1963
	Sullivan	Oct. 1963
	Vermillion	Oct. 1963
Toledo, Ohio-Mich.	Wood, Ohio	Oct. 1963
	Monroe, Mich.	Oct. 1963
Tulsa, Okla.	Osage	Aug. 1960
Washington, D.C.-Md.-Va.	Loudon	March 1967
	Prince William	March 1967
Wichita, Kans.	Butler	Oct. 1963
Wichita Falls, Tex.	Archer	Aug. 1960
Wilmington, Del.-N.J.-Md.	Cecil	Oct. 1963
York, Pa.	Adams	Oct. 1963

Source: Data to 1967 from Office of Statistical Standards, Executive Office of the President, Bureau of the Budget, *Standard Metropolitan Statistical Areas 1967,* Washington, D.C., GPO 1967, 0–257,095. Data from 1967 to 1970 from Statistical Policy Division, Executive Office of the President, Office of Management and the Budget, Data Sheets.

case of a community. It is a set of economic activities linked and spatially related in an urban agglomeration. These activities include the production of goods and services that are consumed in the community or exported from it. Production for consumption and export is measured by the number of people engaged in production as well as by the value of the goods and services produced. The linkage, or relationships, between places of work and places of residence are important in determining the patterns of land use that develop.

That linkage between place of work and place of residence arises from the simple fact that most people have to have jobs, or live with someone who has a job, in order to obtain food, clothing, and shelter. The location of that job provides a stringent limitation on the location of the family's residence. The extent of the limitation is the commuting distance.

Desirable, acceptable, or even tolerable commuting distance changes with the times. Not only does technology permit the distance some people commute to change from that covered by a short walk or ride to that covered by a short flight, but attitudes also change and longer journeys are accepted as routine. Some people commute to work by plane, and many commute between different economies (e.g., Los Angeles–San Diego, Philadelphia–New York). However, most commuting is within one metropolitan area, that is, within a local economy. Ex-

TABLE 7–2
SMSA: 1960 and 1970 Population and Changes

Area	Census Population		Projected Population	Percentage Change	
	1960	1970	1980	1960–1970	1970–1980
Abilene, TX	120,377	113,959	127,500	−5.3	11.8
Akron, OH	605,367	679,239	784,000	12.2	15.4
Albany, GA	75,680	89,639	109,400	18.4	22.0
Albany-Schenectady-Troy, NY	657,503	722,094	827,800	9.8	14.6
Albuquerque, NM	262,199	315,774	415,000	20.4	31.4
Allentown-Bethlehem-Easton, PA-NJ	492,168	543,809	613,300	10.5	12.8
Altoona, PA	137,270	135,358	144,000	−1.4	6.4
Amarillo, TX	149,493	144,396	172,000	−3.4	19.1
Anaheim-Santa Ana-Garden Grove, CA	703,925	1,420,676	1,930,900	101.8	36.0
Anderson, IN	125,819	138,522	163,200	10.1	17.8
Ann Arbor, MI	172,440	234,103	284,300	35.8	21.4
Appleton-Oshkosh, WI	231,990	276,948	NA	19.4	NA
Asheville, NC	130,074	145,056	159,800	11.5	10.2
Atlanta, GA	1,017,188	1,390,247	1,789,700	36.7	28.8
Atlantic City, NJ	160,880	175,043	194,700	8.8	11.2
Augusta, GA-SC	216,639	253,460	312,100	17.0	23.1
Austin, TX	212,136	295,516	388,600	39.3	31.5
Bakersfield, CA	291,984	329,271	375,900	12.8	14.2
Baltimore, MD	1,803,745	2,071,016	2,348,100	14.8	13.4
Baton Rouge, LA	230,058	285,167	373,000	24.0	30.8
Bay City, MI	107,042	117,339	130,500	9.6	11.2
Beaumont-Port Arthur-Orange, TX	306,016	317,572	337,700	3.8	6.4
Billings, MT	79,016	87,367	103,500	10.6	18.5
Biloxi-Gulfport, MS	119,489	134,582	158,000	12.6	17.4
Binghamton, NY-PA	283,600	302,672	342,400	6.7	13.1
Birmingham, AL	721,207	739,274	847,100	2.5	14.6
Bloomington-Normal, IL	83,877	104,389	131,000	24.5	25.5
Boise City, ID	93,460	112,230	133,500	20.1	19.0
Boston, MA	2,595,481	2,753,700	2,986,200	6.1	8.5
Bridgeport, CT	337,983	389,153	471,000	15.1	21.0
Bristol, CT	54,480	65,808	NA	20.8	NA
Brockton, MA	149,458	189,820	214,200	27.0	12.8
Brownsville-Harlingen-San Benito, TX	151,098	140,368	163,700	−7.1	16.6
Bryan-College Station, TX	44,895	57,978	NA	29.1	NA
Buffalo, NY	1,306,957	1,349,211	1,441,700	3.2	6.9
Canton, OH	340,345	372,210	416,200	9.4	11.8
Cedar Rapids, IA	136,899	163,213	193,900	19.2	18.8
Champaign-Urbana, IL	132,436	163,281	197,300	23.3	20.8
Charleston, SC	254,578	303,849	353,100	19.4	16.2
Charleston, WV	252,925	229,515	246,700	−9.3	7.5
Charlotte, NC	316,781	409,370	521,300	29.2	27.3
Chattanooga, TN-GA	283,169	305,768	344,800	8.0	12.8
Chicago, IL	6,220,913	6,977,611	7,890,400	12.2	13.1
Cincinnati, OH-KY-IN	1,268,479	1,384,983	1,542,800	9.2	11.4
Cleveland, OH	1,909,483	2,063,729	2,293,000	8.1	11.1
Colorado Springs, CO	143,742	235,972	284,700	64.2	20.5
Columbia, MO	55,202	80,935	NA	46.6	NA
Columbia, SC	260,828	322,880	398,000	23.8	23.3
Columbus, GA-AL	217,985	238,584	283,600	9.4	18.9
Columbus, OH	754,885	916,228	1,066,500	21.4	16.4
Corpus Christi, TX	266,594	281,832	351,000	6.8	23.2
Dallas, TX	1,119,410	1,556,324	2,069,300	39.0	33.0
Danbury, CT	37,888	78,405	NA	106.9	NA
Davenport-Rock Island-Moline, IA-IL	319,375	362,638	429,400	13.5	18.4

TABLE 7-2 (*Continued*)

Area	Census Population		Projected Population	Percentage Change	
	1960	1970	1980	1960–1970	1970–1980
Dayton, OH	727,121	852,531	1,015,700	17.2	19.1
Decatur, IL	118,257	125,010	147,100	5.7	17.7
Denver, CO	929,383	1,229,798	1,570,900	32.3	27.7
Des Moines, IA	266,315	286,130	310,600	7.4	8.6
Detroit, MI	3,762,360	4,203,548	4,626,700		10.1
Dubuque, IA	80,048	90,609	105,400	13.2	16.3
Duluth-Superior, MN-WI	276,596	265,350	310,000	−4.1	16.8
Durham, NC	154,965	190,388	244,300	22.9	28.3
El Paso, TX	314,070	359,291	442,200	14.4	23.1
Erie, PA	250,682	263,654	313,000	5.2	18.7
Eugene, OR	162,890	215,401	277,400	32.2	28.8
Evansville, IN-KY	222,890	232,775	272,900	4.4	17.2
Fall River, MA-RI	138,156	149,976	157,200	8.6	4.8
Fargo-Moorhead, ND-MN	106,027	120,261	139,400	13.4	15.9
Fayetteville, NC	148,418	212,042	255,200	42.9	20.4
Fitchburg-Leominster, MA	90,158	97,164	110,400	7.8	13.6
Flint, MI	416,239	497,950	556,400	19.6	11.7
Fort Lauderdale-Hollywood, FL	333,946	620,100	780,500	85.7	25.9
Fort Smith, AR-OK	135,110	160,421	191,200	18.7	19.2
Fort Wayne, IN	232,196	280,455	331,600	20.8	18.2
Fort Worth, TX	573,215	762,086	930,300	32.9	22.1
Fresno, CA	365,945	413,329	478,900	12.9	15.9
Gadsden, AL	96,980	94,144	107,700	−2.9	14.4
Gainesville, FL	74,074	104,764	NA	41.4	NA
Galveston-Texas City, TX	140,364	169,812	204,200	21.0	20.3
Gary-Hammond-E. Chicago, IN	573,548	633,367	726,200	10.4	14.7
Grand Rapids, MI	461,906	539,225	599,800	16.7	11.2
Great Falls, MT	73,418	81,804	94,200	11.4	15.2
Green Bay, WI	125,082	158,244	187,100	26.5	18.2
Greensboro-Winston-Salem-High Point, NC	520,249	604,720	704,300	16.2	16.5
Greenville, SC	255,806	299,730	365,400	17.2	21.9
Hamilton-Middletown, OH	199,076	226,207	250,800	13.6	10.9
Harrisburg, PA	371,653	410,505	458,000	10.5	11.6
Hartford, CT	549,249	663,891	794,200	20.9	19.6
Honolulu, HI	500,409	630,528	769,200	26.0	22.0
Houston, TX	1,418,323	1,985,031	2,535,000	40.0	27.7
Huntington-Ashland, WV-KY-OH	254,780	253,743	273,900	−0.4	7.9
Huntsville, AL	153,861	228,239	305,900	48.3	34.0
Indianapolis, IN	944,475	1,111,352	1,299,200	17.7	16.9
Jackson, MI	131,994	143,274	161,000	8.5	12.4
Jackson, MS	221,367	258,906	338,200	17.0	30.6
Jacksonville, FL	455,411	528,865	650,500	16.1	23.0
Jersey City, NJ	610,734	607,839	630,900	−0.5	3.8
Johnstown, PA	280,733	262,822	274,800	−6.4	4.6
Kalamazoo, MI	169,712	201,550	240,000	18.8	19.1
Kansas City, MO-KS	1,092,545	1,256,327	1,470,500	15.0	17.0
Kenosha, WI	100,615	117,917	133,500	17.2	13.2
Knoxville, TN	368,080	400,337	444,800	8.8	11.1
La Crosse, WI	72,465	80,468	NA	11.0	NA
Lafayette, W. Lafayette, IN	89,122	109,378	138,000	22.7	26.2
Lafayette, LA	84,658	111,643	143,600	31.9	28.6
Lake Charles, LA	145,475	145,415	170,500	(Z)	17.3
Lancaster, PA	278,359	320,079	356,600	15.0	11.4
Lansing, MI	298,949	378,423	466,800	26.6	23.4
Laredo, TX	64,791	72,859	84,500	12.5	16.0
Las Vegas, NV	127,016	273,288	360,300	115.2	31.8
Lawrence-Haverhill, MA-NH	199,136	232,415	269,500	16.7	16.0

TABLE 7–2 (*Continued*)

Area	Census Population 1960	Census Population 1970	Projected Population 1980	Percentage Change 1960–1970	Percentage Change 1970–1980
Lawton, OK	90,803	108,144	126,900	19.1	17.3
Lewiston-Auburn, ME	70,295	72,474	77,600	3.1	7.1
Lexington, KY	131,906	174,323	230,500	32.2	32.2
Lima, OH	160,862	171,472	197,000	6.6	14.9
Lincoln, NE	155,272	167,972	194,000	8.2	15.5
Little Rock-N. Little Rock, AR	271,936	323,296	391,400	18.9	21.1
Lorain-Elyria, OH	217,500	256,843	312,900	18.1	21.8
Los Angeles-Long Beach, CA	6,038,771	7,040,697	8,140,000	16.6	15.6
Louisville, KY-IN	725,139	826,553	945,700	14.0	14.4
Lowell, MA	164,243	212,860	241,500	29.6	13.5
Lubbock, TX	156,271	179,295	216,500	14.7	20.8
Lynchburg, VA	110,701	123,474	139,500	11.5	13.0
Macon, GA	180,403	206,342	248,900	14.4	20.6
Madison, WI	222,095	290,272	348,000	30.7	19.9
Manchester, NH	102,861	108,461	127,600	5.4	17.6
Mansfield, OH	117,761	129,997	152,500	10.4	17.3
McAllen-Pharr-Edinburg, TX	180,904	181,535	209,600	0.3	15.5
Memphis, TN-AR	674,583	770,217	918,200	14.2	19.2
Meriden, CT	51,850	55,959	63,700	7.9	13.8
Miami, FL	935,047	1,267,792	1,650,200	35.6	30.2
Midland, TX	67,717	65,433	75,200	–3.4	14.9
Milwaukee, WI	1,278,850	1,403,887	1,599,200	9.8	13.9
Minneapolis-St. Paul, MN	1,482,030	1,813,587	2,185,000	22.4	20.5
Mobile, Al	363,389	376,690	430,400	3.7	14.3
Modesto, CA	157,294	194,506	NA	23.7	NA
Monroe, LA	101,663	115,387	131,300	13.5	13.8
Montgomery, AL	199,734	201,451	240,600	0.9	19.4
Muncie, IN	110,938	129,219	152,700	16.5	18.2
Muskegon-Muskegon Hts, MI	149,943	157,426	171,400	5.0	8.9
Nashua, NH	44,972	66,458	NA	47.8	NA
Nashville-Davidson, TN	463,628	541,142	640,000	16.7	18.3
New Bedford, MA	143,176	152,642	163,600	6.6	7.2
New Britain, CT	129,397	145,269	170,000	12.3	17.2
New Haven, CT	320,836	355,538	406,000	10.8	14.2
New London, Groton, Norwich, CT	170,981	208,718	255,300	22.1	22.3
New Orleans, LA	907,123	1,046,470	1,305,200	15.4	24.7
New York, NY	10,694,633	11,575,740	13,174,600	8.2	13.8
Newark, NJ	1,689,420	1,859,096	2,081,700	10.0	12.0
Newport News-Hampton, VA	224,503	292,159	365,300	30.1	25.0
Norfolk-Portsmouth, VA	578,507	680,600	713,500	17.6	4.8
Norwalk, CT	96,756	120,099	143,700	24.1	19.7
Odessa, TX	90,995	91,805	107,700	0.9	17.3
Ogden, UT	110,744	126,278	148,900	14.0	17.9
Oklahoma City, OK	511,833	641,801	763,200	25.4	18.9
Omaha, NE-IA	457,873	542,646	634,000	18.5	16.8
Orlando, FL	318,487	428,003	545,400	34.4	27.4
Owensboro, KY	70,558	79,486	NA	12.6	NA
Oxnard-Ventura, CA	199,138	378,497	506,000	90.1	33.7
Paterson-Clifton-Passaic, NJ	1,186,873	1,357,930	1,587,400	14.4	16.9
Pensacola, FL	203,376	243,075	286,800	19.5	18.0
Peoria, IL	313,412	341,979	384,700	9.1	12.5
Petersburg-Colonial Hts, VA	106,685	128,809	NA	20.7	NA
Philadelphia, PA-NJ	4,342,897	4,822,245	5,436,600	11.0	12.7
Phoenix, AZ	663,510	968,487	1,294,700	46.0	33.7
Pine Bluff, AR	81,373	85,329	105,100	4.9	23.2
Pittsburgh, PA	2,405,435	2,401,362	2,490,500	–0.2	3.7
Pittsfield, MA	76,772	79,727	89,100	3.8	11.8
Portland, ME	139,122	141,625	162,400	1.8	14.7
Portland, OR-WA	821,897	1,007,130	1,213,800	22.5	20.5

TABLE 7-2 (*Continued*)

Area	Census Population 1960	Census Population 1970	Projected Population 1980	Percentage Change 1960–1970	Percentage Change 1970–1980
Providence-Pawtucket-Warick, RI-MA	821,101	914,110	996,700	11.3	9.0
Provo-Orem, UT	106,991	137,776	174,300	28.8	26.5
Pueblo, CO	118,707	118,238	130,300	–0.4	10.2
Racine, WI	141,781	170,836	195,900	20.5	14.7
Raleigh, NC	169,082	229,006	291,500	35.4	27.3
Reading, PA	275,414	296,382	322,100	7.6	8.7
Reno, NV	83,743	121,068	169,800	42.9	40.3
Richmond, VA	436,044	518,319	611,200	18.9	17.9
Roanoke, VA	158,803	181,436	209,600	14.3	15.5
Rochester, MN	65,532	84,104	NA	28.3	NA
Rochester, NY	732,588	882,667	1,048,800	20.5	18.8
Rockford, IL	230,091	272,063	327,800	18.2	20.5
Sacramento, CA	625,503	803,610	1,040,400	28.5	29.5
Saginaw, MI	190,752	219,743	254,600	15.2	15.9
St. Joseph, MO	90,581	86,915	95,600	–4.0	10.0
St. Louis, MO-IL	2,104,669	2,363,346	2,775,000	12.3	17.4
Salem, OR	147,411	186,658	227,600	26.6	21.9
Salinas-Monterey, CA	198,351	247,450	325,800	24.8	31.7
Salt Lake City, UT	447,795	557,635	698,800	24.5	25.3
San Angelo, TX	64,630	71,047	85,300	9.9	20.1
San Antonio, TX	716,168	864,014	1,053,900	20.6	22.0
San Bernardino, Riverside-Ontario, CA	809,782	1,141,307	1,466,600	40.9	28.6
San Diego, CA	1,033,011	1,357,854	1,612,800	31.4	18.8
San Francisco-Oakland, CA	2,648,762	3,108,026	3,550,300	17.3	14.2
San Jose, CA	642,315	1,066,932	1,474,000	66.1	38.2
Santa Barbara, CA	168,962	264,324	350,500	56.4	32.6
Santa Rosa, CA	147,375	204,885	NA	39.0	NA
Savannah, GA	188,299	187,816	207,600	–0.3	10.5
Scranton, PA	234,531	234,107	247,000	–0.2	5.5
Seattle-Everett, WA	1,107,213	1,424,611	1,742,100	28.7	22.3
Sherman-Denison, TX	73,043	83,225	92,300	13.9	10.9
Shreveport, LA	281,481	293,887	358,900	4.4	22.1
Sioux City, IA-NE	120,017	116,189	131,000	–3.2	12.7
Sioux Falls, SD	86,575	95,209	111,300	10.0	10.9
South Bend, IN	271,057	280,031	314,500	3.3	12.3
Spokane, WA	278,333	287,487	314,000	3.3	9.2
Springfield, IL	146,539	161,335	195,400	10.1	21.1
Springfield, MO	126,276	152,929	180,100	21.1	17.8
Springfield, OH	131,440	157,115	184,900	19.5	17.7
Springfield-Chicopee-Holyoke-MA-CT	493,999	529,922	471,800	7.3	11.0
Stamford, CT	178,409	206,419	248,200	15.7	20.2
Steubenville-Weirton, OH-WV	167,756	165,627	177,600	–1.3	7.2
Stockton, CA	249,989	289,564	342,000	15.8	18.1
Syracuse, NY	563,781	636,596	742,200	12.9	16.6
Tacoma, WA	321,900	411,027	472,000	27.8	14.8
Tallahassee, FL	74,225	103,047	132,600	38.8	28.7
Tampa-St Petersburg, FL	772,453	1,012,594	1,270,300	31.1	25.5
Terre Haute, IN	172,069	175,143	205,700	1.8	17.4
Texarkana, TX-AR	91,657	101,198	130,000	10.4	28.5
Toledo, OH-MI	630,647	692,488	761,500	9.8	10.0
Topeka, KS	141,286	155,322	182,500	9.9	17.5
Trenton, NJ	266,392	304,116	348,400	14.2	14.6
Tucson, AZ	265,660	351,667	430,700	32.4	22.5
Tulsa, OK	418,974	475,264	574,300	13.4	20.8
Tuscaloosa, AL	109,047	116,029	133,300	6.4	14.9
Tyler, TX	86,350	97,096	123,800	12.4	27.5

TABLE 7-2 (*Concluded*)

Area	Census Population 1960	Census Population 1970	Projected Population 1980	Percentage Change 1960–1970	Percentage Change 1970–1980
Utica-Rome, NY	330,771	340,670	383,800	3.0	12.7
Vallejo-Napa, CA	200,487	251,129	304,600	25.3	21.3
Vineland-Millville-Bridgeton, NJ	106,850	121,374	142,000	13.6	17.0
Waco, TX	150,091	147,553	173,600	−1.7	17.7
Washington, DC-MD-VA	2,076,610	2,861,638	3,529,300	37.8	23.3
Waterbury, CT	185,548	208,956	243,400	12.6	16.5
Waterloo, IA	122,482	132,916	148,400	8.5	11.6
West Palm Beach, FL	228,106	348,993	463,500	53.0	32.8
Wheeling, WV-OH	190,342	182,712	201,800	−4.0	10.4
Wichita, KS	381,626	389,352	500,800	2.0	28.6
Wichita Falls, TX	129,638	126,322	149,100	−2.6	18.0
Wilkes-Barre, Hazleton, PA	346,972	342,329	352,700	−1.3	3.0
Wilmington, DE-NJ-MD	414,565	499,493	604,300	20.5	21.0
Wilmington, NC	93,020	107,219	127,300	16.5	18.7
Worcester, MA	328,898	344,320	382,000	4.7	10.9
York, PA	290,242	329,540	380,000	13.5	15.3
Youngstown-Warren, OH	509,006	537,124	596,700	5.5	11.1

NA = Not available.

Sources: 1960 and 1970 data from U.S. Department of Commerce, Bureau of the Census, *County and City Data Book 1972*, pp. 818–19.

1980 projections from Lee, Joe Won and William B. D. Hong, *Income, Savings and Consumption Patterns for Regions, States and Metropolitan Areas 1960–1980: Economic Projections.* Washington, D.C.: National Planning Association, 1971, pp. 527–84.

panding employment opportunities in that economy means that more people can afford to live there. Shrinking employment opportunities means that fewer people can afford to live there.

The simplest theory of city growth is what is called the economic base theory. It holds that the growth of the city is predicated on the growth of employment that produces goods and services *exported* from the community. The logic is that the more goods and services the community can produce and successfully export, the more jobs it can support. Those jobs involved in such export activities are in the "basic" category. All other jobs are in the "nonbasic"—sometimes called "service"—category.

Manufacturing for export is obviously a basic industry. Thus if the outlook for automobile production is excellent, one would expect Detroit to do well. However, not all basic industries are as obvious. A boom in insurance would favorably affect Hartford; an increase in federal programs, Washington, D.C.; an increase in tourism, Washington, D.C., Las Vegas, and Miami; an increase in retirement, Miami and Phoenix. The export may be services as well as products; as long as an activity brings income from outside the borders it is considered basic activity. The retirees in Florida are "basic" employees in that they get their income from outside the borders, from Social Security, from pension checks, and by clipping bond coupons.

In assessing any specific community the procedure is to identify the employment by industry type (as to which is basic and which is not) and to assess the future of the basic industries. As a matter of technique, since most industries are mixed and few are overwhelmingly in one category or another, the detailed analyses will provide an allocation by industry, even though some department stores in Chicago, Dallas, and New York sell a substantial volume of goods to people from outside the community, and some people in Detroit buy cars manufactured in Detroit.

The assessment of the future of the industries, whatever the method, may be used for forecasting population growth. Essentially, a ratio exists at a point in time between basic employees and nonbasic employees, and between basic employees and population. By forecasting change in the number of basic employees one can, with application of the ratio, forecast the total employment and/or population.

Some problems arise in the application of this technique, and its theoretical validity has limitations under the simplistic assumptions ordinarily used. Nevertheless, the concept is relevant and the analysis useful, especially in smaller communities.

Its significance to the land investor is in the identification of the major basic industries. In many communities the planning authority, a development commission, a chamber of commerce, a public utility, or a research organization may have conducted a study that not only identifies the key industries but makes a projection of their growth. By evaluating the work as best they can, investors may reach a conclusion as to whether key industries have prospects that look bright and whether the community has a diversity of employment that provides the minimal risk acceptable.

A more sophisticated technique of analysis is available (input-output analysis), and also another relatively simple method (location quotients). In any case, the investor has to consider the industry that will succeed the current industry, which will be relatively more important than the present one in determining where the new opportunities will be.

Location quotients provide the simplest alternative way of looking at the mix of employment in a local area. Essentially the approach is to compare the mix of employment by category with the average mix for the nation (or any standard). The comparison indicates the industries of greater relative importance. (See Table 7–3.)

Most real estate investors do not do their own economic forecasting and analyzing, although they do go through an evaluation and judgment process. They may use forecasts and analyses made by others in a way that varies from analytical to intuitive. The most critical aspect of it is evaluating the main thrust of events.

The national economy, and to an increasing extent the international economic environment, are important to the economic vigor of the local economy. The larger play of economic forces reverberates through to the local level. Thus an assessment of the vitality of the local economy implies an assessment of the national economy. That assessment must consider what is happening to the gross national product (the value of all the goods and services produced in the nation) and to the whole set of national income accounts. Pragmatically, the typical land investor will follow these events through a weekly newsmagazine such as *Business Week, Time,* or *U.S. News and World Report.* He may also read about them in the *Wall Street Journal* and/or the financial section of a major metropolitan newspaper. What the investor cannot find in these publications is comparable information on the economy at the local level.

To some extent, detailed information at the local level is available from banks, utility companies, and other local sources that publish monthly newsletters reporting on the variations in some economic indicators.

For some investors the foregoing approach is much too simplistic. For those who want to know the strength of the local economy in scientific detail and precision, the answer is to become acquainted with input-output analysis. Input-output analysis builds on economic base theory. It deals with the relationships among industries by explicitly calculating inter-industry transactions, using a matrix.

A matrix is a grid with horizontal and vertical rows. Every industry is listed both horizontally and vertically. The cells within the matrix show what each industry sells to the others. Using the matrix, the analyst can forecast how a change in the output of one industry will affect those that supply it with inputs.

This device helps in understanding a complexity of relationships. While the necessary data are not generally available at the local level, the insights it provides are well worth while for the investor to understand.

For example, automobile employment generates a great deal of other employment that feeds into the production of the auto. This includes people working for companies that supply parts and accessories, as well as for local firms that do printing and provide other business services for the auto industry. Changes in employment in an assembly plant in Detroit have an impact on other employment in Detroit that is much greater than the impact of similar changes in an auto assembly plant in Louisville, Kentucky. This is because Louisville has little local supplying industry in comparison to Detroit. Louisville is supplied by parts and components factories elsewhere.

As a community grows, it is able by virtue of economies of scale to produce components that it formerly imported. Thus the set of relationships within the economy changes with increasing scale. In one sense, this increasing scale causes changes in the key export items to exert a more profound effect because of the high multiplier effect on employment. In another sense, however, the continued integration and expansion provide a capability for new products and a new dimension of stability. They facilitate the formation of new industries.

If the environment is attractive on noneconomic as well as economic grounds, once the economy reaches a certain scale the community on its own will stimulate or improve growth by doing or making for itself what was previously imported, and by providing

TABLE 7–3
Employment Change and Distribution by Major Industry Groups: Washington, D.C. and Comparative U.S. Statistics, 1960 and 1969

Industry	*1960 Annual Employment*	*1960 Percent Distribution*	*1960 U.S. Percent Distribution*	*1969 Annual Employment*	*1969 Percent Distribution*	*1969 U.S. Percent Distribution*	*1960–1969 Percent Change–D.C.*	*Locational Quotient 1960**	*Locational Quotient 1969**
	(000)			(000)					
Manufacturing	20.2	3.77%	30.97%	20.3	2.93%	28.70%	0.3%	.12	.10
Food and Kindred Products	5.4	1.01	3.30	3.5	0.51	2.56	(35.2)†	.31	.20
Printing and Publishing	11.3	2.11	1.68	13.3	1.96	1.56	17.7	1.25	1.25
All Other Manufacturing	3.5	0.65	25.99	3.5	0.51	24.53	0.0	.02	.02
Nonmanufacturing	515.3	96.23	69.03	651.1	97.02	71.30	28.3	1.39	1.36
Contract Construction	20.3	3.83	5.32	18.2	2.67	4.39	(12.5)	.73	.05
Transportation, Communications and Public Utilities	23.2	5.27	7.33	30.9	4.54	6.31	9.6	.71	.72
Wholesale and Retail Trade	34.0	15.69	21.00	85.4	12.53	20.34	1.7	.75	.60
Wholesale Trade	19.5	3.64	5.54	21.0	3.03	5.32	7.7	.66	.53
Retail Trade	64.5	12.05	15.46	54.4	9.45	15.52	(0.2)	.78	.61
Finance, Insurance and Real Estate	27.5	5.13	4.92	31.8	4.57	5.06	15.5	1.04	.92
Services, Miscellaneous and Mining	92.8	17.33	15.01	134.4	19.72	16.33	44.3	1.15	1.17
Hotels and Other Lodging Places	3.7	1.62	1.04	9.4	1.33	1.07	8.0	1.55	1.29
Government‡	262.0	43.93	15.40	360.4	52.37	17.37	37.6	3.18	3.04
Federal‡	236.1	44.09	4.13	317.0	46.52	3.93	34.3	10.55	11.34
Washington, D.C.	25.9	4.34	11.22	43.4	6.37	13.44	67.5	.43	.47
Total Nonagricultural Employment	535.5	100.00%	100.00%	681.4	100.00%	100.00%	27.2		

* Calculated by dividing the local percentage distribution by the U.S. percentage distribution.
† Parentheses denote loss.
‡ Federal employment in the Maryland and Virginia sectors of the SMSA is included in the data for the District of Columbia.
Source: U.S. Department of Commerce.

resources for attracting new industry. If, however, the environment is so mismanaged that it becomes unattractive, the rate of growth will decline and the quality of development will diminish. That is, the population attracted will be of lesser quantity and lesser skill in the sense of economic productivity.

Economic vitality thus involves more than job opportunity; environmental attractiveness is also important.

Political Dimension. The political dimension of local vitality is not as amenable to analysis as the economic, at least not in terms of numbers. But some aspects of it are reasonably amenable to judgment.

Which is preferable—an inept, honest local government or an effective, dishonest local government? What constitutes dishonesty in government—using public office for personal gain, or using public office for personal gain through illegal means such as kickbacks and bribery?

Astute developers, in selecting a new metropolitan area for expansion, have been known to retain professional research assistance to assess the political environment as well as the economic environment. If a community is so sewn up that rezoning is based not on merits but on payoffs, the developer will avoid it. Similarly, many of the more astute business organizations refuse to expand in communities in which they know they would be destined to have environmental problems.

On the positive side, communities with effective leadership that assesses and responds to the goals of their citizens are likely to be relatively safe communities for investment. The political leadership will not be arbitrary and capricious in managing government affairs. It will pursue the development of a quality environment, which will make the community attractive to new firms and to new inhabitants.

The accountability and responsiveness of local government are important to the investor. Communities with the old ward politics are not good places to invest, nor are communities with public agencies that are unresponsive and seemingly unaccountable. In some areas, for example, officials of public works utilities, especially water and sewer systems, are appointed and not elected; once appointed, they take little interest in whether the utility is in fact providing the needed service. Sewer moratoria have occurred and remained in effect because public officials did not do their jobs and were not really subjected to the discipline of the electorate, which then suffered from the misdeeds of the officials.

Political discipline requires an informed constituency. That depends partly on the education and inclination of the constituency and partly on the quality of the news media.

An additional consideration is the extent to which civil liberties are respected and protected. Insofar as freedom offers the best environment for economic progress, the extent to which a free community flourishes in its political dimension will affect its flourishing in an economic dimension.

Social Dimension. To have a viable community, people must feel secure in their daily life. Obviously, a community with a high crime rate is not an ideal location for a real estate investment. Neither is one in which there are riots or other confrontations.

Not so obvious to many is the importance of family structure and the cultural amenities. These elements may be summarized by the catch-all phrase "quality of life." When they are favorable, they help to make communities attractive.

Many smaller metropolitan areas in the United States are developing substantial competitive advantages over the really big cities. Growing numbers of people reject the larger metropolitan areas as places to work because they cannot see them as places to live. For some people these include New York, Chicago, and Los Angeles. For others they include any major city with a great concentration of poor in its center. The move is not back to the farm or to places with just a few thousand people. The move is to communities on a scale that is somewhat more human than the great urban jungles—a scale which will permit some urban amenities but in which the natural aspects of a living environment have not been annihilated.

We hear much about these aspects of living from the environmental movement. The problem is only partly the degradation of air and water quality, and it goes beyond garbage in the streets. A tree growing in Brooklyn is not enough. People have a need for natural beauty, for the softness of growing green things, for seeing animals not in cages and not as nuisances.

The aesthetics of a viable community do not include neon signs and poles and wires and other ugly things. The aesthetics may well include the sloping curve of a graceful access ramp to a freeway, but if the community is all freeway and wall-to-wall rooftops it will draw mostly the people who must come to earn a livelihood.

Sensible urban design makes a city an attractive place to live, and it does not rule out the possibility of being able to earn a living. The assessment of a community by the investor has to begin with how the inhabitants earn their livings, but it does not end until an evaluation has been made as to whether or not it is a good place to live.

Critics will say that the United States really does not have many places that are good to live in. And they may be right. But some communities are making themselves better places to live, and whether they intend it or not they are going to provide competition with other communities for growth and development.

Interestingly enough, many livable communities do not really want much growth, for many of the people who got there first want to keep others out. But that is a side issue. What is most relevant is not growth alone, but rather the character of growth. That will affect the demand for land as well as the quality of life. The next chapter discusses this matter in greater detail.

In summary, community growth is determined by the location of the community and its basic economic strength, plus what its people want and the effectiveness of their leadership. These elements together determine not only which communities grow but the character of that growth.

8

Local Development

When demand for a particular type of land rises substantially, that type of land will increase in value. An excessive restriction of supply will make the land even more valuable. The previous discussion has dealt with general forces and national patterns. This chapter deals with the specifics of the type of land and its location within the local community. It begins with an explanation of the structural forces that influence the location of demand at the local level, and the constraints that limit potential competition.

The second section of the chapter deals with the management of local urban development forces as they affect both the demand for more land and its developability. Specific consideration is given to the trade-offs between development of the land and preservation of the environment—considering environment in the broadest sense.

Finally the chapter deals with the resolution of conflict over rights to use of the land. The objective is to forecast the outcome of the conflict as it affects the developability of land and land value.

Later chapters will provide guidelines on how to seek out land for investment. This chapter assists investors in determining what land to seek out. The land search, of course, is predicated on finding land that gets to be more valuable because it will undergo a *conversion process.* What an investor needs to know is the characteristics of the land that will be demanded for conversion—that is, the land which will turn out to be developable.

STRUCTURAL FORCES

Economic Pulls. Among the structural forces affecting land use are those that we may call the *economic pull.* These result in various types of land use. The types of land use are classifiable by intensity and/or quality, and by location as well as by general character.

A variety of land use classifications are shown in Figure 8-1, which is taken from a planning commission

FIGURE 8–1

Land Use Classifications

After careful consideration of the past work of this Commission, analysis of systems being used by other agencies, past trends of land use in the region, and adaptability for our use, the following list of 20 categories was selected. The list has been classified as a three-digit code to distinguish it from other existing local systems.

RESIDENTIAL

101 Suburban:

.9 DU/gross acre or less

Characterized by:

Individual water supply and sewage disposal

Single-family-estate type development

$40,000 to $60,000 and over

Most predominant lot size is 2 1/2 acres

Rural-type street development

102 Low-Density, 1 and 2.9 DU/gross acre:

In special instances there may be individual water-supply and sewage-disposal facilities

Single-family

$25,000 to $40,000

Most predominant lot size is 1 acre

Generally meet standard urban street requirements

103 Single-Family, 3 to 4.9 DU/gross acre:

Predominant type of development in region (approx. 60% of total)

Single-family

$10,000 to $25,000

Most predominant lot size is 7,000 to 9,000 sq. ft.

Developed to standard subdivision regulations

Depend entirely on public improvements and community facilities

104 Medium-Density, 5 to 14.9 DU/gross acre:

Mixed residential; single-family units on small lots (5,000 sq. ft.), doubles and some apartments

Generally low to middle income, high percentage of rentals

Includes public housing

105 High-Density, 15 DU/gross acre and over:

Predominantly apartments over 2 stories; high-rise and luxury apartments; new multistory apartments mixed with old residential

Medium-to high-income families, childless couples, senior citizens, and apartments for single men and women

BUSINESS

106 Business Districts:

Includes the CBD and major suburban central business districts

107 District Shopping:

Retailing, mainly durable goods, and serving at least two or more neighborhoods

Usually dominated by a large major department store

Examples: University Hills, Englewood, Lakeside, etc.

108 Local Shopping:

Primarily convenience goods, supported by neighborhood old transfer-point locations

FIGURE 8–1 (*Continued*)

109 Other business areas:

The largest percentage of this classification will be strip retail business

General goods, retail establishments which depend on the entire city to support them

Filling stations, automobile dealers, etc.

COMMERCIAL-INDUSTRIAL

110 Light Commercial-Industrial:

Areas more compatible with other land uses generating much less of the above problems

Printing and publishing companies, instrument manufacturers, furniture, etc.

111 Heavy Commercial-Industrial:

Areas producing high percentage of noise, smoke, light, and odor, generally noxious in character

Rail orientation and heavy traffic generation

Railroad yards, packing plants, oil refiners, etc.

PUBLIC AND SEMI-PUBLIC

112 Regional Services:

Institutions, public and private

113 Resident Institutions:

Hospitals

114 Adult Education:

Senior high, college, university, and other educational services

115 Local Services:

Religious, churches, etc.

116 Schools:

Preschool, elementary and junior high

OPEN

117 Agricultural

Farms, agricultural services and forestry

118 Open (Vacant):

Abandoned gravel and clay pits

Flood plains, drainage ditches, etc.

Water areas

PARKS AND RECREATION

119 Parks and Playgrounds:

Public

120 Reservations and regional recreation areas:

Public and private

Regional parks, golf courses, etc.

Major Land-Use Features

Probably one of the most prominent features of the regional land-use pattern is the patchwork of new detached subdivisions. Other salient features can also be recognized, such as the following:

- Industrial corridor following major transportation arteries
- Strip commercial development along major highways
- Old detached cities now part of the Denver urban complex, with only their political boundaries retaining their identity
- Lack of large regional recreation areas within convenient distance to all segments of the region
- High-density residential development encircling well-established central business district
- A round buildable geographic area
- Well-defined, continuous residential areas

Source: Inter-County Regional Planning Commission, Denver. *Survey of 1959 Generalized Land Uses in the Denver Metropolitan Region.* Master plan report No. 11, 1960.

survey in Denver. The industrial classifications are likely to be "basic," i.e., they will include industries that produce products (or services) exported from the community. When communities are especially eager to attract industry they not only zone an ample amount of land for that category, but may even give the land away. Alternatively, various programs have been developed to assist in the financing of the plant and/or in providing tax relief. The heyday of this approach was in previous decades such special inducements were a typically postwar phenomenon. For current practices, see Figure 8–2.

While many areas still have a demand for land for *heavy industry,* the nature of production has shifted in favor of *lighter industry.* Some cities have a substantial strip development of "think factories" on their fringes; many of these were constructed during the boom in the space and engineering segments of the economy. Now industrial parks provide blossoming opportunities. The nature of the production determines the kind of land use.

In most communities "clean industry" is quite welcome, and so ample land is zoned or zonable for such development. Communities with an employment problem may welcome any industry, even "dirty industry," i.e., heavy industry which pollutes the air or water or creates excessive noise. Rezoning for the less desirable land uses is more difficult but more profitable.

The kind and character of the industry influences the price levels at which housing will be demanded. This is so because wage and salary levels affect the ability to purchase housing. Think factories are welcomed not only because they are nonpolluting (except for clogging up the roads), but also because they bring the kind of people the city fathers and the community generally prefer. They are people of higher incomes, less likely to generate a burden on local taxes and more likely to buy in the stores and to provide civic leadership. If a new plant brings blue-collar factory workers, they may be of different ethnic origin than that of the community leadership, in which case the welcome mat may not be out. But in any event, a secondary demand for land will be generated.

That secondary demand will be not only in housing but in the service employment necessary to serve the new population. Service or nonbasic employment includes shopping centers and also office buildings utilized for medical arts, businesses, and professional services for the local populace. Many attorneys, accountants, insurance agents, and others will locate near the people they serve.

Typically, concentrations of office buildings in various parts of a metropolitan area cater to a broad region or at least some at the center of the community do. These main office building districts may have basic employment space as well as nonbasic service space. The regional headquarters of an insurance company or a home office of some regional or national concern will typically be in an office building district. Some cities such as New York, Washington, Chicago, and Los Angeles

FIGURE 8–2
Incentives For Industry

FINANCIAL ASSISTANCE FOR INDUSTRY

	State Sponsored Industrial Development Authority	Privately Sponsored Development Credit Corporation	State Authority or Agency Revenue Bond Financing	State Authority or Agency General Obligation Bond Financing	City and/or County Revenue Bond Financing	City and/or County General Obligation Bond Financing	State Loans for Building Construction	State Loans for Equipment, Machinery	City and/or County Loans for Building Construction	City and/or County Loans for Equipment, Machinery	State Loan Guarantees for Building Construction	State Loan Guarantees for Equipment, Machinery	City and/or County Loan Guarantees for Building Construction	City and/or County Loan Guarantees for Equipment, Machinery	State Financing Aid for Existing Plant Expansions	State Matching Funds for City and/or County Industrial Financing Programs	State Incentive for Establishing Industrial Plants in Areas of High Unemployment	City and/or County Incentive for Establishing Industrial Plants in Areas of High Unemployment
Alabama	●	●			●	●[1]									●[2]			
Alaska	●	●	●	●	●[3]	●[3]	●	●							●			
Arizona	●	[4]		●	●													
Arkansas	●	●			●	●					●	●						
California		●[5]															●[6]	
Colorado		●			●													
Connecticut	●	●	●	●		●	●	●			●	●			●	●		
Delaware	●	[7]	●	●				●							●			
Florida	●	●			●													
Georgia		●	●[3]		●													
Hawaii			●		●	●	●	●							●	●		
Idaho		[4]																
Illinois	●	●			●													
Indiana	●				●						●	●			●	●	●	
Iowa		●			●													
Kansas		●			●													
Kentucky	●	●			●	●	●	●							●			
Louisiana	●	●			●	●	●[8]	●[8]							●[2]			
Maine	●	●	●		●						●	●			●		●	
Maryland	●	●			●	●					●	●			●	●[9]	●[9]	
Massachusetts	●	●			●	●			●	●					●		●	●
Michigan		[4]	[1]		●						[11]	[11]						
Minnesota		●	●		●		●	●	●[12]	●[12]					●		●	
Mississippi	●	●			●	●									●[2]			●
Missouri		●			●	●												
Montana		●			●													
Nebraska		●			●										●[2]			
Nevada					●	●												
New Hampshire	●	●	●				●				●	●			●			
New Jersey	●[9]																	●[10]
New Mexico		●[4]			●													
New York	●	●	●[13]	●	●[13]		●	●[14]	●[13]	●[13]	●[15]	●[15]			●		●[16]	●[16]
North Carolina		●																
North Dakota	●	●		●	●	●	●	●	●	●	●				●[17]		●	
Ohio	●	●	●		●				●	●	●	●			●			
Oklahoma	●		●	●	●	●	●	●	●	●					●	●		
Oregon		●	●[3]				●											
Pennsylvania	●	●	●[18]		●[18]		●[19]		●[19]						●	●[20]	●	●
Rhode Island	●	●	●		●						●	●			●			
South Carolina	●	●			●													
South Dakota					●													
Tennessee	●	●	●	●	●	●					●	●			●[2]			
Texas	●	●	●		●[17]		●	●							●	●		
Utah	●	●	●		●													
Vermont	●	●	●		●						●	●			●	●	●	●
Virginia	●	●			●													
Washington		●			●[3]	●[3]												
West Virginia	●	●			●		●	●							●			
Wisconsin					●	●[21]												
Wyoming		●			●													
STATE TOTALS	30	39	18	8	42	17	14	12	7	6	12	11	0	0	25	8	10	6

FIGURE 8–2 (*Continued*)

	TAX INCENTIVES FOR INDUSTRY												OTHER LAWS							
	Corporate Income Tax Exemption	Personal Income Tax Exemption	Excise Tax Exemption	Tax Exemption or Moratorium on Land, Capital Improvements	Tax Exemption or Moratorium on Equipment, Machinery	Inventory Tax Exemption on Goods in Transit (Freeport)	Tax Exemption on Manufacturers' Inventories	Sales/Use Tax Exemption on New Equipment	Tax Exemption on Raw Materials Used in Manufacturing	Tax Credits for Use of Specified State Products	Tax Stabilization Agreements for Specified Industries	Tax Exemption to Encourage Research and Development	Accelerated Depreciation of Industrial Equipment	State Right-to-Work Law	State Minimum Wage Law	State Fair Employment Practice Code	Statewide Uniform Property Tax Evaluation Law	Statewide Air Pollution Control Law	Statewide Water Pollution Control Law	Statewide Industrial Noise Abatement Law
Alabama	●		●	●	●		●	●	●					●			●	●	●	
Alaska								●	●		●				●	●	●	●	●	
Arizona		●				●	●		●				●	●		●	●	●	●	
Arkansas						●		●	●					●	●		●	●	●	
California							●22	●23	●22				●24		●	●	●	●	●	
Colorado						●25	●26		●26						●	●	●	●	●	●
Connecticut	●27			●28		●	●		●29						●	●		●	●	●30
Delaware			●31		●	●	●	●	●				●		●	●		●	●	
Florida	●	●32				●	●33		●33	●				●			●	●	●	
Georgia								●	●				●24	●	●	●	●	●	●	
Hawaii		●	●		●	●	●	●					●		●	●	●	●	●	
Idaho						●	●	●	●				●		●		●	●	●	
Illinois						●			●						●	●	●	●	●	●
Indiana	●	●	●		●			●	●				●		●	●	●	●	●	
Iowa	●34				35	●	35		●				●36	●		●	●	●	●	
Kansas				●37	●37	●			●38				●36	●		●	●	●	●	
Kentucky				●39	●39	●	●	●	●39				●		●	●	●	●	●	
Louisiana	●40			●41	●	●			●				●					●	●	
Maine						●42		●	●43			●	●36		●	●	●	●	●	●
Maryland				●44	●		●	●45	●			●46			●	●	●	●	●	●
Massachusetts	●47	●	●		●		●								●	●	●	●	●	●
Michigan	●	●		●47	●	●		●	●48						●	●	●	●	●	
Minnesota		●		●24	●	●	●	●49	●		●	●	●36		●	●	●	●	●	●
Mississippi		●		●	●	●	●	●50	●				●36	●				●	●	
Missouri	●	●		●	●	●		●	●							●		●	●	
Montana				●	●	●		●51									●	●	●	
Nebraska						●	●52		●53					●	●	●	●	●	●	
Nevada	●32	●32				●	●							●	●	●	●	●	●	
New Hampshire		●32			●	●	●	●51	●				●36		●	●	●	●	●	
New Jersey		●54				●52	●		●						●	●	●	●	●	●55
New Mexico						●	●		●				●36		●	●	●	●	●	●
New York	●16,56,57	●56		●16	●58	●58	●58	●	●58			●57			●	●	●	●	●	●
North Carolina						●52		●59	●60					●	●	●	●61	●	●	
North Dakota	●		●		●58	●58	●58		●					●	●	●	●	●	●	●
Ohio						●		●	●							●	●	●	●	●
Oklahoma	●	●				●	●	●	●						●	●		●	●	
Oregon	●46,62	●	●62	●63		●	●								●	●	●	●	●	
Pennsylvania					●64	●65	●65	●64	●64			●			●	●	●	●	●	
Rhode Island				●39	●39		●		●		●				●	●		●	●	
South Carolina				●	●	●	●	●	●			●		●	●		●	●	●	
South Dakota	●	●	●		●	●			●					●	●		●	●	●	
Tennessee		●		●39	●39	●	●	●	●	●66			●67	●			●	●	●	
Texas	●32	●32		●68	●68	●								●	●			●	●	
Utah						●	●							●	●	●	●	●	●	
Vermont						●			●		●		●36		●	●	●	●	●	
Virginia								●	●69			70	●71	●				●	●	
Washington				●	●	●			●29						●	●	●	●	●	
West Virginia	●		●					●	●						●	●	●	●	●	
Wisconsin					●72	●	●73	●	●				●		●	●	●	●	●	
Wyoming	●32	●32	●			●	●		●					●	●	●	●	●	●	
STATE TOTALS	18	19	10	18	25	40	30	28	43	2	4	6	20	19	38	38	41	50	50	12

FIGURE 8-2 (*Concluded*)

SPECIAL SERVICES FOR INDUSTRIAL DEVELOPMENT

	State Financed Speculative Building	City and/or County Financed Speculative Building	State Provides Free Land for Industry	Cities and/or Counties Provide Free Land for Industry	State-Owned Industrial Park Sites	City and/or County-Owned Industrial Park Sites	State Funds for City and/or County Development-Related Public Works Projects	State Funds for City and/or County Master Plans	State Funds for City and/or County Recreational Projects	State Funds for Private Recreational Projects	State Program to Promote Research and Development	State Program to Increase Export of Products	University R&D Facilities Available to Industry	State and/or Universities Conduct Feasibility Studies to Attract or Assist New Industry	State Recruiting, Screening of Industrial Employees	State Supported Training of Industrial Employees	State Re-Training of Industrial Employees	State Supported Training of "Hard-Core" Unemployed	State Incentive to Industry to Train "Hard-Core" Unemployed	State Help in Bidding on Federal Procurement Contracts	State Science and/or Technology Advisory Council
Alabama		●		●74		●	●	●	●		●	●	●	●	●	●	●	●			●
Alaska						●	●			●	●	●	●	●	●	●	●	●	●		
Arizona		●				●						●	●	●	●	●	●	●			●
Arkansas						●			●		●		●	●	●	●	●				●
California				●75		●	●		●				●		●	●	●	●			●
Colorado		●74		●74		●	●	●	●			●	●	●	●	●	●	●			
Connecticut						●	●	●			●	●	●	●	●	●	●	●76	●76	●	●
Delaware	●					●	●	●77	●		●		●	●	●	●	●	●	●	●	●
Florida						●			●		●	●	●78	●	●	●79	●79	●79	●79		●
Georgia		●				●	●	●	●		●	●	●	●	●	●	●	●			●
Hawaii					●			●	●	●	●	●		●	●	●	●			●	●
Idaho						●	●		●		●	●	●	●	●	●	●				●
Illinois						●	●	●	●		●	●	●	●	●	●	●			●	●
Indiana				●		●	●	●	●			●	●	●	●	●	●	●	●	●	●
Iowa						●	●	●	●			●	●	●	●	●	●	●			●
Kansas		●80				●					●	●	●81	●	●	●					●
Kentucky						●	●	●			●	●	●	●	●	●	●	●		●	●
Louisiana				●		●			●		●	●	●78	●	●	●	●	●			●
Maine	●			●82		●				●83		●	●78	●	●	●	●	●			●
Maryland						●	●	84	●	85		●		●	●	●	●	●	●		●
Massachusetts		●				●	●	●			●	●	●	●	●	●	●	●		●	●
Michigan						●		●	●		●	●	●	●	●	●	●			●	●
Minnesota						●	●	●	●	●		●	●	●	●	●	●	●	●	●	●
Mississippi		●		●86	●	●					●	●	●	●	●	●	●	●	●	●	●
Missouri						●						●	●	●	●	●87	●	●	●		●
Montana						●						●	●	●	●	●	●				●
Nebraska		●88		●88		●		●	●		●	●	●	●	●	●	●			●	●
Nevada						●							●	●	●	●			●		
New Hampshire	●				●	●	●	●	●	●	●	●	●	●	●	●	●			●	●
New Jersey						●	●	●	●		●	●	●	●	●	●	●	●	●	●	●
New Mexico		●				●						●	●	●	●	●	●			●	●
New York						●	●	●	●		●	●	●	●	●	●	●	●	●16	●	●
North Carolina						●	●	●	●		●	●	●	●	●	●	●	●	●	●	●
North Dakota				●		●			●		●	●	●	●	●	●	●			●	●
Ohio							●				●	●	●	●	●	●	●	●	●	●	●
Oklahoma		●		●	●	●		●	●		●	●	●	●	●	●	●	●	●	●	●
Oregon					●	●	●		●		●	●	●	●	●	●	●	●	●	●	●
Pennsylvania		●				●	●	●	●		●	●	●	●	●	●	●	●	●		●
Rhode Island					●	●		●	●	●		●	●	●	●	●	●			●	●
South Carolina				●74		●		●	●		●	●	●	●	●	●	●	●			●
South Dakota		●		●86		●						●	●	●	●	●				●	●
Tennessee		●			●	●	●89	●89	●89		●	●	●	●	●	●	●	●	●	●	●
Texas						●	●	●	●			●	●	●	●	●	●				●
Utah						●					●	●	●	●	●	●	●				●
Vermont	●					●	●	●	●		●	●	●	●	●	●	●	●	●	●	●
Virginia		●80				●80	●89	●	●			●	●	●	●	●	●				●
Washington						●90	●		●			●	●	●	●	●	●	●	●	●	●
West Virginia						●				●			●	●	●	●	●	●			
Wisconsin						●	●	●	●		●	●	●	●	●	●	●	●			●
Wyoming						●			●		●	●	●	●	●	●	●	●		●	●
STATE TOTALS	4	14	0	12	7	48	28	27	34	7	32	45	48	49	50	50	47	33	19	27	46

Source: Reproduced from the November/December issue of *Industrial Development*, pp. 8–10 (copyright 1973), by permission of the publisher, Conway Research, Inc., Atlanta, Ga. No further reproduction of this copyrighted material is authorized.

have substantial numbers of office building concentrations. More and more communities are getting such facilities, especially near airports. The broad forces for change discussed earlier have much to do with this. For example, intercity travel by air has stimulated office and motel development near airports.

The space used for basic activities takes various configurations in the land use patterns. These configurations differ, of course, by type of community. Large-scale industrial districts are prevalent in metropolitan areas which depend upon heavy industry, e.g., Pittsburg. "Think factories" have different types of industrial land-use patterns, such as Boston, Route 128. Washington, D.C. "factories" are strung along Constitution and Independence Avenues in the form of large buildings housing government agencies.

Seeing the configurations as types of space in land use rather than as types of basic space activity is easier. Industrial types of space may in many cases be predominantly basic. Commercial space may be basic or nonbasic. Sometimes a single building will have a mix of tenants some of which are primarily local and others of which are regional or national.

The downtown of the smaller community contains its business and financial center. The growth of those communities has typically been upward and outward. Upward growth is a shift to high-rise buildings. It occurs when demand is strong, land scarce, and local officials permissive. Outward growth typically emphasizes a single direction for the high income sector, for example to the west in Los Angeles and to the northwest in Washington, D.C.

Some smaller communities get neither outward nor upward growth because they do not prosper. Those that do prosper become bigger communities and then central cities, as in the case of Los Angeles and Washington, D.C. Both these cities engulfed neighboring smaller communities in their growth, as did most other cities of substantial size. Those communities also had centers, and some of them flourished. Many more communities now at the periphery of growth will flourish, but they will be in the metropolitan areas that grow and can handle the development problems.

Not all the land converted to office space has been in engulfed communities. Airport office structures are excellent examples, as are office buildings in new communities. The opportunities have been even more widespread in shopping centers.

In some communities most of the shopping is still done downtown. But the trend is toward *regional shopping centers,* especially covered malls. The location of development is in suburbia, in many cases on what was recently farmland.

These regional malls serve somewhat the same function as the old downtown of the small community of an earlier era. Not only is the shopping done there, but the teenagers also hang out there. The young people even have their proms in the malls, and also utilize them for various "town center" activities as does the adult population. Art shows, exhibits, voter registrations, and many of the varied and sundry activities associated with a small downtown center take place in the shopping malls.

Office buildings are sometimes built in the same development as the shopping center. Other times they are built nearby. High-rise apartment buildings are included in some of the more densely developed areas.

Thus the configuration of land use has changed. The basic demand forces still work, but they have been channeled into different patterns by new concepts of work environment as well as by the simple availability of facilities and the accidents of terrain and development.

The basic forces are for economic segregation, with the highest income uses going to land in the most desirable locations. The lesser income uses are also sorted out by the market. This economic segregation becomes a substantial social problem when the scale of the community gets very large. If whole segments of the population are wealthy or poor and if they are in different political jurisdictions, trouble is bound to follow. They will have unequal ability to afford schools, police protection, and a whole host of services. Those that have it better will try to keep their advantage.

Where growth will occur is relatively predictable. Once an area is established as a high-income one, it typically grows by expanding upward or outward into more high-income uses. The less well-to-do cannot compete at that location, and the affluent are not likely to go elsewhere. A sector pattern develops. (The segregation of housing by value and rent levels makes for a land-use pattern explained by Homer Hoyt in his "sector theory.")

The exact growth pattern varies in areas of different urban design. Communities having multiple nuclei may repeat the sector pattern so that some of the upper-income uses are located in the engulfed older communities. Then, the metropolitan area as a whole gets a variation of the sector pattern. Investors who put their money on the broader metropolitan-wide pattern will fare best because the character of the community tends to change as a whole. Thus, communities with mixed income levels and a broad range of housing become high-priced communities when engulfed by a high-income sector.

When a wedge and corridor pattern is used, communities usually attempt to scale the density down outward from the corridor. But they will have high-income corridors and low-income corridors. The demand forces of Hoyt's sector theory are still in force. The configuration changes because master plans force a different dimension.

The old pulls of transportation still affect the growth pattern. Lack of transportation can be a growth constraint. Political power is still correlated with income, so the higher-income areas can reasonably be expected to have better transportation.

The lower-income areas may also grow, and they may also be the locality of good investments, especially if the character of the demand is at the lower end of the price spectrum. The market analyst not only tries to forecast population growth, but he segments it by income so as to determine at what price levels housing will be demanded. In many cases the demand is at the blue-collar wage levels. The reason land used for higher-priced housing is better than land used for lower-priced housing is that it sells for more. All land starts out selling as farmland or at some other nonurban price level, and moves. Some properties move farther than others, but the important thing is to buy them at the right time, just before the move.

Facilities Constraints. The right time to buy is predicated on an increase in demand and/or the removal of a facilities constraint. If the area has plenty of good roads, good well water, porous land, and low water tables permitting septic tanks, plus nonexclusionary zoning that permits adequate land for all uses, then the question is simply one of demand. Changes in employment, together with the kind of land use conversion they require, and its location, are fairly predictable.

But those conditions rarely exist. As demand increases, it pushes up the price of land. That is what makes it so profitable, after all. In the meantime various public authorities will be working on facilities, each in its own way. The changes they make may be of prime importance to the investor.

The federal government has been fostering an interstate highway system for national defense. Commuter usage of it is high. When a highway official is given the choice of paying 100 percent for a local feeder road or contributing 10 percent to an interstate highway, he obviously will take the better buy. Accordingly, over the last decade land investors have needed to know three fundamental things: (*a*) which communities were about to grow; (*b*) the general direction of growth according to types of land uses permitted; and (*c*) where the interstate highways were to be built. Although the situation is a little more complicated in reality, knowledge of these things would give most investors ample edge.

New opportunities generated by mass transit are now appearing. The story here will be similar but much more complicated. It will involve the variables of environmental impact and community conflict, to be discussed later in the chapter. These variables will make selection of land more difficult but more profitable, at least for those who do it wisely.

Transportation is a pulling force for development as well as a constraint. It is a pulling force because as improved transportation reduces travel time, the location gets better. In fact, the accessibility of a location is a determinant of the demand for it. Improved transportation also removes a constraint to the degree that land already in strong demand becomes more accessible. Thus shortages or imbalances in transportation can channel development into land use patterns that are less efficient than could reasonably be achieved.

Public sewage treatment facilities are another constraint. Some land cannot be developed without such facilities. Their existence is not, like transportation, a pulling force for development. They are not a determinant underlying demand unless lack of them creates a shortage. Sewage facilities do not improve accessibility for the public. But they do permit some land to be developed which might otherwise remain unimproved. The demand, however, must already be present. Thus a shortage of sewage treatment facilities may create structural problems that channel growth to some less efficient pattern of development.

The difficulty for the community, and the opportunity, arise in that the demand may be so strong relative to availability of developable land that determination of the land to be developed depends on where the sewer lines will go. Thus close-in land may be skipped over in favor of far-out land because the latter has sewer availability. In some localities the constraint may be water. It could be any of a number of variables—even zoning.

Apartment house construction tends to gravitate to locations having access to jobs, shopping, and transportation, as well as a variety of neighborhood and demand characteristics. But apartment houses are not necessarily constructed at the most sensible locations because of zoning constraints. If the zoning is restrictive enough, developers will build apartment houses anywhere they can as long as they can make a profit, and the sites may not be near transportation or jobs or shopping.

To forecast where a community will grow, one must therefore forecast the availability of facilities. Its transportation plan may already exist as a published document, perhaps even with a time schedule for completion. Most communities have, or will have, a capital improvements program for the construction of sewer, water, and other facilities. Such plans are not always carried out, but they provide a place to start when looking at development constraints.

LOCAL GOALS

The investor looking for land to develop does not end his search with programs for public improvements. The next step is to look at local goals to see what the community wants to achieve. If it has a negative attitude toward development, then the would-be developer may consider legal action.

Growth and No Growth as Goals. Growth in itself is not a goal. It is a mechanism through which other goals such as greater employment opportunities and rising levels of income are achieved. No growth may be a goal in that it represents a desired condition of no change. Another set of desired conditions is represented by the popular term, *quality of life*. The dimensions of quality of life include economic, social, and political conditions, and also the environment, both natural and man-made.

A community seeking to improve its quality of life is likely to consider the economic sector of prime importance, although the greater the community's economic success the less importance it may give to developing its economy further. Thus communities that are growing too slowly because of lack of appropriate economic base activities will seek out industry. They will even accept pollution and company domination because they want more food on the table. If, however, the economic development of the community is proceeding at a satisfactory rate, people may turn their attention to such things as work satisfaction, income distribution, and economic security.

People who live in communities that

measure high economically are relatively more concerned about their political environment, or at least they manage to have a stronger voice in it through electoral and nonelectoral participation. They are better informed, have higher standards of civil liberty, and hold the government to greater accountability. Indeed, this accountability may be the means by which the affluence was generated.

Communities also have goals of a social nature. A "family" community may be distressed to find unrelated individuals sharing a house. The distress may be even greater at the thought of "halfway houses" for people from mental or penal institutions. Its attitudes may include economic discrimination and/or racial and ethnic discrimination. Most communities have their share of bigots, and narrowness of mind is an affliction of epidemic proportions.

Zoning regulations have been used to exclude people, as have other measures. The degree of the intent to exclude may well be related to pressures of growth and the relative number of "undesirables." If the community is not under great growth pressure, no one has to watch the gates. But if it is under pressure it may resort to tactics such as those of some towns in Connecticut, where public beaches are reserved for local residents. Out-of-state cars, particularly from New York, are not welcome. They are not even allowed entrance as visitors. The message is, "Don't come to visit and don't move in." The last people to move into the lovely neighborhood want to be just that—the last people to move in.

The desire is understandable. The air and water are already polluted, and more people mean more pollution. Traffic is congested, and more people mean more congestion. Public facilities are heavily used, and building new schools is expensive. The attitude is, "Thanks a lot for wanting to move to our community, but who needs you?" Or, "We made it, now don't ruin it for us."

The problem occurs because the rate of growth is more rapid than the community is prepared to handle. It doesn't matter whether the source of the problem is (*a*) the rapid pace of change as discussed earlier, or (*b*) the lack of a federal urban growth strategy that would guide employment location, or (*c*) a lack of effective administrators and/or innovative techniques for administration, or (*d*) a lack of statesmanship by local politicians. The point is that in many cases the system works poorly. And it has been getting worse.

Investors, particularly in an area with multiple jurisdictions, need to assess the intent of the public leadership and the community's attitudes in each jurisdiction. Mismanagement, for whatever reason, will drive up land prices if the land is developable. On the other hand, improvement of management will make undevelopable land developable because bringing the land into use makes sense for the community.

Some land now under a sewer moratorium may be built upon eventually because it is absurd to make people drive ten extra miles twice a day. How that will come about will depend in part on the community. Investors can either put their money in land with few problems and wait a short time for modest profits; or they can put their money in land with many problems and wait until they are solved, or possibly help to solve them. The rewards in such cases are quite substantial.

Environmental and Other Impacts. The solution to many of these resource problems is going to depend on public attitudes on environmental questions. As this is being written, some new shopping centers are running into problems with *environmental impact statements.* Persons who do not want the centers allege that they cause pollution and other undesirable effects by virtue of the traffic they generate. That argument may have some merit, but the consumption of services purchased at neighborhood shopping centers is not going to change significantly because a particular shopping center is not built. The consumer will simply drive farther, and perhaps less frequently. The analysts making recommendations against building a shopping center probably do not think of that, nor do the politicians, who may yield to pressures of the moment. But in the course of time, a decision that does not make sense will be reversed, assuming the land is still available. The investor should ask himself whether the community really needs the shopping center. If it does, and if the price is attractive (and it should be because everyone else has been scared away), then it may be wise to buy such land and hold it until opinions change.

In some cases the question will be answered in court. Winning in court may be easier in the case of residential land, a matter that is discussed in the next section. But buying land for future residential land use does not have to wait upon a court battle.

With the price of land escalating, the logical thing to do is to economize—that is, to develop at a higher density. The higher the density permitted, the higher the value for a given piece of land.

Some communities provide for a variety of densities. Land zoned for higher density residential development may not be located where it would be in most demand in the marketplace. If investors believe that very little land will be available at higher density in the better locations, they may purchase land in the less desirable locations and just wait until the market is driven there. Or well-located land that logically should be developed may be bought in anticipation of changes even though the zoning does not currently permit the high density.

Future mass transit stops are a good example to consider. In many instances these locations will be developed with high density. Some will not, and that is a risk investors must take. But in locations where development makes sense from an urban design point of view, investment is a good bet.

Land at future mass transit stops may already have been developed for residential use in the 1920s or earlier. Such houses make good rental units. Bought early enough, they can be obtained at house prices. Later they will sell by the square foot of land, and the price curve will move upward from cents per square foot to a few dollars or more. A final purchase may be made at a fantastic price contingent upon rezoning, but the buyer will fight the zoning battle; the investor will have bought earlier at the lower prices.

In suburban areas this kind of land may be developed for commercial or other nonresidential land uses, but most of the opportunities are in residential uses because they require a lot of land. The transition to higher density may be from five-acre zoning to half-acre zoning or from one-acre zoning to quarter-acre zoning, or from 4 units to the acre to 10 or 20 units to the acre.

The land to buy, of course, is land in the path of growth. If a community has a master plan, the "ultimate paths" may show on it. If not, the investor can look at what would make sense from the community's point of view.

Sometimes the land may be in an area beyond that which has been master planned. In that case the investor's question is again whether developing the land makes economic sense, and if so, when. The answers again are determined by the structure of city growth.

Any property's prospects should be evaluated from the standpoint of the community. Does the community have the capacity to service it with schools, transportation, sewers, and water? What does the community's capital improvements program call for? How much land might the developer be required to donate to the government to facilitate development (i.e., for schools, parks, etc.)? Perhaps most important of all, does the public want that kind of development? If it does, and the only question is one of time, one can buy and wait. If it doesn't, the investor's decision must be whether to pass or to fight.

RESOLUTION OF CONFLICT

The investor's decision to pass or to fight is only one part of the conflict over the rights to use of land. Another part involves the rights of residents of the community as opposed to the rights of those who do not live in the community.

Rights of Others. As a matter of national policy every American family has a right to a decent home and a suitable living environment. This right is stated in the Housing Act of 1949 (see Figure 8–3). Unfortunately, the implementation of that act has left much to be desired.

Part of the attempt to implement it has involved public housing and the impediments frequently associated with social discrimination. Some of these cases have resulted in new laws on equal opportunity in housing, and in the enforcement of existing laws against discrimination.

Citizens of the United States are free to travel from state to state as they see fit. The ease with which they do so sometimes astonishes Europeans who expect to encounter checkpoints when crossing state lines. Not only do the states have no checkpoints, but they are prohibited by law from limiting the movement of persons from one permanent residence to another.

The right to travel to seek economic opportunity has been upheld by the Supreme Court of the United States. During the Great Depression, Cali-

FIGURE 8–3

Be it enacted by the Senate and House of Representatives of the United States of America in Congress assembled, That this Act may be cited as the "Housing Act of 1949."

Declaration of National Housing Policy

SEC. 2. The Congress hereby declares that the general welfare and security of the Nation and the health and living standards of its people require housing production and related community development sufficient to remedy the serious housing shortage, the elimination of substandard and other inadequate housing through the clearance of slums and blighted areas, and the realization as soon as feasible of the goal of a decent home and a suitable living environment for every American family, thus contributing to the development and redevelopment of communities and to the advancement of the growth, wealth, and security of the Nation. The Congress further declares that such production is necessary to enable the housing industry to make its full contribution toward an economy of maximum employment, production, and purchasing power. The policy to be followed in attaining the national housing objective hereby established shall be: (1) private enterprise shall be encouraged to serve as large a part of the total need as it can; (2) governmental assistance shall be utilized where feasible to enable private enterprise to serve more of the total need; (3) appropriate local public bodies shall be encouraged and assisted to undertake positive programs of encouraging and assisting the development of well-planned, integrated residential neighborhoods, the development and redevelopment of communities, and the production, at lower costs, of housing of sound standards of design, construction, livability, and size for adequate family life; (4) governmental assistance to eliminate substandard and other inadequate housing through the clearance of slums and blighted areas, to facilitate community development and redevelopment, and to provide adequate housing for urban and rural nonfarm families with incomes so low that they are not being decently housed in new or existing housing shall be extended to those localities which estimate their own needs and demonstrate that these needs are not being met through reliance solely upon private enterprise, and without such aid; and (5) governmental assistance for decent, safe, and sanitary farm dwellings and related facilities shall be extended where the farm owner demonstrates that he lacks sufficient resources to provide such housing on his own account and is unable to secure necessary credit for such housing from other sources on terms and conditions which he could reasonably be expected to fulfill. The Housing and Home Finance Agency and its constituent agencies, and any other departments or agencies of the Federal Government having powers, functions, or duties with respect to housing, shall exercise their powers, functions, and duties under this or any other law, consistently with the national housing policy declared by this Act and in such manner as will facilitate sustained progress in attaining the national housing objective.

Source: U.S. Congress, *Housing Act of 1949,* Public Law 171, 81st Congress, 1st session, July 15, 1949.

FIGURE 8–4

More recently, the U.S. Supreme Court struck down state-imposed residency requirements for welfare benefits as a restraint on this same fundamental right. In the welfare case, the court observed that "the nature of our Federal Union and our constitutional concepts of personal liberty unite to require that all citizens be free to travel throughout the length and breadth of our land." Although in law this freedom —which is implied by the creation of the Federal Union rather than expressly articulated in the Constitution—is called "the right to travel," it means the right to migrate and settle. Two lower federal courts have applied this principle to invalidate *local* residency requirements for initial occupancy of public housing.

Thus, the principle of freedom of choice as a right flowing from constitutional concepts of personal liberty cannot be restricted by a state, or a locality exercising state-delegated powers, in controlling the use of land for housing. Although the influx of indigents into California may have created fiscal burdens for the state, as an influx of low- or moderate-income people is assumed to do in many localities today, this does not provide an unconditional basis for "closing the door." When a locality proposes not to close the door altogether but to keep it somewhat ajar, as it were, the question arises as to who is able to stand in line waiting to go through. The *Ramapo* court was not concerned, or was not aware, that those in line to enter Ramapo will be mainly people able to afford expensive houses on large lots. Other courts and other local legislatures may view the matter differently if the community's zoning and development plan are fully analyzed from this perspective.

Source: Herbert M. Franklin, *Controlling Urban Growth—But For Whom?* The Potomac Institute, Inc., Washington, D.C., March 1973, p. 24.

fornia tried to stop immigration from the dust bowl in Oklahoma. At that time the migration from Oklahoma was particularly troublesome because it increased the costs of local government, but those costs were not deemed a sufficient reason to exclude the newcomers.

The use of residency requirements by states in dispensing welfare benefits has also been struck down by the U.S. Supreme Court, and lower courts have applied that precedent to requirements for obtaining entry to public housing. (See Figure 8–4.)

The application of the same right to private housing is more difficult because such housing may just not be available. The local development process may be managed in such a way as to exclude the provision of such housing.

Court Action and Rezoning. Landowners sometimes resort to legal action to get their land rezoned so as to make a profit, but, on the legitimate grounds of making available a more balanced choice of housing in the community. Figure 8–5 gives excerpts from court testimony in one such proceeding. In this case, the request was for rezoning in accordance with a master plan. That type of request, of course, is much stronger than the request for an exception of sorts. The legal issues are complicated by the concept of *exclusionary action* and the intent to exclude.

Some local officials make little secret of their intent to exclude. Sometimes they speak out for environment and quality of life. Actually they may mean their own environment and their own quality of life. At the same time, their

FIGURE 8–5

Excerpt from Testimony of Maury Seldin on Balanced Housing in a Community

Q: How does the present zoning, restrictive nature of the present zoning, impact on this housing cost problem?

A: Well, housing costs have been moving up. The restrictive nature of the zoning is that the houses that are being built are very expensive houses. The land that is available is being developed for these very expensive houses and people who can afford to pay even the $50,000 prices begin to run into problems; that is, I am not talking about low-moderate income but the people of substantial income are being driven out of the market by the rising prices because there is not enough land in what we consider normal, moderate size suburban development. One acre is a fairly luxurious site.

Q: Is there, in your opinion, a sufficient supply of land zoned for the R-12-5-R-17 categories in the Pohick Watershed?

A: No. The whole pattern of large-lot zoning has been exclusionary as a way of—

MR. SYMANSKI: Objection, Your Honor; that is testifying to a legal conclusion.

MR. HAZEL: I don't think it is a legal conclusion. Mr. Symanski is sensitive about the use of the word but—

THE COURT: It is a word of art in effect. It is a conclusion I may or may not come to ultimately but it is an ultimate finding.

MR. HAZEL: I didn't know it was a word of art.

THE COURT: I think it can be. If we are talking about constitutional rights, it can be.

MR. HAZEL: We hope the Court will find it is exclusionary.

THE COURT: The objection is sustained.

THE WITNESS: I can answer the question without using that word.

MR HAZEL: He says he can answer the question without using that word.

THE COURT: I am sure there are paraphrases.

THE WITNESS: In many areas, they have used large-lot zoning in order to influence the price of housing which would be built. In some cases, two acres and five acres, and these areas, by being zoned for very large lots have, in my opinion, knowingly concluded that the only houses that anybody could afford to build on there would be expensive and that the only people that could afford to buy them would be super affluent and, therefore, the only people that would be moving into their neighborhood would be of that kind of income class.

The availability of land in Fairfax County is now such that in the one-acre and up category there is a great deal of land and so the way in which the land is being managed, only those with substantial means can afford to move into the County. People who would, let us say, earn in the $20,000 a year category, people who would buy houses in the $50,000 category, do not have adequate opportunity, and people under 40 get very thin, and under that you can forget.

BY MR. HAZEL:

Q: You mean under $40,000 or under 40 years? I guess it is both.

A: If you are going to buy a house in Fairfax County today, if you want to come, if you want to come into the County, if you are looking at the development of the County, the way the land use system is being managed, you pretty well have to be able to afford housing, some in the 50s and the like.

There are some townhouses in the 40s, but if you are talking about single-family detached, most of it is now being built for the super affluent.

Q: You anticipate that is beyond the $50,000 bracket in cost of the house?

A: Most of those are beyond the 60s and more. A lot of it is being at $70,000 and $80,000.

Q: And with specific reference to the Pohick Watershed, you found that condition to prevail?

A: Yes, sir.

MR. HAZEL: I have no further questions.

Source: Testimony given in the following consolidated cases in the Circuit Court of Fairfax County Virginia: *Thomas R. Williams et al.* v. *Board of Supervisors of Fairfax County, Virginia, et al.*; *A. G. Van Meetre Associates, Inc.* v. *Board of Supervisors of Fairfax County, Virginia.*

These cases were appealed by Fairfax County and at the time of writing were being considered by the Supreme Court of Virginia.

actions may in fact delay the cleaning up of water pollution because of the way in which they maintain the sewage treatment facilities and/or fail to upgrade the quality of waste water treatment.

Court action may be an expensive although possibly profitable route. But when the local officials keep losing in the courts, they begin to expose themselves to personal liability from lawsuits charging misfeasance or malfeasance. They are also liable to the discipline of the ballot box if the costs to the community become too high.

Failure to provide for development may choke off the growth of the local economy. The construction industry is important in rapidly growing communities, and its strangulation generates a substantial secondary impact on the local economy. The loss in economic vitality is felt in the local government's revenue. When taxes are raised to balance the books, the citizenry get upset. When they get upset enough, they "throw the rascals out."

A community goal of no growth simply does not make sense. Some development is necessary for viability. The question becomes one of how much, what kind, and where. For this reason most communities with favorable economic prospects sooner or later come around to a sensible policy. Whether the discipline is supplied by the courts, the ballot, or some aspect of federal policy is of concern to the potential investor only as to expectations. He needs to decide whether any particular community seems likely to prosper. If it does, then an investment in the right land in that community will be profitable—very profitable.

No investment is without hazard. Choosing the right parcel of land is of considerable importance, as is getting in and getting out at the right times. An investor must be able to wait.

Timing and waiting are dealt with in the next section, comprised of three chapters. Chapter 9, "Interim Land Uses," deals with income sources that reduce the financial burden of holding the land. Chapter 10, "Analyses of Predevelopment Land," deals with the information required to evaluate developability potential and profitability. Chapter 11, "Analyses of Development," is concerned with the evaluation and development of land for immediate use. That section explains land use conversion so as to assist the investor in knowing what to look for. Finding and buying are covered in the ensuing section.

Part three
Land Conversion

9

Interim Land Uses

Land investors who want to make high profits look for situations in which the land will undergo a change in use. The profit is made because conditions change and problems are solved. Sometimes land investors solve them by getting zoning approval or sewerage connection permits. Sometimes, however, they do not have to do anything but wait.

Waiting is not easy. And waiting is not simply a question of patience. It costs money. Investors have to pay property taxes, interest, and usually some of the principal on their mortgages. The longer they wait, the larger the increase in value necessary for the desired rate of return on their investments.

The analyses of the preceding chapters have indicated that investors should pick the right time to invest and then use the interim to their advantage. The longer they stay in, the more the dollar profits on their investments and perhaps even the higher the rates of return.

However, investors have to keep putting in cash. Some investors do so out of their own earnings. Others use investment income, e.g., the cash flow from other real estate. But there is at least one other way of meeting their waiting expenses: they can get income from the property itself.

Such income is said to be derived from an interim land use. Frequently the land is committed to a low-value use many years before the urbanization process reaches it. It may be a farm not far from the edge of town, or a miniature golf course on what was once an arterial road of a suburban community and will someday be the location of an office building development. Perhaps the land has been developed with a low-density garden apartment project and now has more value in reuse for high-rise development than the combined value of the land and buildings if the land were to remain in its current use.

While numerous types of interim land uses are possible (including agricultural, extractive, recreational, residential, commercial, and industrial), the vast majority are either agricultural or urban (residential, commercial, or industrial). This chapter will discuss agricultural uses and generalized urban interim uses. The somewhat significant omission from land investment is recreational land.

Recreational land bought for recreational use without expectation for change to another use does not qualify as an interim land use. It may provide a fine investment, especially if it is developed and used. With the growing popularity of recreation, despite the energy crisis, such land has potential use for a second home with resale of the second home for a large profit, just as with the primary residence.

Recreational land can be an excellent investment if it is bought wholesale, cut up in pieces, and sold. Buying the pieces subsequently sold "for investment" could also turn out to be profitable. But the results depend very heavily on the land realistically being used for recreation. Thus this topic is not included because, in this author's view, the best reason for buying recreational land is to use it—and this book is about buying land that someone else is going to use.

AGRICULTURAL LAND

Investment in agricultural land generally is an investment in a business. The intent of this book is not to explain how to run such a business but to explain how investment in land used for that business may be made; particularly how land used in that business may within a reasonable time come to be used for some urban purpose. Such conversions create big profits.

If the land is located at the urban fringe, the price will already have risen so high that the income from farming will be negligible. The time to have bought that land was five or ten years earlier. The time horizon for such purchases is more likely to be five to ten years than the two to four years for land about ready for conversion. The difference is that the farmland is drawn into the pattern over a long period of time, and anticipation of that change pushes prices above farmland values. Thus the longer intermediate-term investor (five to seven years) gets in at close to farmland prices, and the short-term investor (two to four years) speculates on zoning changes or sewer installations. (See the next chapter for a discussion of zoning and sewers.)

Investors do not have to work farmland to get an income from it. As a matter of fact, with the increasing scale of farming, combining ownership and operation of small farms is becoming more and more difficult. Usually the landowner can find a neighboring farmer who will, if the economics are right, be glad to pay to use the land. Also, larger commercial organizations may want to farm the land, or sharecropping arrangements may be made with a tenant farmer. If something of value is for sale (such as the use of good farmland) and a market exists for it, investors can profit from owning a farm and having someone else run it. The question is, which farm to own.

Farm Size. If ten acres or more is used for agricultural production, it can

TABLE 9-1
Number of Farms and Value of Farm Products Sold by Kind of Farm Organization: United States, 1964

Kind of Farm Organization	*Total Value of Sales*	*Number of Farms* (thousands)	(percent)	*Value of Farm Products Sold* (millions)	(percent)
Commercial					
Elite	$100,000 and over	31.4	1.0	$ 8,539	24.2
Blue ribbon	40,000–99,999	110.5	3.5	6,533	18.5
Upper middle	20,000–39,999	259.9	8.2	7,114	20.1
Lower middle	10,000–19,999	467.1	14.8	6,614	18.7
Low income	5,000– 9,999	504.6	16.0	3,653	10.3
(Subtotal)		(1,373.5)	(43.5)	(32,453)	(91.8)
Subsistence*	50– 4,999	792.2	25.1	1,975	5.6
Part-time†	50– 4,999	639.4	20.2	495	1.4
Partial Retirement‡	50– 2,499	352.8	11.2	430	1.2
Total, All Farms		3,157.9	100.0	$34,369	100.0

* Income received from nonfarm sources was less than value of farm products sold. Farm operator was also less than 65 years of age, and he did not work off-farm 100 or more days.

† Income received from nonfarm sources was greater than value of farm products sold. Farm operator was under 65 years of age and worked off-farm 100 or more days.

‡ Farm operator was over 65 years of age. Category includes 2,180 abnormal farms.

Source: *Census of Agriculture,* Vol. 2, Chap. 6, United States, 1964.

legitimately be called a farm. Small farms are typically subsistence or part-time operations (see Table 9–1). The United States has over a million such farms, and according to the census of agriculture (1964) they comprised 56 percent of the number of units but accounted for only 8 percent of the value of the farm products sold. Thus, economically, these small farms are frequently more practicable investments for those who will be actively involved.

The commercial farm is more of a business. It involves the major portion of a person's time, promotes enough income to support a family, and utilizes enough capital to have a reasonably efficient operation. An idea of scale is provided in Table 9–2 and in Figure 9–1. It shows that a few hundred acres requires several hundred thousand dollars of capital investment, most of which is in the land. Since the farms are financeable, investors with down payments in the low five figures can realistically afford such a farm. Or a small group could handle a fair-sized parcel.

A square mile contains 640 acres. Divided into four quarters it provides four 160-acre parcels, which measure one half mile on each side. Each parcel has enough land for a 500-house subdivision (at 3 units to the acre) with lots that would average more than 80 feet wide. One tenth of the land in a quarter of a square mile, or 16 acres, is enough for a neighborhood shopping center, and one half of the land in a quarter square mile parcel or 80 acres is enough for a regional shopping mall. For those kinds of uses the prices are quoted in dollars per square foot rather than dollars per acre. Even 40 acres can turn out to be a lot of land in an urban use.

The transition of farmland, be it 40

TABLE 9–2
Land, Labor, Capital Resources, and Operator's Income: High- and Low-Income; Small, Medium, and Large Commercial Farms; Central Indiana, 1970

Size of Farm:	*Small*		*Medium*		*Large*	
Tillable Acres:	*Less than 260*		*260 to 400*		*400 and Over*	
Income Grouping:	*Low*	*High*	*Low*	*High*	*Low*	*High*
Number of Farms:	*7*	*8*	*7*	*7*	*14*	*16*
Total farm acres	240	274	405	385	669	671
Months of labor	17.4	17.4	25.2	18.8	28.2	30.1
Total days productive work*	290	478	535	512	745	874
Days of productive work per man	201	329	255	327	317	348
Capital investment						
Land, building, and improvement	$ 85,205	$104,968	$174,343	$151,509	$279,000	$229,798
Livestock	14,239	20,208	25,249	26,648	43,152	42,901
Machinery and equipment	12,038	13,360	26,740	22,078	35,374	35,442
Feed, grain, supplies	11,295	13,953	24,386	29,666	39,772	57,115
Total	$122,777	$152,489	$250,718	$229,901	$397,248	$429,256
Capital investment per man	$ 94,248	$105,220	$119,410	$146,813	$169,132	$170,828
Total value of sales†	$ 40,035	$ 47,990	$ 75,261	$ 76,063	$107,983	$115,077
Operator's labor income‡	$ −2,464	$ 11,266	$ −1,999	$ 12,962	$ −3,632	$ 29,288

*A productive work unit is equal to the amount of productive work one man can accomplish in a 10-hour day under average conditions.

†Cash farm receipts.

‡Operator's labor income is what the operator receives for his labor and management after paying all operating expenses and interest on all capital invested.

Source: *Indiana Farm Business Summaries*, 1970.

or 160 acres, to developable urban land typically takes a long time; the question of what the land can produce until it is ready for urban use is answered in the next section. But one last word about size: land that can be farmed intensively may be available in relatively small parcels; land that is farmed extensively is typically available in large parcels. But a tree farm (extensive use) in a smaller parcel is not unreasonable. The key question is

FIGURE 9–1
Capital Investment in Indiana Farms, 1970
(average per farm)

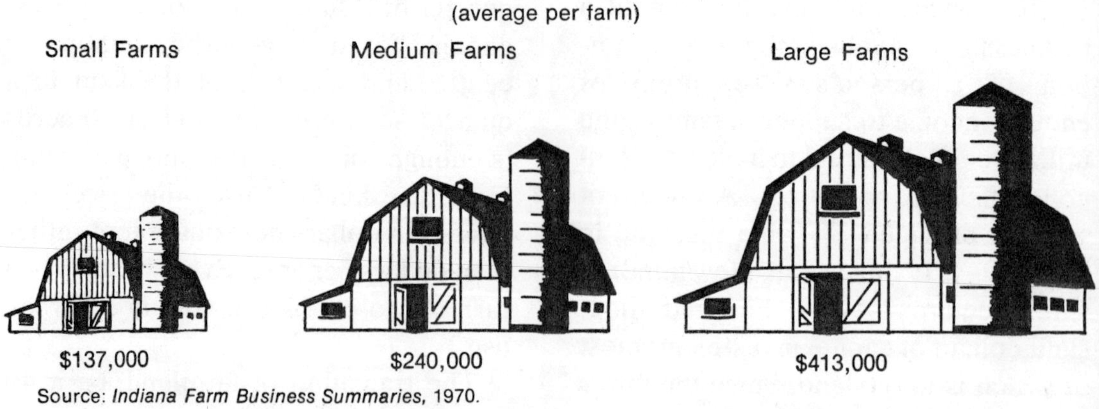

Source: *Indiana Farm Business Summaries*, 1970.

whether a market exists for the use of the land, at whatever the size of the parcel.

Land for Farming. Location is always important, even in farming. Aside from the natural environment, the location affects accessibility to the market and to other activities. In the case of farmland for investment, the closer in the location the greater the potential.

At any given location climate will affect the agricultural productivity of the land. The elements to consider in climate are rainfall, frost-free dates, and temperature ranges. Human beings have as yet been unable to do much about climate. One implication of this fact is that the potential competition in growing some crops is severely limited by climatic conditions.

Climate is not enough. Soil is required. And soil may be the most important single factor in determining the type of farming that may be done on the land. The soil may be viewed as a natural body or medium that can be modified to be usable for growing crops or increasing yield.

The county farm agent has a wealth of information. Finding the right land is the subject of a later chapter, but note that when evaluating farmland for investment the first questions may well be, "Where is it?" and "What can you do with it?" A look at a soil map in consultation with the farm agent would give a pretty good picture of what crops are growing where, especially in relation to locations of particular interest. (See Figure 9–2.)

Topography is another major consideration. This means the lay of the land—its slope and physical contour. This kind of information is shown on a contour map. (See Figure 9–3.) Topography is important not only from the standpoint of moving machinery but also draining the land. Topography is also an important cost factor in developing land, but with urban land the cost of modifying the slope and contour may not be prohibitive.

Based upon location, including climate and physical features of the land and especially soil and topography, a particular farm may produce particular products. Whatever they are, whether grain, green beans, or grass (for feeding cattle), the product will be exposed to a market. Conditions in that market affect the value of the land.

Labor and Capital. Farms require labor and capital just as do other businesses. A small farm may include the farm family and possibly one or two hired hands. The family owns and operates the business, which may even be incorporated.

The large-scale farm or ranch operation may have numerous hired laborers and thus develop some management organization. This type of operation exists where conditions are favorable to overseeing numerous laborers in production efforts. Such large-scale farming is sometimes referred to as agribusiness, since it is a combination of agriculture and business. Large enterprises may have vertical as well as horizontal integration. Vertically integrated agribusiness covers various stages of production ranging from growing food to process-

FIGURE 9-2
Montgomery County, Maryland

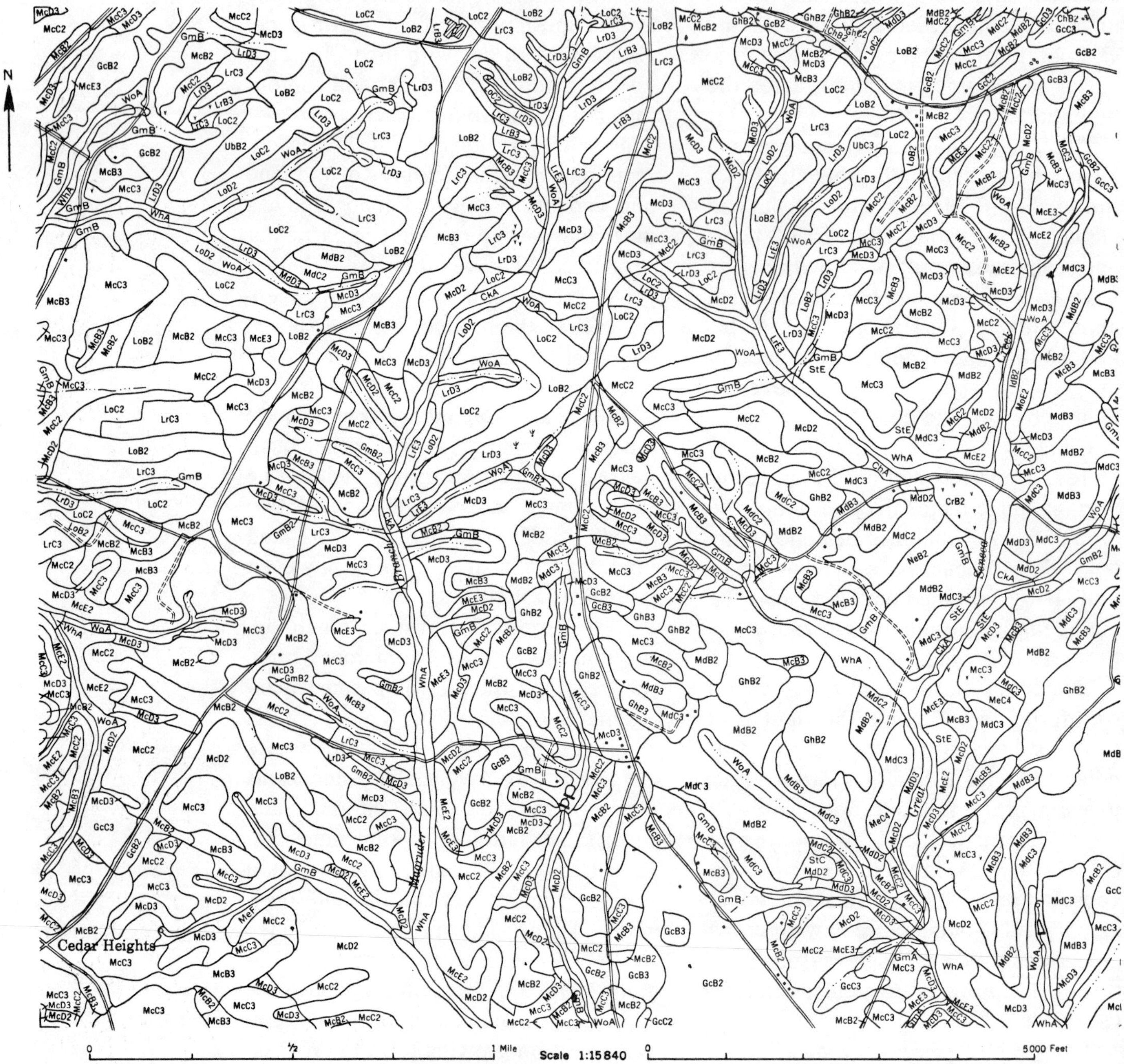

Source: The Maryland National Capital Park and Planning Commission.

FIGURE 9-2 (*Continued*)
Explanation of Soil Map Symbols

Map symbol	Soil	Depth to seasonally high water table (feet)	Depth to bedrock (feet)	Brief description of site and soil	Depth from surface (typical profile) (inches)	USDA (textural class)
LhC3	Lewisberry sandy loam, shallow, 8 to 15 percent slopes, severely eroded.	(3)	1 to 2			
LhD2	Lewisberry sandy loam, shallow, 15 to 25 percent slopes, moderately eroded.	(3)	3			
LhD3	Lewisberry sandy loam, shallow, 15 to 25 percent slopes, severely eroded.	(3)	1 to 2			
LhE3	Lewisberry sandy loam, shallow, 25 to 45 percent slopes, moderately and severely eroded.	(3)	1 to 2			
LnA	Lindside silt loam, 0 to 3 percent slopes.	1 to 2	(3)	Moderately well drained soils on the flood plains; developed in alluvium derived from limestone. Occasionally flooded.	0 to 4 4 to 18 18 to 48+	Silt loam...... Silt loam...... Silt loam......
LoB2	Linganore channery silt loam, 3 to 8 percent slopes, moderately eroded.	(3)	2	Well drained to excessively drained, shallow upland soils that developed in residuum derived from hard, phyllitic schist and that contain much skeletal material. The severely eroded soils have lost most, and in places all, of the original surface soil, and the subsoil is mixed with any remaining surface soil; a few to many gullies, some to bedrock.	0 to 6	Channery silt loam.
LoC2	Linganore channery silt loam, 8 to 15 percent slopes, moderately eroded.	(3)	2		6 to 20	Channery silty clay.
LoD2	Linganore channery silt loam, 15 to 25 percent slopes, moderately eroded.	(3)	2		20 to 24	Very channery silty clay.
LrB3	Linganore channery silty clay loam, 3 to 8 percent slopes, severely eroded.	(3)	1		24+	....
LrC3	Linganore channery silty clay loam, 8 to 15 percent slopes, severely eroded.	(3)	1			
LrD3	Linganore channery silty clay loam, 15 to 25 percent slopes, severely eroded.	(3)	1			
LrE3	Linganore channery silty clay loam, 25 to 45 percent slopes, moderately and severely eroded.	(3)	1			
McB2	Manor channery silt loam, 3 to 8 percent slopes, moderately eroded.	(3)	2 to 6	The channery silt loams are somewhat excessively drained, shallow upland soils that developed in residuum weathered from hard schist; much skeletal material that increases in coarseness with depth. The severely eroded channery silt loams have lost most, and in places all, of the original surface soil; a few to many gullies, some to bedrock. The silt loams developed in residuum from softer schist and are nearly free of skeletal material; the saprolite is weathered to much greater depth; ML to about 9 inches, then ML to MH to bedrock. The severely eroded silt loams have lost most, and in places all, of the original surface soil; a few shallow to deep gullies. In the very severely eroded soils, highly micaceous parent material is exposed, and a few deep gullies have formed; bedrock is exposed in some places.	0 to 7	Channery silt loam.
McB3	Manor channery silt loam, 3 to 8 percent slopes, severely eroded.	(3)	1 to 4		7 to 18	Channery silty clay loam.
McC2	Manor channery silt loam, 8 to 15 percent slopes, moderately eroded.	(3)	2 to 6		18 to 36+	Channery silty clay loam.
McC3	Manor channery silt loam, 8 to 15 percent slopes, severely eroded.	(3)	1 to 4			
McD2	Manor channery silt loam, 15 to 25 percent slopes, moderately eroded.	(3)	2 to 6			
McD3	Manor channery silt loam, 15 to 25 percent slopes, severely eroded.	(3)	1 to 4			
McE2	Manor channery silt loam, 25 to 45 percent slopes, moderately eroded.	(3)	2 to 6			
McE3	Manor channery silt loam, 25 to 45 percent slopes, severely eroded.	(3)	1 to 4			
MdB2	Manor silt loam, 3 to 8 percent slopes, moderately eroded.	(3)	6 to 12			
MdB3	Manor silt loam, 3 to 8 percent slopes, severely eroded.	(3)	5 to 10			

Source: U.S. Department of Agriculture Soil Conservation Service. Maryland Agricultural Experiment Station.

FIGURE 9–3
Contour Map

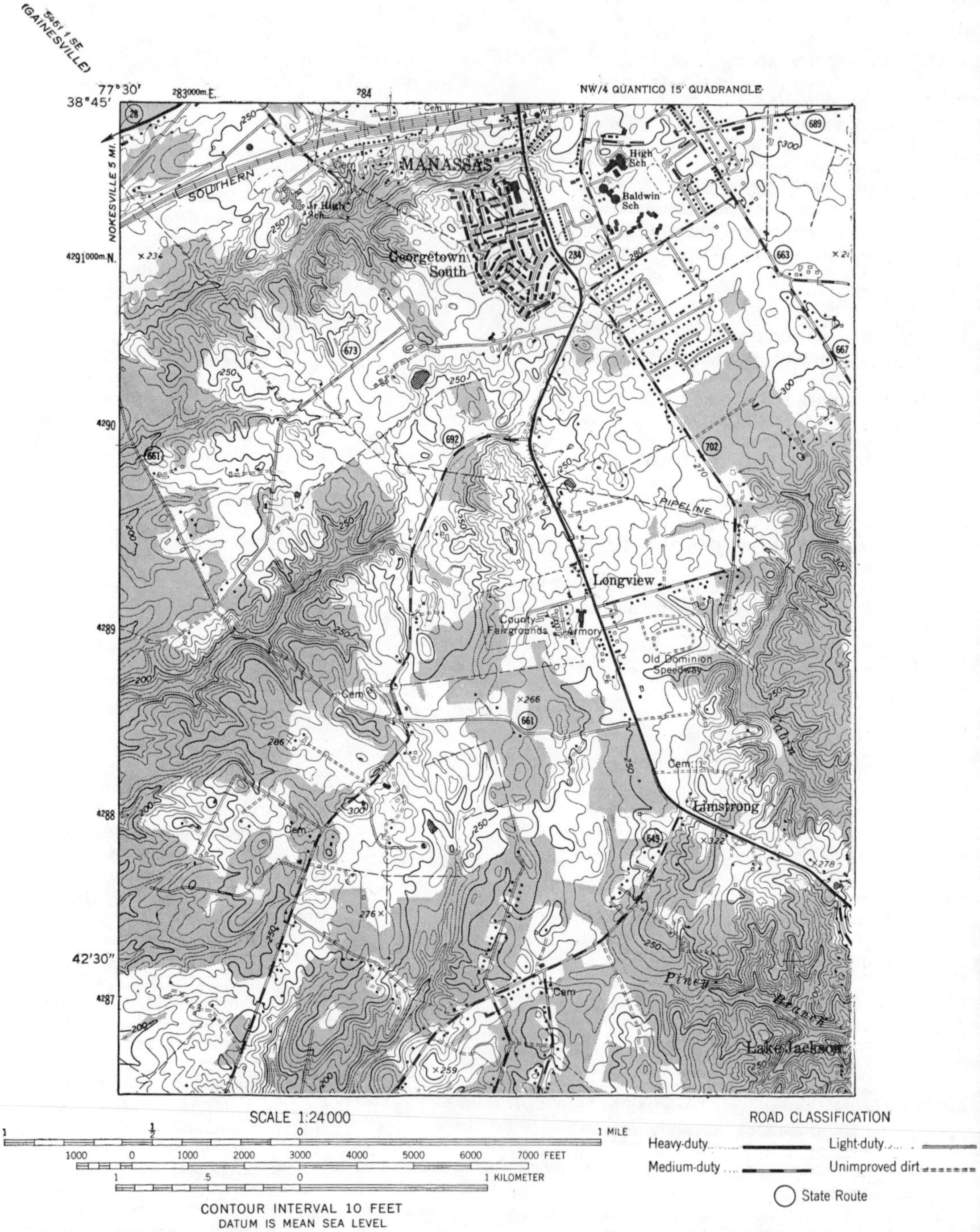

Source: U.S. Department of the Interior, Geological Survey, map of Independent Hill Quadrangle, Virginia, 7–5 minute series.

ing, canning, and wholesaling. On a horizontal scale it combines activities at the same stage of production; thus various crops may be grown at various locations and with changing crop mixes.

The firm that owns the enterprise may own the real estate. But just as many business firms lease their plants, so many farmers or farm enterprises lease their land.

The use of land may be paid for under a lease by a fixed fee in cash to cover a stipulated period of time. Or the landowner and the farmer may crop share with payment for land depending upon the proceeds of sale of the crop.

Under the lease arrangement, when payment is made in cash the rent is fixed on a per-acre basis (or for the whole farm) and the tenant assumes the risks of the farming business. Thus, crop failures or low yields hit the tenant first and hardest and may hit the landlord only if the tenant cannot pay the rent. Theoretically, rental rates should follow crop prices. However, land prices (and rents) increase steadily each year (see Figure 9–4).

The crop-share arrangement calls for the rent on the land to be a share of the crop (50–50 or 60–40). In such an arrangement the landlord contributes the use of the land, buildings, and other improvements such as fences. Sometimes he pays the real estate taxes, insurance on buildings, upkeep on buildings and fences, and perhaps even a share of the seed cost, fertilizer cost, and other expenses of operating the enterprise. The tenant furnishes all the labor, power, and machinery. Thus the tenant has to put up the money for major machinery, repairs, and fuel, as well as his share of seed and fertilizer costs and other operating expenses. A cash payment may even be a part of the deal, in which case the arrangement is a crop-share-cash arrangement.

As with most real estate deals, terms are negotiable. An inquiry into local practices as they relate to particular crops will indicate what the usual arrangements are. Going with the usual pattern frequently is easiest, although some price items may be negotiable.

Another important variation is the share lease for crop or livestock. Under this arrangement the landlord and tenant own the livestock or crops jointly. They each put up half of the money for the livestock, or make their

FIGURE 9–4

Indexes of Farm Real Estate Value per Acre, Prices Received by Farmers for Crops, and All Farm Products (March 1, 1967 = 100 percent)

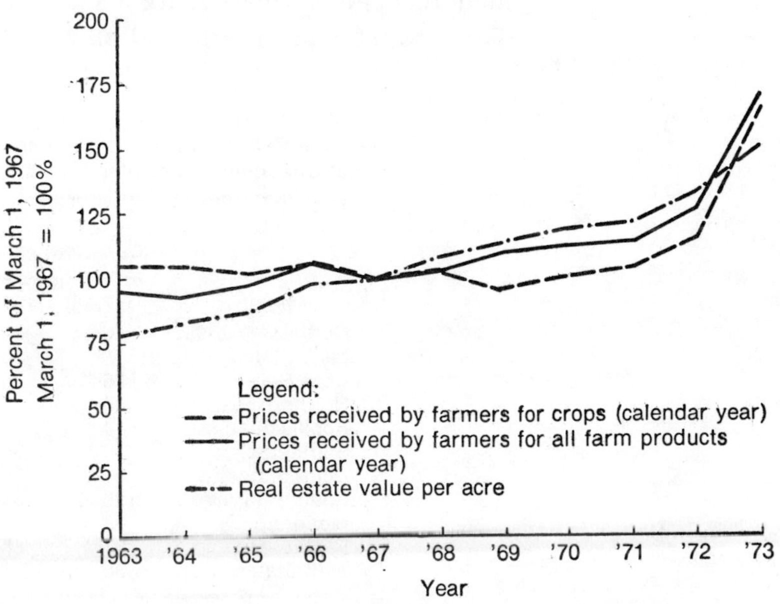

Source: William D. Crowley, United States Department of Agriculture. Compiled from agricultural prices.

contribution in kind. Additionally, the landlord contributes the use of land, buildings, and permanent improvements. Usually he also pays the real estate taxes and insurance, and frequently will pay for half of the equipment, for example, feed grinders, manure spreaders, or milking machines. The tenant furnishes all the labor, power, and machinery and pays for all hired labor, machinery repairs, and half of the general operating expenses.

Sometimes the tenant under the arrangement will also own some land and will pool that land with that of other landlords. In that case the tenant pays the property taxes and insurance on his own land.

Because of mechanization the trend is toward large farms, and so a farm enterprise may expand its operation by leasing land in one form or another from others in the area. (See Table 9–3.) The market for the use of that land reflects the market for its crops. Thus investment in farmland may well be worth while based upon rising farmland values. (See Table 9–4.)

Naturally, the big investment winner will be farmland that undergoes a transition in land use. The price to pay for that speculation may be low compared to the potential return.

The operation of the business of farming requires capital as does the ownership of the land. The amount of capital needed for the business may range from as little as one half to as much as twice that required for land. The ratio varies with location and type of farm.

The source of capital may be equity funds or borrowed money, and generally both sources are used. The borrowed money may be a long-term loan in the 10 to 40-year range with the real estate and farm equipment covered under the mortgage. Under such a package mortgage, personal property used in the business is pledged along with the real property as security for the loan.

If the farm is purchased with a low

TABLE 9–3
Farm Real Estate Transfers: Percentage of Purchases by Intended Method of Operation, Year Ending March 1, 1972 and 1973

	Complete Farm		*Part of Another Farm**		*Part-Time Farm*	
Region	*1972*	*1973*	*1972*	*1973*	*1972*	*1973*
Northeast	46	52	30	28	24	20
Lake States	41	36	43	44	16	20
Corn Belt	25	25	63	64	12	11
Northern Plains	15	17	80	79	5	4
Appalachian	44	41	38	38	18	21
Southeast	28	34	54	49	18	17
Delta States	31	35	49	55	20	10
Southern Plains	28	33	58	53	14	14
Mountain	33	40	54	50	13	10
Pacific	37	36	43	46	20	18
48 States	30	31	56	56	14	13

Based on farmland sales reported by farm realtors and others.
* To be operated with land already owned or leased.

TABLE 9-3 (*Continued*)
Farm Real Estate Transfers: Percentage of Purchases by Method of Operation before and after Sale, 48 States, Year Ending March 1, 1970–1973

Type of Operation	*1970*	*1971*	*1972*	*1973*
Complete farm before sale				
Bought for operation as:				
A complete farm	19	21	25	26
Part of another farm	25	21	21	23
Part-time farm	5	4	4	3
Total	49	46	50	52
Part of another farm before sale,				
Bought for operation as:				
A complete farm	4	4	4	4
Part of another farm	32	34	32	31
Part-time farm	4	6	5	4
Total	40	44	41	39
Part-time farm before sale				
Bought for operation as:*				
A complete farm	2	1	1	1
Part of another farm	4	4	3	3
Part-time farm	5	5	9	9
Total	11	10	9	5
All transfers	100	100	100	100

Based on sales reported by farm realtors and others.

* The data for properties that were part-time before sale are biased downward because reporters are instructed to include only those properties of 10 acres or more used primarily for farming purposes. This limitation excludes many part-time farms.

Source: Economic Research Service, U.S. Department of Agriculture, *Farm Real Estate Market Developments*, July 1973, p. 25.

down payment the seller may retain title but execute a land contract or contract for deed; thus the document is both a credit instrument and an instrument of transfer. The purchaser is in a lesser position than if he had a deed. In some states the land contract is generally acceptable in cases of low down payment.

Most real estate loans, aside from those provided by sellers, are extended by commercial banks, savings and loan associations, life insurance companies, federal land bank associations, and through the Farmers Home Administration.

An operating farm is a financial asset. It provides income that is available for repayment of loans. Vacant land not used in any production, and thus not producing income, is not desired by lending institutions as security for a loan. Lenders want to see where the money to repay them is going to come from. Income is a good source.

On the basis of income, intermediate term financing—e.g., for three to eight years—is also available. Those loans are used for capital equipment or other expenditures that will assist in income production.

Short-term capital, money borrowed for a few months or perhaps a year, is designed to bridge the gap in cash requirements until the crop is sold. This kind of borrowing is strictly for short-term operation of the business and not part of its permanent or long-term capital.

A farm business is like any other business in that the enhancement or loss of capital depends to a great extent on the quality of management. In some conditions even the poorest manage-

TABLE 9-4

Farm Real Estate: Indexes of Average Value Per Acre, by State, Grouped by Farm Production Region, 1960, 1965, and 1970–73* (1967 = 100)

State	*1960*	*1965*	*1970*	*1971*	*1972*	*1973*
Northeast						
Maine	79	89	128	146		
New Hampshire	66	86	149	178		
Vermont	70	83	155	177		
Massachusetts	72	89	126	139	174	198
Rhode Island	67	89	132	145		
Connecticut	68	87	134	149		
New York	73	90	123	132	155	176
New Jersey	58	82	144	155	180	211
Pennsylvania	70	88	145	154	167	201
Delaware	63	92	116	131	134	155
Maryland	61	85	138	150	162	191
Lake States						
Michigan	72	84	113	115	127	150
Wisconsin	76	85	124	137	148	179
Minnesota	80	90	118	121	127	144
Corn Belt						
Ohio	73	86	115	120	127	147
Indiana	69	80	104	109	113	131
Illinois	71	84	107	108	116	129
Iowa	73	79	114	114	122	141
Missouri	63	82	124	130	143	160
Northern Plains						
North Dakota	69	87	120	122	127	142
South Dakota	74	86	112	114	118	130
Nebraska	69	86	115	117	127	145
Kansas	72	88	107	109	118	137
Appalachian						
Virginia	67	85	121	132	149	171
West Virginia	66	93	137	153	177	211
North Carolina	69	91	113	128	138	164
Kentucky	71	93	116	123	137	153
Tennessee	66	88	123	128	142	167
Southeast						
South Carolina	68	88	124	135	162	179
Georgia	55	80	138	152	175	201
Florida	74	100	121	128	136	(†)
Alabama	57	85	121	139	146	167
Delta States						
Mississippi	53	81	125	127	129	144
Arkansas	54	84	129	127	143	159
Louisiana	66	80	116	127	139	148
Southern Plains						
Oklahoma	61	87	115	122	131	150
Texas	67	89	119	125	138	156
Mountain						
Montana	71	89	124	131	142	159
Idaho	76	91	120	128	141	159
Wyoming	62	88	116	119	134	153
Colorado	69	88	105	114	128	152
New Mexico	62	88	120	127	136	151
Arizona	56	85	127	139	159	170
Utah	80	89	137	154	173	186
Nevada	67	83	155	181	213	251
Pacific						
Washington	73	88	124	124	130	145
Oregon	52	91	137	152	170	187
California	72	91	110	109	112	115
48 States‡	68	86	117	122	132	150

* March 1 values Includes Improvements. Revised data relate to series published in Supp. 2 to CD-77, June 1973, which supersedes all previously published real estate index series.

† Insufficient data for publication.

‡ Excludes Florida after 1972.

Source: Economic Research Service, U.S. Department of Agriculture, *Farm Real Estate Market Development*, July 1973, p. 15.

ment can survive. But sooner or later the quality of management tells in profit and capital accumulation. Two examples are often given to show the importance of good management. One is that of a hired hand who saves four years to purchase 80 acres. Sixteen years later he owns 320 acres and rents an additional 400 acres. By way of contrast another fellow inherits a section and a half (960 acres). In 10 years he has sold off pieces of the land to pay his debts—first 160 acres, then 80 acres, and then 240 until he has only 480 heavily mortgaged acres remaining. In short, if an investor is going to share the risk in the business, as is often the case, he should make a careful assessment of the quality of the farm management. Otherwise it is better to take a cash lease and hope for the best.

Other Factors. Hoping for the best is not a financial exercise, only an emotional one. Other factors than hope need to be present. These include the accessibility of the farm enterprise to necessary services, credit institutions that will lend money, farm supplies, buildings, contractors, farm machine dealers, and grain and feed. Agricultural markets may require shipping points, grain elevators, cotton gins, canning factories, tobacco auctions, and livestock yards. The adequacy of these facilities as well as the market for the product affect the profitability of operation.

Many people buy farms to make money. But for others they are a nonmonetary source of satisfaction. The satisfaction of using home-grown products is as important to some people as the money saved in raising the food. Pride of ownership and recreation are other types of satisfaction. From the investment point of view, owning a house and land is also a good hedge against inflation. However, the emphasis in this book is on the economic benefits.

Only the experienced farmer can realistically expect profitable results from being an owner-operator. A farmette on the suburban fringe will provide some income, but the owner-operator will probably have to have a job as well. Such a real estate investment can do quite well, but the money will be made on the land appreciation, not the farming income.

An absentee owner with a tenant can do all right. But the farm is a business, and the landlord will have various risks depending on whether the arrangement is one of shares or a cash lease. The cash lease has the least business risk.

The most risky course is to buy a farm and employ a resident manager with hired labor. Such investors are advised to learn something elsewhere about farming, for this book is about land investment, not farming.

Investment Analysis. Whether the owner of the land is going to operate the farm through a crop share agreement or lease it for cash, he needs to know something about its value as an investment property. As with any investment, its value may be predicated on what comparable property is selling for. But if that is the only method used, the investor has no way of knowing whether the market is overpriced. Disillusioned stock market investors can tell a lot about their experiences in overpaying.

Obviously an investor will not pay more than the prevailing price. But neither will he want to pay more than the present value of the future benefits.

Two methods can be used to calculate the present value of future benefits. The difference between them lies in the choice of capitalizing all the income earned by the business or in capitalizing the income earned by the land.

The first method treats the farm as a going business. In many instances income and expense statements for the farm are available. The first thing to do with such statements is to evaluate the numbers that go into them, as to their reasonableness for future projections. This evaluation involves not only the question of changing conditions but also the kind of accounting treatment. How are capital outlays treated? Are they expensed? Is the depreciation reasonable? Are management fees included? Are any items omitted? These and other questions will provide the basis for estimating a reasonable future income and expense statement.

Most agricultural colleges have data on typical operating statements of various types of farms in their area so that a potential investor can check a statement for reasonableness. He can also assess through the agricultural school the future for the farm's crop. The amount of free advice available to farmers is enormous, and its quality is very good. The information includes prices, farm size or volume, crop yield or rate of livestock production, and labor utilization. Analyses are available by crop as well—e.g., alfalfa, hay, dairy cattle, and feeder cattle.

The net income earned by the enterprise is subject to federal income taxation. Some items, however, are expensed without a cash outlay. For example, depreciation is treated as an expense for income taxes without the owner having to put out cash. The result is that part of the benefit of farm investment is in tax shelter as well as in cash.

The particular tax advantages may be reflected in the capitalization rate. Beyond that, other techniques are available for calculating the present value of the projected income from the farm. It is like valuing a business on the basis of its earnings. Comparing price/earnings ratios is a rather simplistic technique. Discounted cash flow is more refined. In both cases the investor makes a projection of future income and an estimate of what he should pay now for the right to that income.

The alternative to valuing the business is to value the land based upon the rent that would be paid for it. That rent, of course, is related to what a reasonably well-run business can afford to pay. The land may have a premium value above that capitalization because of its potential for an urban use. An investor needs to identify how much of the value is based upon income and how much on speculation for conversion in land use.

The idea of interim use is that the income will carry the land—that is, the rental income will reduce the negative cash flow or even permit an investment that requires no additional cash after the down payment. The investor may wait five or ten years for his proceeds of sale, which may be a very large chunk of money taxed at a favorable long-term capital gains rate. Therefore, farming can be a valuable interim use for land.

OTHER INTERIM LAND USES

Investment in farms and other agricultural land may be viewed as investment in interim land uses when the land is expected to go through some transition in use. Premiums are paid for such farmland. The size of the premiums reflect the speculative value of the potential of land conversion.

Most land investments are primarily based upon that speculative value. As previously noted, such investments require that one keep investing, because vacant land produces a negative cash flow. The investor must keep adding to the investment. Constant negative cash flow can be a problem for some investors because they prefer to make lump-sum investments from time to time without committing themselves further. They may not need a positive cash flow from their investments, but just do not want a negative cash flow.

Investments in land with an interim use are well suited for such investors. The income from such current use may be enough to carry the land, i.e., produce neither a positive nor a negative cash flow. Total cash receipts and total cash expenditures would nearly balance.

Such interim land uses include, of course, the farm that is surrounded by urban land uses. Later that farm may be subdivided for single-family homes. Sometimes, however, more intense and valuable uses are made of the land and the "farmer" is able to hold off selling for quite some time. The farm income helps to pay rising taxes. In some states preferential tax assessment policies permit the "farmer" to pay taxes on the land as farmland rather than according to the value at which it would sell. The incentive is thus to hold the land for further price rises.

In many jurisdictions the county assessor values the land according to its current zoning. At the same time the planning and zoning authority will wait for the owner to apply for rezoning, even when it knows that the expected use is one it would reasonably be expected to grant. As a result, the investor may pay less property tax than he would otherwise.

Other possible interim uses include single-family detached houses that will be torn down later for apartments or other uses. Much of the land near new metro or rapid-rail subway locations in towns has potential interim uses. Additionally, light industrial and office building properties in suburban areas that are being engulfed by urbanization are candidates for investment with the intention of razing the buildings at some future date in order to reuse the land.

Value in Current Use. The value of the current use is predicated on current income and the expectation that that income will continue. Thus in a given neighborhood a 25-year-old, three-bedroom, 1,200-square-foot house on a 60x150-foot lot might sell for $20,000. But for similar houses fronting on the main street—which has been rezoned as commercial and is undergoing development—the price might be $36,000 (which is $600 per front foot or $4 per square foot). That increase to the $36,000 price did not happen all at once. A few years earlier most of the houses were selling for $18,000, but those with the speculative use before rezoning were selling at about $24,000. And a few years before that the houses might all have sold for $15,000 each with little if any differential in price by location on or off the main road.

As things turned out, people who bought homes that happened to be on the main street at $15,000 were lucky. Usually those houses are less desirable because of traffic noise and hazard. Investors who started paying premiums for the houses on land that had potential for rezoning turned out to be smart. If they paid an extra few thousand dollars for the chance of a substantial increase, it was well worth it. Buying a house at $24,000 and watching it move to $36,000 over a few years is quite satisfactory if only a few thousand dollars are invested in the down payment.

Such houses on the rental market would bring anywhere from $150 a month to $180 per month, more or less. Cash flow would be very small, perhaps negative, depending on the price, kind of house, taxes, and expenses of upkeep. If large premiums were paid for the potential of reuse, the cash flow would most assuredly be negative.

At the time that the houses with speculative potential mentioned above are selling for $24,000, while the others are still selling at $18,000, the property is a good buy. The value in its current use is $18,000. The value considering the potential use is $24,000. A $6,000 premium is paid for speculating. But interim use of this property provides an excellent vehicle for financing the operation.

If an investor bought a lot for $24,000 it would have to increase in value by at least 10 percent per year in order to cover interest and taxes. But, if he buys land with an interim use, the income that is produced offsets part of that 10 percent (in this case $2,400). The rent at say $160 a month or about $2,000 a year will even, after taxes and operating expenses, leave something to reduce carrying costs. That money can be used to pay the interest on the mortgage. Thus, for instance, $1,400 a year of income after expenses but before mortgage payments reduces the amount of money that will have to be invested each year *and* reduces the required amount of appreciation. Instead of the value having to increase by $2,400 for a minimum return, the $1,400 in cash reduces the minimum required appreciation to $1,000. That is, the rented house will have to increase in value only $1,000 per year to give the same result as an investment in vacant land.

If one bases ones estimate of value on the returns to investment property in current use, the result will usually be less than the prevailing market price. This is because the prevailing market price includes a premium for the future potential.

The way to value such an investment is first to examine its value in its current uses. For instance, what is a fair rental for the old office building? What is the value base on that rent? What is the net lease payment for the miniature golf course? What is it worth as a golf course? What is the old FHA 608 low-density garden apartment project worth on the basis of its rental income? Having calculated comparable values in current use, the next step is to assess the future potential.

This is done by choosing a point in the not too distant future and determining an expected value based upon the reuse of the land at that time. Based upon the waiting time, the cash investment to be made, and the costs of holding, a warranted price can be calculated. The warranted price will usually be higher than what the property is worth in its current use, and hopefully higher than the price that would have to be paid to buy it. The idea is to find property that owners, and the market in general, undervalue in terms of future expectations.

Future Use and Expectations. Future use depends on patterns of growth and forces of change. The easiest way to get a picture of patterns of growth is to take half a dozen population (dot) maps at five or ten year intervals and arrange them by years. Examining them is a bit like watching the flicks in a penny arcade in which changing pictures give an illusion of motion.

Lay investors can successfully deal with major events such as a new highway, a new mass transit system and its stations, or any significant change in transportation. For example, the energy crisis will alter the relative merits of many locations. Other major events could be a new sewage treatment facility, extension of a sewer

TABLE 9–5
Example of Land with and without Interim Use

		With Improvements (value $50,000)		*Vacant (value $42,000)*
Income	$ 3,600			-0-
Less: Expenses (property tax)	800			$ 660
Income before mortgage payments		$ 2,800		−660
Less: Mortgage payments on $38,000/32,000		4,200		3,600
Cash flow		−$ 1,400		−$ 4,260
Purchase price		$50,000		$42,000
Down payment		12,000		10,000
Mortgage balance		$38,000		$32,000
Paid off in 5 years		$ 7,000		$ 6,000
Sales price		$68,000		$68,000
Less: Mortgage		31,000		26,000
Cash received		$37,000		$42,000
Cash invested				
Down payment	$12,000		$10,000	
Carrying cost	7,000		21,300	
		$19,000		$31,300
Excess of cash received over cash invested		$18,000		$10,700

main, or a replanning of an area under a master plan. Additionally, an upsurge in employment because of government or business expansion at new locations nearby could make a significant difference. Such events trigger sharply rising prices.

A strategy for investment in such land with interim uses and potential changes, especially when the potential change is risky, is to use time to advantage. By buying well in advance of general expectations—five or more years in advance—and being *able to wait,* investors can make time work for them. If the land has an interim use and if the premiums on speculation are still small, investors can afford to wait seven, eight, or even ten years. If the land is vacant, however, a potential change that takes ten years instead of five can be ruinous. The interim use provides more than an ability to wait (because of the cash flow); it also provides a modest return while waiting. See Table 9–5 for an example.

How to analyze land in the predevelopment stage is the subject of the next chapter. The discussion applies to land with an interim use as well as to vacant land.

10

Analysis of Predevelopment Land

Investors in predevelopment land are speculators. They speculate on the rate and direction of growth of the community plus the developability of the particular parcel of land.

The previous chapters have provided a basis for understanding the rate and direction of growth. This chapter deals with the analysis of a specific parcel of land as it is being included in the *supply* of developable land. The next chapter emphasizes the *demand* aspects as they relate to the absorption of the improved property in the market, i.e., how fast anything built on the land can be sold or rented.

This chapter, in dealing with the analysis of specific parcels of land, focuses first on its permitted potential use. The permitted aspect derives from land use regulations and the provision of public facilities. The second section, on profitable potential uses, focuses upon the analyses of land by type of land use—that is, which kinds of land use will be in demand and what areas the extreme shortages are likely to occur in.

POTENTIAL OF LAND USE

The potential of land use is restricted by various legal limitations such as zoning and by the necessity of having available public facilities such as sewers. Local government is usually the authority for land use regulations. Lately, however, other agencies (state and national) have been getting into the act.

Many local government officials labor under the misconception that they have the authority and the tools to decide how fast the community will develop and which land will be developed. As discussed earlier, local government officials as part of the community leadership may influence the rate of growth by encouraging or discouraging industrial and other employer locations. They may also influence growth by the effectiveness with which they manage. The more attractive the community, the better the service, and the lower the costs for services provided, the greater the inmigration.

FIGURE 10–1

California Ruling Hits Cities' Growth Curb Plans
By Rasa Gustaitis
Special to The Washington Post

PETALUMA, Calif.—Two years ago, this mushrooming community seemed to have come to grips with the urban-sprawl problem when it adopted a growth-management plan limiting subdivision units to 500 a year.

Today, Petaluma's future is uncertain again following a federal court decision that its plan is unconstitutional.

In a decision that may hit cities nationwide. U.S. District Court Judge Lloyd H. Burke ruled Jan. 17 that the Petaluma law infringes on the constitutional right to travel. It was the first time a federal judge had ruled on a phased, local growth-control program.

Plaintiffs were landowners and builders, including the Construction Industry Association of Sonoma County and the San Francisco, Peninsula and Redwood Empire Building Industry Association.

They claimed that the Petaluma plan violated the landowners' right to due process, exceeded local power to legislate, and violated the right to travel.

James L. Beyers, an attorney for the plaintiffs, estimated that without the current restrictions, developers would realize $70 million more in business during the next five years.

Ruling in the developers' favor, Judge Burke said that "no city may regulate its population growth numerically so as to preclude residents from any other area from traveling into the region."

He warned Petaluma it must not resort to any "ruse" to circumvent his decision, and said he would stand ready to review cases in which a ruse might be involved.

"He set himself up as planning director and final authority over the council," commented City Manager Robert H. Meyer.

To Meyer, it was ironic that Petaluma's growth program was stopped while nearby communities were permitting no new construction at all by claiming inadequate water and sewer facilities.

Petaluma had the option of that same course, he said. But instead of acting "under the table," he said, "we tried to manage growth, taking into account everyone's interest. And by so doing and getting citizens involved, we got hauled into court."

At stake, according to proponents of the plan, Petaluma's future as a balanced community. Without some kind of control over development, they say, it is certain to become primarily a commuter bedroom town.

Until about a dozen years ago, it was a rural center surrounded by poultry farms and dairies. Automated poultry handling drove Petaluma's farmers out of business just as developers began to eye the land. Only 45 freeway minutes north of San Francisco, it is easily accessible for commuters.

Population jumped from 14,000 in 1960 to 30,000 this year. Tract houses and mobile-home parks spread out from the old Victorian center, mostly on lush farmland east of the freeway.

The city annexed land liberally and was open-handed with developers until, in 1971, it took a look at its overcrowded schools and overladen community services and imposed a 15-month moratorium on construction.

Then, Petaluma asked its citizens what kind of town they wanted in questionnaires sent out with water bills, made available at public offices and printed in the local newspaper.

A conference, resulted, from which emerged recommendations leading to a five-year plan designed to prepare the way for implementation of an existing 20 year general plan.

The population estimate for the year 2000 remained the same—77,000. But for the next five years subdivision units were to be limited to 500 a year.

The limit affected only projects of more than five units. Anything smaller continued to be approved in the accustomed manner.

FIGURE 10–1 (*Continued*)

Potential builders of the large units were to submit plans to a specially selected 17-member board in October for the following construction year. The citizens would choose 500 that seemed most in harmony with Petaluma's needs.

The board was uniquely designed. Each of four school boards chose one member. Drawn from a hat were the names of two city council members and two planning-commission members. The rest were elected citizens.

To make sure of the community's approval, the council put the plan to an informal vote. And received a resounding yes.

For 1972–73, the board selected from among 2,000 building-permit applications. But last fall it had only 1400.

"We were getting better quality housing," said Meyer. "Knowing they were in competition with others, builders were more generous with open space, with bicycle paths. They provided better treatment of creeks. They were encouraged to provide lower-cost housing."

The limit on new construction proved to be an incentive for restoration of older homes. Some of these attracted young people from San Francisco who wished both to live and work in Petaluma.

When the developers sued, Mayor Helen Putnam appealed for help to other municipalities in the state, asking for contributions of $250 toward legal expenses. About $10,000 came in.

Source: Rasa Gustaitis in *The Washington Post*, February 11, 1974

Officials such as those of Petaluma, California (see Figure 10–1), may attempt to transform these plans for growth into regulations limiting the number of building permits, but they run afoul of the law in so doing. Essentially, the courts in interpreting the Constitution have held that citizens have the "right to travel," which is the right to move to locations where they have better opportunity. While the costs of housing in particular neighborhoods may exclude them, a community may not systematically exclude them. The intent to discriminate is as illegal on an economic basis as it is on a racial or ethnic basis.

At this writing the courts are just beginning to make these interpretations. Heretofore the exclusionary regulations, if not challenged, have held up. But more and more local government officials are seeing their land regulations set aside by the courts (Figure 10–3). Some officials have been heard to complain that the courts will not let them manage the county's growth.

Before we turn to a discussion of land use regulation, let us first examine another powerful tool for managing urban growth. This is the provision of public facilities, or more accurately the withholding of the provision of public facilities (Figure 10–2). Since development requires facilities, a jurisdiction may deter development by not providing them, or by legislating an "adequate facilities ordinance" to limit development. (See Figure 10–4 for discussion of the Ramapo case.) Sometimes the intention of the officials may be to use such limited facilities as a means to implement a no-growth or a slow-growth policy.

The truth is that no one really

FIGURE 10–2

Court Shatters Moratorium;
'Water Ban Can't Slow Growth'
By Leila Davis, Associate Editor

San Rafael, Calif.—A Marin County Superior Court has kicked out another prop from under the no-growth platform by ruling that towns cannot use water moratoria as a pretext for banning development.

The controversial ruling was the result of a suit brought against the Marin Municipal Water District by the McCarthy Co. of Northern California. McCarthy Co., a San Rafael builder, was unable to obtain water connections for a 54-acre development here.

Superior Court Judge E. Warren McGurie rules against the year-old moratorium. He is expected soon to issue an in-depth written decision. Judge McGuire said the state legislature has not given any municipal water district any jurisdictional power in the field of zoning, land use or population control.

William McFarland, president of McCarthy Co., is pleased with the decision, and he sees it as a test of the whole concept of no-growth through water moratoria. He concludes from the case that "you can't use a water moratorium as a means of growth control."

The company has been held up for a year in its plan to construct 124 townhouses and 168 apartments. He expects to get the necessary short pipeline extension and home hook-ups by the end of the year.

Among those who are convinced that the water moratorium is part of a plot to minimize growth in the San Francisco Bay area is Bill Leonard, executive vice president of the Associated Building Industries of Northern California (ABI) in Haywood. ABI went to court with McCarthy to overturn the ban.

Voters Reject Bond

"These things happen all the time," said Leonard. "They might say they are short of water or anything else, but the real purpose is to stop growth.

"People talk about manufactured shortages such as the gasoline shortage or the energy crisis. But this is a case of communities manufacturing shortages in terms of interstructure. We're dealing here with real shortages in terms of turning down bond issues to provide the interstructure, and also with false shortages where they claim there is a shortage but there really isn't."

Interstructure, as Leonard defines it, is the patchwork of roads, sewers, water and other utility networks that precede the development of an area. Leonard claims that communities are balking at providing the interstructure network in order to limit their growth.

Marin County voters twice rejected a bond issue to increase the water supply. Leonard said the failure to pass this type of bond issue is the most effective measure in the no-growth arsenal.

Another measure which Leonard thinks some communities are practicing illegally concerns the failure of towns to pass comprehensive master plans. California state law had ordered every municipality to adopt such a plan. One of the nine elements to be included in the plan was to concern the environment of the area. Deadlines are long passed and many communities have failed to assemble a reasonable environmental package to complete their plan.

Politics On Tap

Leonard reported that the state attorney general has told the tardy communities that until the complete adoption of their master plans they don't have to approve any new development. The attorney general may have meant this as a penalty in the hope that it would speed along the adoption, but Leonard sees it as a boon to the no-growth advocates.

"The penalty is what they wanted in the first place," he said.

Leonard said the net effect of the Marin water moratorium has been to

FIGURE 10–2 (*Continued*)

hold up the Marin operations of between 10 and 15 builders for about a year. The question that remains now concerns the future of the water district in fighting the court decision.

Tom Thorner is attorney for the Marin Municipal Water District. He does not know whether he will be called upon to challenge Judge McGuire's decision. Whether he is or not depends on how the voters respond in elections this year for a new five-man board of directors of the district.

The five-man board only has four active members now. Those four are equally divided between supporters of the ban and opponents of it. There is to be a special election on June 4 to fill the empty fifth chair. This election will determine the immediate stance of the board in regard to the moratorium issue, but it will not be until the end of the year after the entire board comes up for re-election that some sort of consistent stand will be determined.

Apparently, there is a groundswell of popular demand for limited or planned growth. This is indicated by the considerable support that the anti-moratorium forces are able to muster on the board and for the upcoming elections.

Sees Real Shortage

Thorner said he does not agree with the court's decision. The judge ruled that the water board was arbitrary and capricious in that it imposed the moratorium before a shortage actually arose. The judge said a moratorium is justified only when there is an actual shortage, not a projected one. Thorner said there is actually a shortage at hand, as well as the possibility for a far worse one if controls are not used.

"Our net safe yield is 26,000 area feet of water, and we are now using 32,500. We're 25 percent beyond our net safe yield." said Thorner.

The net safe yield is the amount of water you can rely on from the annual rainfall. Thorner said the reservoirs are full now, but this is the result of excellent rainfall over the last couple of years. The net safe yield is an historical average and it takes into account the droughts of the 1930's. There would be serious problems if the area were to be struck by an extended drought now.

An administrator at the water district put it this way: "If we had a couple of bad dry spells we'd run out of water.

Source: Leila Davis in *Homebuilding Business,* May 1974, p. 1.

manages the urban development process, at least not in the United States. Under some socialist and communist systems the development of land is carefully controlled, since the intention is to avoid using the market mechanism. Under the market system prevailing in the United States, though the operation of market forces is severely constrained by regulation and limited availability of public facilities, the market does serve to determine which land will be used, and when, how, and by whom, within the framework of the limitations.

Nothing is wrong with regulating the system to guide market forces to achieve society's goals. On the contrary, that has been called the American Way. It has been sullied by corruption and ineffectiveness, but that is not unique to any system. The proper functioning of the market system would protect the rights of all the people and resolve conflicts in accordance with the hierarchy of law.

Rights guaranteed by the federal Constitution prevail over what some state or local politician thinks, legislates, or practices. Thus unreasonable search and seizure, taking private property without due process and just compensation, and discriminatory exclusion are illegal because they are unconstitutional.

Unconstitutional practices by local authorities are sometimes corrected on other grounds. Landowners may get their land rezoned or serviced with utilities after going to a court of law on the ground that they are being treated arbitrarily and capriciously, or that others are being excluded, or that community interests call for development of the site. It is good strategy for investors to allow other people's interests to work in behalf of their investments. Thus, while local laws are passed and illegal practices prevail, forces for correction build up.

Strategy is the subject of the last chapter in this book. Before studying strategy, investors need to know the legal rules and prevailing practices.

FIGURE 10–3

Court Order,
Township Response

In January 1973, Judge George Gelman of the Superior Court, New Jersey, Law Division held that the then existing Washington Township zoning ordinance was invalid insofar as it had imposed a two-acre minimum lot size restriction on residential use on the subject property, and insofar as it failed to make provision for multifamily and/or rental housing within the municipality. He ordered the municipality to "proceed with reasonable promptness" to amend the ordinance and to make provision for multiple-family and/or rental housing.

Shortly thereafter, the Township amended its ordinance by providing for multifamily dwelling use, but on a site other than the property owned by the plaintiff. The amended ordinance of the Township also imposed numerous restrictions: A requirement that 70 percent of the dwelling units not have more than one bedroom, and the balance not more than two bedrooms; a minimum floor space requirement of 1,000 square feet for one-bedroom units and 1,200 square feet for two-bedroom units; a density limitation based on building heights, ranging from 6 units per acre for two-story buildings to 15 units per acre for four-story (elevator) buildings; and several other cost-raising requirements.

Most of the land in the district rezoned for multifamily and nonprofit uses was owned by the Township, the Young Men's Hebrew Association, and a fraternal order. In a subsequent proceeding, Judge Gelman noted that affidavits had been filed with the court "Which suggest that the rezoning of a large acreage which they chose for this purpose was not in good faith."

In his decision holding the Township zoning ordinance invalid, Judge Gelman summarized the basic issue—whether the Township of Washington can continue its zoning policy of excluding all multifamily and rental housing within its borders. "Can it, in other words, zone out people—including its own residents—who have a need for this type of housing, or is there a statutory requirement to provide as part of a comprehensive plan for a well-balanced community at least some area, however limited it must be under the circumstances present here, where such housing may be constructed?"

Source: *Urban Land,* May 1974, p. 15.

FIGURE 10-4

Ramapo Case

On May 3, 1972, the New York Court of Appeals, the highest court in that state, upheld the legality of a "development timing" or "controlled growth" ordinance passed by the Town of Ramapo.

The town amended its zoning ordinance to prevent the development of land for new housing unless the developer of such housing receives a "special permit," regardless of the existing residential zoning of his land. This permit is granted only if the land to be developed is located in an area of the town which will be served by a minimum level of certain community facilities. Installation of these facilities is scheduled in accordance with the town's capital improvement program. This capital improvement program (CIP) covers the provision of the following facilities: sewerage, drainage, parks and recreation areas, roads, and firehouses.

The CIP spans an 18-year period. Thus, land which will not be served with such facilities for as long as 18 years may not be developed for residential purposes, and the tax on such land is to be reduced to reflect its diminished value because of the deferred development potential.

This decision has occasioned great interest in planning, legal, local government, and housing circles,[1] and may spawn ordinances that attempt to slow urban growth through similar means. The genesis of controlled growth policies may be found in the adverse reaction in many communities to rapid residential expansion. This growth has produced three sources of concern: (1) housing has been developed that is not supported by adequate community facilities, such as roads and schools, which have become overcrowded as a result; (2) the public financing of these facilities has occasioned a rapid increase in real property taxation, particularly for earlier arrivals to the community; and (3) the failure to provide some facilities, such as sewers and waste treatment plants, has contributed to deterioration of the quality of ground water or nearby streams, lakes or other bodies of water.

"Slow growth" or "no growth" policies are therefore being adopted or considered with increasing frequency to reduce the volume of housing and public facilities in many localities that have experienced or fear rapid population growth. These policies take various forms. "Moratoriums" on residential building permits, sewer hookups, or new sewer construction are commonly employed. Other policies sometimes purport to place specific numerical limits on the ultimate population in a locality without any plan for more efficient use of resources. More conventional policies, such as underzoning of land for residential use generally or apartments in particular, or limiting the number of bedrooms in an apartment—so-called fiscal zoning—have of course been common for many years. In addition, the transfer of costs for sewage, drainage, roads, or recreation from municipalities to residential developers can provide a means to assure that more expensive housing, or less housing altogether, will result.

Although there often is a valid temporary health and safety basis for some local policies—avoiding pollution of the ground water, for example—many localities may use newly popular ecological reasons for "slow growth" or "no growth" policies that in reality are intended to serve fiscal purposes. Increases in local real estate taxes can be forestalled in the short run by limiting the entry into the community of new residents, particularly low- or moderate-income residents with school-age children, or limiting the entry of any new residents who may use community facilities.

The existing system of land conversion to urban uses in metropolitan areas can produce serious environmental "overloads." An inefficient and regressive method of financing public facilities for urban growth, and the failure of public planning to control both the timing and nature of private residential development, often leads to this result. The private developer thus becomes the visible political target of an aroused populace that is only dimly

FIGURE 10-4 (*Continued*)

aware of how to reform public processes to avoid the exploitation of land for private profit.

Consequently, certain measures aimed at ecological problems appear to be attractive even though their remedial effect on the environment will be minimal compared to their potential economic and social effects. For example, the existing sewage effluent in a sanitary district or locality may fall well below acceptable water quality standards, and the affected surface water may be badly polluted. A common official reaction to this situation is to "temporarily" ban the connection of more housing units to sewers. Such a ban, however, may do little to improve water quality, because the increased pollution resulting from incremental urbanization is trivial in relation to the total problem facing the inadequate sewage treatment capacity. A ban in such circumstances may therefore have a depressant effect on the availability of housing out of reasonable proportion to its remedial effect on environmental quality. Once water quality has badly deteriorated, the most reasonable solution may unfortunately be the most costly one: rapid and substantial upgrading of treatment facilities. It may be more expedient, however, to declare a moratorium on urbanization than to confront the difficult question of paying for such facilities.

Source: Herbert M. Franklin, *Controlling Urban Growth—But For Whom?* Washington, D.C.: The Potomac Institute, March 1973, pp. 3–5.

Land Use Controls. Zoning is one of three land use control mechanisms. The other two are nuisance litigation and restrictive covenants.

Nuisance litigation is the oldest, stemming from common law. This control consists essentially of action by one landowner against another for an alleged infringement of property rights. For example, one landowner infringes on the rights of another by burning leaves or manufacturing explosives. A lawsuit is a means of settling the dispute, and it may result in a regulation of land use.

The second mechanism, restrictive covenants, makes use of private agreements. All the landowners in a neighborhood can get together and mutually promise that they will not build houses smaller than 2,000 square feet, or closer than 30 feet to the street, or engage in manufacturing or commercial activities on their sites. Such agreements may be made as covenants that run with the land so that subsequent landowners are also bound. Frequently, restrictive covenants are put on by the subdivider so as to protect the character of the neighborhood until after he has got his money out and longer, perhaps 20 or 30 years. Sometimes restrictive covenants go so far as to specify items of design such as tile roofs, or even provide for architectural review committees.

Recently a house built without approval from an architectural review committee (which never functioned) was ordered torn down for that reason. It was subsequently removed from the site. This was a very contemporary house with a high blank wall abutting on more conventional housing. While the action seems harsh, such covenants are enforceable. They would not be if they were against public policy.

Restrictive covenants that exclude

occupancy on racial criteria are clearly against public policy. They have been held to be unconstitutional by the Supreme Court, whatever the nature of state legislation.

Zoning, the most widely used restrictive device, is also the most comprehensive. Its effectiveness in achieving societal objectives is debatable. And its misuse may well have created more problems than it has solved, albeit the costs were not borne by the same people who benefited from it.

Zoning is based on the state's authority to impose regulations necessary to safeguard the public health, morals, and safety and to promote the general welfare. The state does not become the owner of the land, and does not have to pay the owner whose property declines in value because of a zoning decision.

The use of zoning as an exclusionary device has been ruled against in a series of court cases. Aside from exclusion on racial grounds, courts have held against exclusionary practices based on minimum building size and minimum lot size.

In one of the minimum building size cases (cited in *The Structure of Urban Zoning,* by Norman Williams, Jr., p. 125), the court held:

> The provisions of the present ordinance virtually exclude from the municipality every individual who desires the privacy and other advantages of his own little home, not to mention both young and old couples who, by reason of health or economic status, prefer a small servantless dwelling. In view of the fact that low-cost housing is a burning issue of the day and the dwellings erected and approved by the governmental housing agencies are themselves below the minimum-size requirements of the ordinance, the specification appears indefensible. . . .
>
> The ordinance, in its present form, practically provides that no house costing less than a certain sum may be erected in the entire community, let alone a specified area, and this it cannot legally do. . . .
>
> No person under the zoning power can legally be deprived of his rights to build a house on his land merely because the cost of that house is less than the cost of his neighbor's house.

On the subject of large lot zoning, sometimes called "snob zoning," the following statement of the court (again as quoted in *The Structure of Urban Zoning,* pp. 142 and 149) gives a picture of intent to exclude.

> Can it be said that the zoining ordinance in question has any relation to health, welfare or morals? I think not. At most, it is an attempt to protect the large estates in the village. There was never any plan to encourage the building of houses on two-acre plots.
>
> It follows, therefore, that the zoning ordinance is unconstitutional and void. . . .
>
> Moreover, such an unconstitutional concept and application of the police power would likewise apply to *every* suburban area, district, township and county and would stifle and in reality effectually block the expansion of our country's rapidly growing population into any suburban township or county, or would herd the poor and medium income people into specified areas, and effectively and intentionally limit parts or all of a county to the rich or well-to-do. Such an intentional and exclusionary interdiction is contrary to our constitutional guarantees and to the American Way of Life.

The present case is a concrete local example of the cry for land and homes which, because of the rapidly increasing and expanding population, is worldwide. In this case the fight has taken the form of a battle between the State, which is constantly attempting to expand the power of Government, and the rights of individuals to own, enjoy, use and protect their own property in any way they desire, so long as it does not interfere with their neighbor's property—an ageless ever-lasting struggle which began before Magna Carta and is now intensely vexing peoples and governments all over the world.

The present Ordinance is obviously and intentionally intended to exclude from this area the poor and medium income people.

Few cases are simple and clear cut, and the issues are still being fought. At this writing there is some evidence that court action is beating down local government action deemed to be exclusionary.

Comprehensive Planning. The use of zoning as an enforceable control device generally requires that it be in accordance with some comprehensive plan. That comprehensive plan includes a mapping of land use and some element of planning for development or development policy, the exact requirements of which are somewhat uncertain. In general, however, a comprehensive plan should include the provision of public facilities. The idea is to plan land use for some time in the future and to coordinate the provision of facilities with land use.

Unfortunately, the comprehensive plan seldom works well. Instead of really programming for a coordination of facilities and development, the plans are usually just pretty pictures of land use and supposed facilities at some point in time.

More on this process later. The important point here is that the comprehensive plan will ordinarily have a master land use plan designating how the land is "ultimately" to be used. A zoning map indicates the current use permitted. It also indicates plans as to what will be permitted when the zoning is changed.

Frequently land is zoned for a low-density use pending the "right" timing for rezoning. That low-density use may be agricultural, but frequently it is one or two acres per dwelling unit and sometimes five acres. Land is then rezoned in accordance with the master plan, usually upon petition of the landowner or contract purchaser.

The laws and procedures vary by state. In some states not all of the land area is zoned or planned. Often the land is zoned and/or planned in accordance with a master plan as the jurisdiction expands in a territory, as with a city, or economically as with a county. Where a master plan is established, rezoning for a use not in accord with the plan can be very difficult. In some cases the applicant has to show that a mistake was made in the original plan or that conditions have changed since the plan was made. Some jurisdictions require periodic updating or review of the plans, say every five years.

Rezoning in accordance with a master plan is generally not difficult unless the jurisdiction is vigorously pursuing a no-growth or slow-growth policy. Then the battle may be fought in the courts and generally won. A related element in the rezoning is timing. Some jurisdictions attempt to control urban sprawl by restricting premature development, i.e., development at locations before the appropriate time.

What is the appropriate time for a location may well be debatable. In some cases the absence of public facilities is deemed to constitute premature conditions. Ordinances are sometimes designed to deal with these processes.

As an alternative to the public facilities ordinances some jurisdictions use the time-phased development plan. They classify all the areas in three categories: developed, developing, and holding. The developed areas are already urbanized and have the necessary public facilities. Filling in undeveloped land in these areas will generally be encouraged, since it is the most economical location for further development. The next most economical, and usually the most practicable for a growing community, is the area undergoing a transition in land use. It is where the infrastructure (pipes, wires, and roads to service land) is being developed. The holding zone is considered not ready for development until some later time.

All these various approaches have some merit. But just as zoning has been abused over the years, public facilities ordinances and staged growth (that is, time-phased development) may also be abused. Such devices lend themselves to economic discrimination and exclusion.

The investor needs to know what the leadership of the community intends to do, particularly what the relevant public officials will do. If the investor is satisfied that he has an adequate picture of the politics, he is ready to make his economic analyses. If not, some further study of the political scene is necessary.

A review of previous zoning action will tell whether or not the local government officials have followed the plan. Such information may be common knowledge. The success of various zoning attorneys may also be assessed for a pattern of rezonings in accord with or in conflict with the master plan. A general look at local politics will also give some picture as to how predictable rezoning actions are, and whether they are likely to be based upon merit or upon other criteria.

Now let us look at economic criteria. The master plan will call for some amount of land for each kind of land use. Land categories that are underzoned (i.e., not providing enough land for the type of use) will rise the fastest in price. Local government will in effect be restricting the supply of that type of land and forcing up the price, although that may not be its intention.

One way to make money is to invest in land that is likely to be rezoned to one of the underzoned land categories, before the general market recognizes that likelihood. That requires buying the land at prices comparable to those for land that will not get the restricted zoning. Such land should be purchased well in advance of the time for its development.

A good way to select such land is to study the master plan for land that is likely to be rezoned. Buying the land zoned makes sense under some circumstances. Under other circumstances buying land for a use different from that called for by the master plan is worthwhile. The principle is to look for land that just needs to be held for awhile, but which is well located.

Obviously investors can make money by selecting land that will be used in a way different from that generally expected. That is good to do. But investors can also make money by buying land that will be developable *sooner* than expected.

The land may be developable sooner for two reasons. One is demand, the subject of the next chapter. The other is the availability of facilities, the next topic in this chapter.

Facilities. The availability of facilities acts as a land use control when the facilities are critical for development. For example, if a public sewer is required for any development beyond a certain density, and if an artificial restriction on the availability of sewer is created by the monopolistic suppliers of the service, growth will go where the sewer lines go.

Under these conditions, all that needs to be done is to forecast where the sewer lines will go. If demand is strong enough the market will absorb the development even at less than the best locations for that particular type of land use. It will do so because it is the only game in town, and some people have to play—they need a place to live or to open a business or for some other urgent purpose.

Many developers have made more money on their land than on building, especially when they engage in advance land acquisition. The approach is obvious. Investors need only find out where the sewer lines will go, and buy land. Certainly, the better locations will rise more in value than the poorer locations. That is a demand consideration. But the timing of development will be influenced by the sewer lines.

The case with roads is somewhat similar but not as constraining. Wherever the road goes, some rising values will accrue to that land. Accessibility will be improved. The change in values will depend on the gain in competitive advantage with other locations of potential development.

Public officials have sometimes used information to which they were privy for their personal profit. Obviously, controlling developability is controlling profitability, and only a little imagination is needed to figure out ways to make money from violating a public trust, although, some schemers have been quite imaginative.

The dishonesty is probably less of a problem now than it used to be. This is not because morality has improved (it may have declined) but because better planning has been necessary to meet the pressing conditions of growth, and that planning has led to the release of information well in advance of the letting of contracts for public works.

When a sewage treatment plant is built, it is fairly easy to provide for expansion of capacity later on. But providing for the expansion of the pipes that will feed into the plant is expensive. Still, the marginal cost of laying larger pipe for increased capacity is relatively low compared with the cost of going back later and substituting a larger pipe or putting in a parallel line. Considering that letting the effluent flow by gravity is generally cheapest, planners need to have a good forecast of what the population of an area will be before the pipe is put in the ground. They also need to have a good idea of the timing of development so that both capacity and lines may be programmed in an efficient manner.

The sad fact is that the vast majority of administrators responsible for the provision of these facilities have proved unequal to the task. Sewer moratoria are living evidence that the administrators could not handle their job. If they were in private business many would have been bankrupt. But a monopoly permits a great deal of inefficiency.

The efficient method is to plan decades in advance and to program in detail at least five years in advance, possibly even ten. Thus a capital improvement program becomes an announced public policy and everyone can see what is expected well in advance. More and more of this programming is being done of late.

The next step is the implementation, that is, letting the construction contracts. In some cases that step is preceded by provision of bonding authority and obtaining the capital commitments. In any event, the expansion plans are public information.

Public information, and the right to it, are guardians of honest government. Superior information can create profit. That profit is illegal when it is taken in violation of a public trust. But when information is made available so that superior private enterprise can earn a profit, that profit is not only legal but highly desirable.

So private enterprise analysts/investors find out where the sewer lines are going and when. They match that timing with any of the critical restraints on development and with projected demand. And *voila!*—the information for making a profit is there.

Additional facilities that may constrain developability include water and roads, and perhaps others. But facilities such as schools, libraries, firehouses, and the like generally follow development. Local governments will sometimes try to restrain development by not providing sufficient facilities, but that is generally difficult to do. Such techniques were mentioned under land use control.

Transportation is another major public improvement that will affect developability and profitability. The improvement of transportation may take the form of a road network or a rail network, as in a rapid rail system. It may even be a bus system. (The reader is referred back to Chapter 5, "Forces for Change.")

In working at his analysis, the investor should get maps and maps and more maps. The transportation planning authorities, whether highway or public transportation, have made plans. They have capital improvement programs. One should find out what they are.

PROFITABLE POTENTIAL USES

As a practical matter, most investors are presented with specific opportunities by someone who wants to sell them something. Logically it is better to make systematic analyses of what to buy and where to buy it, and then go out and look for it. But that is not the way most investors go about it.

Land Use Category. In evaluating a specific parcel of land, investors need to know what it can be used for and when. This section seeks to help them answer those questions. But first they must get answers to other questions: What is it zoned for? What is it master-planned for? What would be the reasonable expectation as to its use? Given that answer, What is the competition?

For any type of land use, only so much competition exists at any particular location. The master planning documents may identify the acreage available, and may even have totaled up the acres. A review of the maps will indicate the competitive situation.

The next chapter will give the methods of analysis as they relate to timing of development. The analysis for predevelopment decisions begins in the same way as for development decisions. A brief general discussion is presented here, with more detailed discussion in the next chapter.

Supply. The supply of land in any category of use will undergo some expansion as land is rezoned and facilities provided. For any given land use category, investors must answer these essential questions on supply: What is the attitude of local government toward permitting additions? How large is the current stock relative to long-range demand?

The local government is going to make money for land investors if it rations supply. The greater the market pressures, the more the price will rise. But first, investors must assess the current supply and the potential supply.

This is done by making an inventory of the total quantity of land in any particular category and reviewing the amount of land that has been absorbed annually over the last decade. Ordinarily, at least a three-year supply of developable land is needed to avoid an unduly restrictive market, and frequently a five-year supply or more. The ratio varies with the strength of the market and the attitudes of landowners who hold their land off the market. High concentrations of ownership and strong demand are combinations that will push prices up. The hope for even more profit is a strong force for holding land off the market. Competition will cut the monopolistic or oligopolistic edge, and the extent of potential competition depends on the amount of overt or covert collusion among landowners.

The kind of land to own is the kind that will be available for the uses which are in short supply and which will be in demand. A look at past activities gives a good picture of the constraints on supply.

The demand for an addition to any category of land is based upon the character of the growth of the community. Essentially, if more heavy industry comes to town more land will be used for heavy industry, and for other activities that are linked to it. For example, if heavy industry will buy goods and services locally, the kind of firm from which the industry buys will expand in volume. Substantial expansion in volume means more demand for land for industry and offices or whatever the business use of space happens to be.

The employees of the new and, of course, expanded industry have to live somewhere. New industry may hire some employees from the local work force, but as substantial additions to employment opportunities occur new employees migrate to the area. Some analytic techniques make detailed estimates of the future size of the work force.

If the new industry employs many blue-collar workers, then housing will be demanded for families at that income level. Usually some of the demand can be satisfied from the existing stock, but if the increase is substantial then construction of new housing will begin at prices the blue-collar worker can afford, or sometimes at higher levels. With some simplification, the new employees and those who will gain employment as an indirect result of the initial expansion will make necessary an addition to the housing stock. By looking at their income levels, one can see what kind of housing needs to be built.

With that information, investors have a pretty good idea as to the kind of land that will be needed. The prices of housing and land are related. The availability of the particular type of land may then be assessed. That assessment takes into account location. Where will the development take place? The details of how to conduct such an analysis are given in the next chapter.

The key points of this chapter are that predevelopment land is selected first on the potential of its becoming developable and then, if developable, on the extent of the demand for it. The techniques for estimating demand discussed in the next chapter may also be used to assess the demand for predevelopment land.

11

Analysis of Development Land

Analysis of development land or land that is rapidly approaching development requires data for an informed decision. The information needed relates to (*a*) demand for a particular type of land and (*b*) demand for land at a specific location.

The problem with most so-called analyses is that they do not focus on reaching a decision. Typically the analysis "takes a look at" something, or else falls into a standard format of economic base analysis, neighborhood analysis, or market analysis without really getting to the investment problem.

The first questions to ask are as follows:

1. Does the community have the economic base to warrant a long-term commitment (in land investment, construction, or ownership)?
2. What is the changing character of the community as it affects a basic shift in demand?
3. What will be the pattern in market segmentation over the near and intermediate future?
4. What will the land requirements be by quantity and type? (How will the absorption pattern change from the historical?)
5. Where in the metropolitan area will the change take place (by jurisdiction and within jurisdiction)?
6. What land is developable and what land is already in the pipeline for development?
7. What other land can be brought into the supply?

The answers to these questions will indicate which land will become more valuable because its use will be most needed.

The next set of questions focuses on a specific parcel of land that is ready to go or that will soon be ready to go, i.e., will become developable. The questions vary according to the investor, but may be along the following lines.

1. When is the most propitious time to develop this site?
2. At that time (or whenever the development is to take place) what is the most profitable use to which the land can be put?

3. Specifically, what are the characteristics of the product? If the product is to be housing, what will be its size, style, features, and price range? If the product is to be office space, will it be for rental or for sale? Will the buildings be low, medium or high rise? What other characteristics will the product have?
4. How rapidly will the market absorb the development?
5. How long can the land be held without missing the market?

The following discussion describes the analytical methods that can answer these questions.

This chapter is organized into two major parts: long-run investment and short-run feasibility. The part on long-run investment deals with the analysis of the local economy to determine the trend in volume and character of new building, and the analysis of the structure of urban growth to identify the location of development. The second section focuses on the developability of specific parcels. It draws upon the results of the first part but adds the analysis of specific uses of a site and the analysis of the competition to determine the strength of the market. The purpose here is to determine the timing of development and the amount of time needed for the market to absorb the new construction.

LONG-RUN INVESTMENT

Analysis of the Local Economy. The key to the analysis of the local economy is the analysis of employment. Employment is important because it determines both the extent of growth and the character of growth.

Earlier discussion (see Chapter 8) has identified the various techniques of analysis, especially economic base analysis, and has given the background for dealing with the broad forces at work. The purpose here is to provide the reader with explanations and illustrations of how the tools are used. Professionally trained analysts will make their own calculations, and professional investors will evaluate the work of the analysts and draw their own conclusions.

The prime source of data on employment is the U.S. Department of Labor, which issues monthly reports by metropolitan area. Table 11–1 shows an excerpt from a report for the Washington Metropolitan Area.

State employment commissions also provide data, broken down by county. Figure 11–1 shows a sample of that data.

Definitions and reporting practices used in compiling employment statistics vary among jurisdictions. Thus, in compiling statistics for a metropolitan area such as Washington, D.C., merely adding up the employment figures for the various jurisdictions in Virginia, Maryland, and the District of Columbia will not necessarily provide the right totals. Great care must always be exercised when mixing data sources.

The aforementioned employment data relate to place of employment, i.e., they are broken down by location of work. The alternative is a breakdown of employment by place of residence. The U.S. Bureau of the Census has compiled such data for the decennial

TABLE 11–1
Employment in Washington, D.C., Metropolitan Area, December 1973

Industry Division	Dec.* 1973	Nov.† 1973	Dec.‡ 1972	Net change from Nov. 1973	Net change from Dec. 1972
Civilian Work Force	1,435,300	1,435,800	1,404,500	–500	30,800
Total Unemployment	38,300	43,000	34,400	–4,700	3,900
Unemployment Rate (unadjusted)	2.7	3.0	2.4	xxx	xxx
Unemployment Rate (seasonally adjusted)	3.1	2.8	2.9	xxx	xxx
Total Employment	1,396,900	1,392,700	1,370,100	4,200	26,800
Nonfarm Wage & Sal. Empl.	1,287,200	1,283,200	1,260,100	4,000	27,100
Construction	77,000	80,600	78,500	–3,600	–1,500
Manufacturing	46,400	46,000	44,400	400	2,000
Food & Kindred Products	6,200	6,000	5,700	200	500
Printing & Publishing	19,200	19,200	19,100	0	100
All Others	21,000	20,800	19,600	200	1,400
Trans., Comm., Pub. Util.	62,800	63,000	60,200	–200	2,600
Interstate Railroads	3,700	3,700	3,700	0	0
Other Transportation	28,700	28,900	26,000	–200	2,700
Comm. & Pub. Util.	30,400	30,400	30,500	0	–100
Trade	264,100	258,600	257,300	5,500	6,800
Wholesale	40,700	40,100	39,900	600	800
Retail	223,400	218,500	217,400	4,900	6,000
General Merchandise	50,300	46,200	48,000	4,100	2,300
Food	29,800	29,700	29,900	100	–100
Automotive	28,800	29,000	28,500	–200	300
Apparel & Access.	17,200	16,200	16,300	1,000	900
Eating & Drinking	49,500	50,200	48,700	–700	800
Miscellaneous	47,800	47,200	46,000	600	1,800
Finance, Ins. & Real Estate	78,700	78,200	73,700	500	5,000
Banking	15,400	15,300	14,100	100	1,300
All Other	63,300	62,900	59,600	400	3,700
Service	276,000	275,500	270,100	500	5,900
Hotels & Lodging Places	16,300	16,400	14,600	–100	1,700
Personal Services	16,700	16,800	17,200	–100	–500
All Others	243,000	242,300	238,300	700	4,700
Government	482,200	481,300	475,900	900	6,300
Federal Government	328,300	327,600	325,100	700	3,200
State & Local	153,900	153,700	150,800	200	3,100
All Other Employment††	109,700	109,500	110,000	200	–300

Note: Figures may not add to totals due to independent rounding.
* Preliminary.
† Revised.
‡ Includes total agricultural employment and nonagricultural self-employed, unpaid family, and domestic household workers.

Source: D.C. Manpower Administration, ***Washington, D.C. Metro Area Labor Summary,*** February 1974, p. 4. The Washington, D.C. Metropolitan Area includes the District of Columbia; the Virginia cities of Alexandria, Fairfax, and Falls Church; the counties of Fairfax, Arlington, Prince William, and Loudoun in Virginia; and Montgomery and Prince Georges counties in Maryland.

census. An example is shown in Table 11–2.

Various regional and local planning authorities and commercial institutions, especially banks, regularly report employment data. In some cases, local governments and/or institutions publish their own data and/or analyses. Figure 11–2 shows excerpts from a bank newsletter (*Monthly Report,*

FIGURE 11-1
Employment: Selected Counties in Virginia, September 1973

Subject	Fairfax	Fauquier	Floyd	Fluvanna
I. Population	482,100	27,100	10,100	8,100
II. Civilian Work Force (Sum of III, IV & V)	125,556	9,501	2,425	2,274
III. Unemployment	4,617	183	72	68
IV. Employment, Total (Sum of a & b)	120,939	9,318	2,353	2,206
(a) Nonagricultural, Total (Sum of 1, 2 & 3)	120,368	7,558	1,767	1,944
(1) Manufacturing	3,861	313	521	417
Durable Goods	2,717	211	72	206
Lumber	100	19	66	102
Furniture	100			
Stone, Clay & Glass Prod.	734	59		
Primary Metal Prod.		*		
Fabricated Metal Prod.	294	*		
Machinery, except Electrical	282			
Electrical Machinery	824			
Transportation Equipment				
Miscellaneous Manufacturing				
All Other Durable Goods 2/	383	133	6	104
Nondurable Goods	1,144	102	449	211
Food	510			
Tobacco				
Textile				*
Apparel			444	*
Paper	*			
Printing	601	53		
Chemicals	*			
Rubber & Plastics	*			
All Other Nondurable Goods 3/	33	49	5	211
(2) Nonmanufacturing	103,194	5,153	825	1,006
Mining	191	*		
Contract Construction	11,558	735	74	231
Transportation & Public Uitlities	3,985	288	39	90
Wholesale & Retail Trade	25,761	1,329	190	96
Finance, Insurance & Real Estate	8,055	248	32	29
Service	22,000	958	97	248
Government	31,037	1,551	381	312
Federal	11,841	566	63	
State	1,832	190	116	
Local	17,364	795	202	
All Other Nonmanufacturing 4/	607	44	12	
(3) All Other Nonagricultural Employment 5/	13,313	2,092	421	521
(b) Agriculture	571	1,760	586	262
V. Persons involved in labor-management disputes				

1/ For explanation of data see reverse side. Some industrial groups may not be broken out either because there was no employment in these groups or in order not to identify individual firms.

2/ Includes the sum of all industries in the manufacture of durable goods denoted by an asterisk and/or not otherwise specified.

3/ Includes the sum of all industries in the manufacture of nondurable goods denoted by an asterisk and/ or not otherwise specified.

4/ Includes the sum of all industries in nonmanufacturing denoted by an asterisk and/or not otherwise specified.

5/ Includes nonagricultural, self-employed and unpaid family workers, and domestic workers in private households.

Source: Manpower Research, Virginia Employment Commission, April 1974.

TABLE 11–2
Population, Employment, and Housing: James City County, Virginia

	1970 Census	*1995 Estimates*
Total Population	17,853	44,000
SFD and duplex population	14,460	30,500
Multi-family population	922	11,000
Group quarters population	2,471	2,500
Housing units	5,073	13,200
Employment by place of work		
Total employment	3,589	11,500
Blue collar employment	2,129	7,750
White collar employment	1,397	3,750
Military employment	0	0
Retail trade employment	370	2,140
Government employment	1,373	2,900
Agricultural employment	0	60
Offices and services employment	208	1,200
Manufacturing employment	1,124	3,700
Miscellaneous employment	514	1,500
Employment by place of residence		
Total employment	5,587	13,240
Blue collar employment	3,367	8,810
White collar employment	1,754	4,140
Military employment	466	290

Source: 1970 Census; Peninsula Planning District Commission Forecasts, 1971.

Security Pacific National Bank, Los Angeles).

Investor/analysts need a consistent series of figures that they can keep an eye on, together with a projection of future employment. Such projections are often made for local planning authorities. Other local authorities or businesses will sometimes make such projections. Investors who use them should understand the underlying assumptions.

Any technician can project the past trends of gross employment figures into the future. Such extrapolations are hazardous and may even be worse than useless. If employment forecasting is done by simply projecting past employment increases, no real analysis of potential change is made. Turning points will be missed, and the investor who follows such guidance may get in at the wrong time or stay too long.

By way of illustration, a forecast of employment in the Los Angeles area in the early 60s made by extrapolating past trends would have projected great employment increases for the ensuing decade. Analysis of changing employment, however, showed that the space industry was tapering rather sharply and that Los Angeles was losing its relative share of what was to be a declining space budget. Everybody found this out when the major layoffs occurred. But a charting of the data would have provided an early warning.

Investors watching the newspapers as well as the numbers, looking at the clogged roads that were getting more clogged every day without any sign of improvement in transportation facilities, and seeing the yellow cloud of smog more and more often, could well

FIGURE 11–2

SECURITY PACIFIC BANK

MONTHLY SUMMARY OF BUSINESS CONDITIONS IN SOUTHERN CALIFORNIA

RESEARCH DEPARTMENT NOVEMBER 1973 VOLUME 52 NUMBER 11

MONTH IN REVIEW

The pace of business activity in Southern California slowed in October. On a seasonally adjusted basis, the Bank's monthly business index registered an estimated 159.5 (1967=100), down 0.8 percent from September's revised 160.8 level, but 8.1 percent above the year-ago reading. The September-to-October decline is the second in as many months and may signal the beginning of the forecast economic slowdown.

For the first time in at least two years, all four of the major index components weakened. Bank debits, building permits, real estate activity and department store sales all softened last month, though compared with year-ago readings, department store sales and bank debits still showed substantial increases. Pointing up the very slow housing situation due to high money and material costs, building permit activity and real estate sales were both below the October 1972 levels.

Total civilian employment in the Southland increased to a record-high 5,104,800 workers last month. The seasonally adjusted figure for October was 26,400 ahead of September and 203,900 more than were employed in October 1972, a gain of 4.2 percent.

The number of jobless workers in Southern California contracted last month. Unemployment was estimated at 252,800, comparing favorably with September's 254,800 and a year-ago reading of 285,800. Because employment growth last month outpaced labor force growth, the unemployment rate moved downward to 4.7 percent, following four consecutive months at 4.8 percent. By comparison, the October jobless rates in the state and nation were 5.2 percent and 4.5 percent respectively.

INDEX OF BUSINESS ACTIVITY
SOUTHERN CALIFORNIA
1967=100

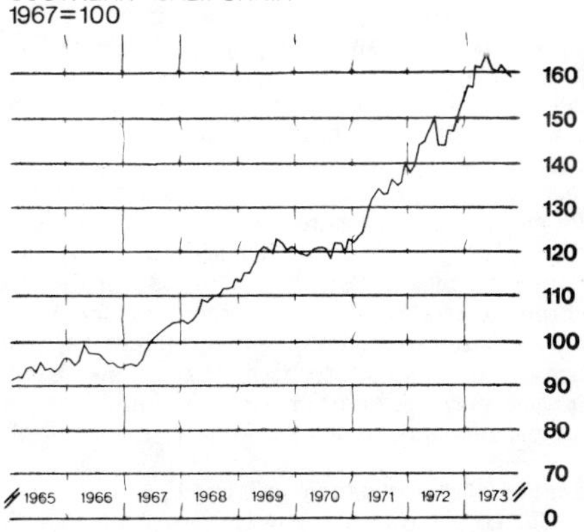

PERSONAL INCOME

Overview

The most comprehensive measure of activity within the U.S. economy is Gross National Product, defined as the final market value, in current prices, of all goods produced and services performed. For geographic areas within the U.S., however, no such broad barometers generally exist. Hence, economic trends in states, regions, counties and cities are commonly analyzed using as a yardstick the broadest indicator usually available on a less-than-national basis – personal income.

Personal income is derived by subtracting from GNP corporate sector activities (capital consumption, indirect business taxes, corporate net earnings, corporate profits taxes, and social insurance contributions) and by adding into the total all government transfer payments to individuals.

Persons desiring the MONTHLY SUMMARY sent regularly may receive it free of charge upon request to the Research Department, Security Pacific National Bank, Box 2097, Terminal Annex, Los Angeles, Calif. 90051. Permission is granted publications to reprint, with credit.

FIGURE 11-2 (*Continued*)

Stated another way, personal income is simply the total of: wages and salaries paid to workers; income to individuals from property owned, including rents; transfer payments, such as welfare and unemployment benefits; net income from farming and unincorporated businesses; and finally fringe benefits and other similar payments to labor. As a benchmark, personal income accounts for approximately 80 percent of GNP, though between regions, cities and other smaller areas this proportion may not remain constant.

The factors affecting the growth of personal income are obviously the business conditions having impact on the basic components of this indicator, but especially (due to the very high proportion accounted for by wages and salaries) employment trends. Hence, on a less-than-national basis, geographic labor shifts are very significant. Importantly, this shift factor suggests one of the most significant considerations in the use of personal income data as a measure of business activity on a regional level. For example, county personal income data measures income earned by persons living in that county, rather than income generated by activities in that county. Thus, county business trends may not parallel personal income trends exactly. Another *caveat* regarding the use of personal income data is that, depending on the proportion of total business activity in a particular region that is accounted for by the corporate sector, personal income may understate or overstate true overall growth trends. A final consideration is that, for some purposes, per capita income may be a more meaningful indicator than aggregate income trends.

Southern California Income Trends

The large movement of wage earners into Southern California in the 1950's and early 1960's had a direct impact on total personal income in the Southland. Importantly, immigration from other regions of the country has slowed dramatically,

causing regional income growth to be more closely aligned with growth rates for the rest of the nation.

Security Pacific Bank estimates place the income of persons residing in Southern California at $65.6 billion for 1973, a gain of 9.9 percent over 1972's reading. The ten county region accounts for nearly 59 percent of total California personal income and 6.4 percent of the national total.

Per capita income in Southern California is estimated at $5,395, a figure nearly double that recorded in 1960. The Southland, with its concentration of highly paid manufacturing wage earners has historically registered per capita income levels slightly higher than the rest of the state and considerably higher than the national average. In the latter 1960's, however, the relationship changed, as progress in the aerospace industry, which had buoyed the Southland's economy since World War II, began to flag. Since 1967, the region and the state have followed similar per capita trends. Compared with the national average, the local area's per capita income is nearly 10 percent higher, but the gap is closing fast. By contrast, in 1960 regional income in the Southland was nearly a third higher than the comparable U.S. figure.

TOTAL PERSONAL INCOME, SOUTHERN CALIFORNIA, CALIFORNIA AND THE NATION ($000,000)

	1960	1965	1970	1971	1972	1973	Percent Change 71-72	Percent Change 72-73
Imperial County	$ 183.2	$ 223.5	$ 291.1	$ 332.2	$ 335.0	$ 389.0	7.0	9.6
Inyo County	25.0	37.2	52.9	58.5	62.0	66.0	6.0	6.5
Los Angeles County	18,071.5	24,288.0	34,282.9	35,300.6	37,786.0	41,278.0	7.0	9.2
Orange County	1,702.0	3,373.1	5,968.3	6,291.2	6,971.0	7,766.0	10.8	11.4
Riverside County	665.7	1,036.8	1,635.6	1,771.5	1,954.0	2,166.0	10.3	10.6
San Bernardino County	1,079.4	1,567.7	2,366.3	2,721.0	2,966.0	3,274.0	9.0	10.4
San Diego County	2,590.2	3,273.8	5,662.4	5,925.0	6,535.0	7,267.0	10.3	11.2
San Luis Obispo County	159.2	219.8	348.0	375.8	410.0	452.0	9.1	10.3
Santa Barbara County	445.1	746.3	1,098.6	1,160.4	1,264.0	1,389.0	9.0	9.9
Ventura County	473.5	758.0	1,220.8	1,314.8	1,437.0	1,596.0	9.3	11.1
Southern California Total	25,395.8	35,524.2	52,925.3	55,251.0	59,726.0	65,638.0	8.1	9.9
Remainder of State	17,584.2	24,709.8	36,386.7	39,161.0	42,374.0	46,462.0	8.2	9.6
California Total	42,980.0	60,234.0	89,312.0	94,412.0	102,100.0	112,100.0	8.1	9.8
United States Total	400,953.0	538,893.0	808,290.0	863,515.0	939,161.0	1,033,200.0	8.8	10.0

Source: Security Pacific Bank, California Department of Finance, Williams Research Associates, U.S. Department of Commerce.

2

conclude that a slowdown was coming. As time went on the forecasts began to reflect it.

The early warnings are to be found in the statistics because one can look at the structure of employment and then analyze the key industries. An industry analysis is, as the name implies, a study of the market for a related group of products and of the firms that produce the products. The investor wants to know which firms are involved and how well they are doing. A study of the industry is a first step. But it may be followed by a look at particular firms.

Table 11–3 gives excerpts from a table showing major manufacturing firms in the Norfolk–Virginia Beach–Portsmouth Metropolitan Area. That table is from a composite of sources, and has some announced location plans. Generally, a state industrial directory provides the raw data on each firm, the nature of its business, and its employment.

In some cases the best procedure is to inquire directly of a firm regarding its expansion plans. One can discover the intentions of new firms through the local industrial development authority, Chamber of Commerce, or similar body. Plans and intentions will not necessarily be expressed in numbers, but they will facilitate an informed judgment as to future expectations.

The development of an area depends not only on the expansion of existing industries but on the transition to new industries. Los Angeles, for example, made a successful transition from moviemaking to television and from airframe manufacturing to space industries. A forecast should consider both the emerging new industry and the declining old one, as well as conditions influencing the development of job opportunities.

In some cases the community's expectations in these matters are reflected in official employment and population forecasts. In other cases, analysis of the environment is necessary.

The employment forecast is used as a basis for forecasting population. It would be a rare local jurisdiction that did not make some population forecast. The quality of the forecast is, however, quite another matter. The investor would do well to seek out several sources.

Among sources other than local governments are the state governments and regional authorities. The National Planning Association makes forecasts (quoted in Chapter 7) as do numerous research-oriented organizations. In essence, the investor will want to identify the forecasters' assumptions with regard to growth in employment and ratios of employment to population. The latter ratios can change because of changes in work force participation rates, which in turn reflect changes in age composition and average family size. Economic opportunity is also a variable.

For example, the expected increase in employment in the Washington, D.C., area is in office space use. Note that, while the federal component was losing relative ground, state and local governments were expanding rapidly.

TABLE 11-3
Major Manufacturing Firms* in the Norfolk–Virginia Beach–Portsmouth Metropolitan Area, 1971

Name of Firm	*Location*	*Year Established*	*Product or Major Activity*	*Approximate 1971 Employment*
Norfolk City				
Penrod, Jurden & Clark Co.	Norfolk	Pre-1950	Veneer and plywood	110
Mitchell & Smith, Div of Shelter Manufacturing Corp.	Norfolk	Pre-1950	Cork products	400
Southland Cork Co., Inc.	Norfolk	Pre-1950	Cork products	200
Atlantic Furniture Manufacturing Co., Inc.	Norfolk	Pre-1950	Wooden upholstered furniture	65
Paramount Bedding Corp.	Norfolk	Pre-1950	Mattresses—bedsprings	60
Landmark Communications, Inc.	Norfolk	Pre-1950	Newspapers	1,000
The Guide Publishing Co., Inc.	Norfolk	Pre-1950	Newspapers	50
Smith-Douglas, Division of Borden Chemical Co.	Norfolk	Pre-1950	Industrial chemicals	200
Swift Agricultural Chemicals Corp. (Acquired Swift and Co. of Chesapeake in 1969)	Norfolk	Pre-1950	Agricultural Chemicals	300
F. S. Royster Guano Co.	Norfolk	Pre-1950	Fertilizers	110
Southern Block & Pipe Corp.	Norfolk	Pre-1950	Concrete block and pipe	250
United States Gypsum Co.	Norfolk	Pre-1950	Gypsum products	150
Southern Materials Co., Inc.	Norfolk	Pre-1950	Gravel, crushed stone, concrete	215
Berkeley Machine Works & Foundry Co.	Norfolk	Pre-1950	Iron and non-ferrous castings	125
Richard Foundry Corp.	Norfolk	Pre-1950	Iron castings	110
Hall-Hodges Co., Inc.	Norfolk	Pre-1950	Fabricated structural steel	75
Globe Iron Construction Co., Inc.	Norfolk	Pre-1950	Fabricated structural steel	220
Air-A-Plane Corp.	Norfolk	Pre-1950	Refrigeration and air conditioning units	90
Tabet Manufacturing Co., Inc.	Norfolk	Pre-1950	Measuring-dispensing pumps	200
Ford Motor Co.	Norfolk	Pre-1950	Motor vehicles	1,800
Colonna's Shipyard, Inc.	Norfolk	Pre-1950	Ship building and repairing	150–250
Moon Engineering Co., Inc.	Norfolk	Pre-1950	Ship building and repairing	125
Norfolk Shipbuilding & Drydock Corp.	Norfolk	Pre-1950	Ship building and repairing	1,800–2,100
Norfolk City, continued				
Royal Silver Manufacturing Co., Inc.	Norfolk	Pre-1950	Silver and plated ware	100
Tidewater Steel Co., Inc.	Norfolk	1950	Steel fabrications	60
Anjay Fashion Manufacturing Co., Inc.	Norfolk	1958	Women's suits and coats	60
Southland Manufacturing Co., Inc.	Norfolk	1958	Oil absorbent pads for freight cars	65
General Foam Plastics Corp.	Norfolk	1959	"Genafoam" plastic for insulation	400
Chesapeake City				
C. W. Priddy and Co., Inc.	Chesapeake	Pre-1950	Fertilizer mixing	25–55
F. S. Royster Guano Co. (2 locations)	Chesapeake	Pre-1950	Fertilizers	180–210
Lone Star Cement Corp.	Chesapeake	Pre-1950	Cement	150
The J. G. Wilson Corp.	Chesapeake	Pre-1950	Metal doors, frames, etc.	230
Borden, Inc.	Chesapeake	Pre-1950	Agricultural Chemicals	350
Tidewater Equipment	Chesapeake	1960	Boat building and repair	50
Portsmouth City				
Proctor & Gamble Manufacturing Co.	Portsmouth	Pre-1950	Peanut butter	60
Corn Products Co.	Portsmouth	Pre-1950	Peanut butter	130
Portsmouth Lumber Corp.	Portsmouth	Pre-1950	Lumber and millwork	55
Norfolk Veneer Mill, Inc.	Portsmouth	Pre-1950	Veneer and plywood	75
Landmark Communications, Inc.	Portsmouth	Pre-1950	Newspaper	75
Georgia-Pacific Corp. (Acquired American Package Corporation in September 1965)	Portsmouth	Pre-1950	Wooden containers	220
Atlantic Creosoting Co., Inc.	Portsmouth	Pre-1950	Wood preserving	115

TABLE 11-3 (*Continued*)

Name of Firm	Location	Year Established	Product or Major Activity	Approximate 1971 Employment
Star Band Co., Inc.	Portsmouth	Pre-1950	Masks, Xmas decorations	100–1,000
Virginia Chemicals, Inc.	Portsmouth	Pre-1950	Industrial chemicals	550
Associated Naval Architects	Portsmouth	Pre-1950	Boat building and repair	80
Norfolk Bag Co.	Portsmouth	Pre-1950	Textile bags	50
Murro Chemical Co., Inc.	Portsmouth	1953	Soap, cleaning compounds	50
Virginia Crusty Pie Co., Inc.	Portsmouth	1957	Baked pies	95
Coronet Casuals, Inc.	Portsmouth	1958	Mens–boys shirts	130
Suffolk City and Nansemond County				
William H. Sheffield	Suffolk	Pre-1950	Lumber	60
National Screen Co., Inc.	Suffolk	Pre-1950	Millwork	140
Benthall Machine Co., Inc.	Suffolk	Pre-1950	Farm machinery	50
Ferguson Manufacturing Co., Inc.	Suffolk	Pre-1950	Farm machinery	50
Virginia Packing Co., Inc.	Suffolk	Pre-1950	Meat packing	50
Nansemond-Adams Oyster Co., Inc.	Crittenden	Pre-1950	Fresh and frozen fish	10–80
Kirk Lumber Co.	Suffolk	Pre-1950	Lumber	70
Webster Brick Co., Inc.	Suffolk	Pre-1950	Bricks	80
T. J. Lipton, Inc.	Suffolk	1954	Tea	300
George Schmitt and Co.	Suffolk Area	1960	Commercial printing	50
General Electric Co.	Northeast corner of Nansemond County adjoining Portsmouth City	1966	Portable television sets	2,200

* Includes only firms which employed 50 or more in the spring of 1970, or seasonal firms which reached 50 or more during 1970.
Sources: Virginia Employment Commission; Virginia State Chamber of Commerce, *Industrial Director of Virginia 1971–1972,* (1971); Virginia Division of Industrial Development.

The net result was a strong office building market, particularly evident in suburban locations.

If the expected increase in employment is in some manufacturing industry, then of course industrial-type land will be in demand. Most local planning agencies and/or land development consultants have a pretty good idea of the land requirements for the type of employment that is growing in the local area. The more sophisticated among them will know what the total zoned and developed land is, and what kind of land is available where. They will also know the absorption rate, i.e., how fast the market is taking the land into use. This kind of information indicates the future requirements for each type of land.

Types of land may be further broken down into subclassifications, Industrial subclassifications may be light, medium, or heavy. Commercial may be stores or office space, and the office space in turn may be subclassified as high, medium, or low rise. Residential subclassifications may be apartments (high, medium, or low rise), townhouses, or detached dwellings. Just as land requirements vary with industry, so do they vary with housing.

Housing also varies by income level. Investors are concerned with wage and income levels as they will affect the price of housing that will be demanded. The results of such an analysis will indicate whether trends are changing. In recent years, for example, the structure of employment in Birmingham,

Alabama, has changed substantially. Table 11–4 shows the shift toward higher average income levels with increases in employment in the service industries.

What investors are looking for is, first, an underlying current of demand. Information of the kind described above should be enough to indicate whether a community has the basic economic strengths to warrant a long-term investment. It may also provide clues to some exceptional opportunities.

Analysis of the Structure of Urban Growth. Analysis of the structure of urban growth is becoming more difficult because of the constraints being put on market forces. The series of population distribution maps shown in Chapter 7 indicate population movement over time. Maps showing income and value distribution indicate economic segregation. With the zoning restraints that were typical of the past, a projection of the location of future growth was quite simple. It was only a matter of determining the price class in which the growth was going to take place, and where the available land was to be found in the community.

The introduction of beltways into the general interurbanization pattern has obscured some of the orderliness in the patterns of urban growth. Constraints on the developability of land have further altered patterns and obscured what orderliness was left. Thus the problem of limited supply of developable land is back again.

With this limitation of supply in mind, the demand analysis can proceed to answer the first question: What land is available for development or will become available for development in each segment of the market? Each subcategory of permitted land use has a finite but changing supply. The demand will be filled from this supply, and if the supply is severely restricted, price rises will cause curtailment of the quantity of land used and/or shifts in location.

The location of the development that will ultimately take place will be determined partly by landowners who decide not to sell or develop. Sometimes these decisions are rooted in personal objectives such as staying on the old homestead. Sometimes no incentive for sale exists because a particular investment fits comfortably into a portfolio, and the rise of the prevailing price level provides reassurance that holding on is a good investment. If the market is very strong, and the supply very tight, some investors will be induced to hold their land indefinitely by the lure of ever higher profits. To some extent their belief that prices will go up helps to make them go up—a self-fulfilling prophecy. Land held by this kind of investor may not come on the market until the death of the owner. Meanwhile, development will have moved out even farther.

The availability of developable land relative to the annual absorption requirement is thus quite variable. A three-to-one ratio is very low and a five-to-one ratio may also be low. Possibly even a ten-to-one ratio would be low, but that kind of ratio would break loose some of the holdouts if they saw a weakening in price.

In forecasting where growth is going

TABLE 11–4
Estimated Civilian Work Force: Birmingham, Alabama SMSA, 1960–1973 (in thousands)

	1960	*1961*	*1962*	*1963*	*1964*	*1965*	*1966*	*1967*	*1968*	*1969*	*1970*	*1971*	*1972*	*Jan–Nov 1973*	*Ave. Increase per Year (1965–1973)*
Total Civilian Work Force	275.0	272.6	268.7	268.0	271.8	280.2	287.6	290.8	293.9	301.0	308.1	313.2	324.5	329.8	5,511
Total unemployment	19.8	23.2	19.6	16.7	12.9	12.2	12.1	11.9	12.7	10.5	12.5	15.6	16.1	13.6	156
Unemployment rate	7.2	8.5	7.3	6.2	4.7	4.4	4.2	4.1	4.3	3.5	4.1	5.0	5.0	4.1	–
Total employment	255.2	249.4	249.1	251.3	258.9	268.0	275.5	278.9	281.2	290.5	295.6	297.6	308.4	316.2	5,355
Nonagricultural employment	251.8	246.4	245.9	248.0	255.7	264.9	272.7	276.8	279.2	288.5	293.8	295.9	306.7	314.6	5,522
Wage and salary	215.1	210.1	211.0	214.0	220.8	229.8	238.9	244.3	247.8	256.9	259.9	262.8	274.1	281.8	5,777
Manufacturing	63.8	61.1	62.7	64.0	66.0	69.5	70.0	69.5	68.3	72.0	72.1	70.2	69.3	70.6	122
Durable goods	49.3	46.8	48.6	50.0	51.3	54.4	54.7	54.3	52.6	55.7	55.5	54.4	53.2	54.5	11
Lumber and wood (exc furn)	1.8	1.7	1.6	1.6	1.7	1.7	1.7	1.5	1.5	1.6	1.6	1.7	1.7	1.9	22
Furniture and fixtures	0.9	0.9	1.3	1.3	1.5	1.6	1.7	1.7	1.7	1.9	1.8	1.8	2.0	2.2	77
Stone clay and glass products	3.9	3.7	3.6	3.4	3.4	3.5	3.6	3.3	3.1	3.3	3.3	3.1	3.3	3.4	– 9
Primary metal industries	27.9	26.7	26.0	26.1	27.5	27.6	27.3	27.6	27.2	27.2	27.1	26.3	26.6	26.5	-122
Fabricated metal products	7.1	7.0	6.9	7.3	7.5	7.8	8.0	8.6	8.4	9.3	9.4	9.0	8.9	9.6	200
Machinery (excl. elec)	1.6	1.4	1.4	1.5	1.6	1.9	2.3	2.4	2.3	2.3	2.5	2.9	2.8	3.1	133
Transportation equipment	4.4	3.6	6.0	6.9	5.9	7.8	7.4	6.3	5.5	6.9	6.5	6.4	4.8	4.9	–322
Other durable goods	1.7	1.8	1.8	1.9	2.2	2.5	2.7	2.9	2.9	3.2	3.2	3.2	3.1	2.9	44
Nondurable goods	14.5	14.3	14.1	14.0	14.7	15.1	15.3	15.2	15.7	16.3	16.6	15.8	16.1	16.2	122
Food and kindred products	6.5	6.7	6.4	6.6	6.8	6.8	6.8	6.7	6.9	7.1	7.3	6.5	6.8	6.8	0
Apparel and related products	1.3	1.2	1.3	1.5	1.7	2.0	2.1	2.0	2.1	2.2	2.3	2.3	2.3	2.3	33
Printing, public and allied	2.4	2.5	2.5	2.5	2.6	2.6	2.6	2.7	2.8	3.1	3.2	3.2	3.4	3.2	67
Chemicals and petro. products	1.4	1.4	1.4	1.3	1.4	1.5	1.6	1.5	1.6	1.6	1.4	1.3	1.3	1.3	– 22
Other nondurable goods	2.9	2.5	2.5	2.1	2.2	2.2	2.2	2.3	2.3	2.3	2.4	2.5	2.3	2.5	33
Nonmanufacturing	151.3	149.0	148.3	150.0	154.8	160.3	168.9	174.8	179.5	184.9	187.8	192.6	204.8	211.2	5,655
Mining and quarrying	10.0	8.9	7.4	6.1	6.3	6.1	5.6	5.6	5.5	5.4	5.6	4.6	5.2	5.5	– 66
Contract construction	13.6	11.7	11.1	11.2	12.3	13.3	13.8	13.3	14.6	15.2	12.9	15.7	17.0	17.2	433
Trans., commerce and utilities	17.4	16.9	16.8	17.3	17.3	17.6	18.0	18.2	18.0	18.6	18.9	18.9	20.1	21.3	411
Trade	49.2	49.0	49.4	49.7	50.5	51.9	54.9	56.1	57.6	59.2	60.3	60.2	63.7	65.2	1,477
Finance, insurance and real estate	13.9	14.2	14.3	14.5	14.8	15.4	15.8	16.5	16.6	17.0	16.6	17.3	17.5	18.2	311
Service and miscellaneous	24.2	24.9	25.7	26.7	27.7	28.7	30.0	32.5	33.8	35.3	37.1	38.1	40.7	41.7	1,444
Government	23.0	23.4	23.6	24.5	25.9	27.3	30.8	32.6	33.4	34.2	36.4	37.8	40.6	42.3	1,666
All other nonagricultural employment	36.0	36.1	34.8	33.9	34.6	34.3	32.9	32.1	31.0	31.4	31.6	32.0	32.2	29.9	–488
Agricultural employment	3.4	3.0	3.2	3.3	3.2	3.1	2.8	2.1	2.0	2.0	1.8	1.7	1.7	1.6	–166

Source: Alabama Department of Industrial Relations and Metro Metrics, Inc.

to take place, the investor has to allow for developable land that is not going to be developed at the normal time. It will be skipped over, even though its time is right. Within that pattern, some land is likely to come into development each year. As more land is required, some of the skipped-over land will be brought in, while some additional outward movement will also occur.

Several paths of outward movement exist, and each path represents a segment of the market. Thus, other things being equal (which they never are), a forecast for the segment of the market with increasing demand will forecast the extent of growth in a particular direction.

Among the factors that change, of course, is the desirability of neighborhoods. So if housing for modest-income families is severely restricted because of zoning and a scarcity of land, that segment will get sharply rising prices and some would-be homeowners will be priced out of the market. The area to which the successful buyers come will upgrade, which means that larger and ever more expensive housing will be built on such land as is available in that area.

FIGURE 11–3

Minimum Population Needed to Support Classes of Shopping Centers

Regional (with one department store as largest tenant): 150,000 or more people

Community (with junior department store as major tenant): 40,000 to 150,000 people

Neighborhood (with supermarket as major tenant): 5,000 to 40,000 people

Source: J. Ross McKeever, ed. *The Community Builder's Handbook*. Washington, D.C.: The Urban Land Institute, 1968, p. 327.

The analysis of the structure of residential growth will follow the paths of development. These paths tend to fan out as one follows arterial roads outward. The exact configuration will be determined by zoning and perhaps by sewer availability, as well as by road construction.

Commercial development typically follows residential development. For any particular type of shopping center, depending upon its size and the mix of stores, some minimum volume of purchasing power will be necessary. That volume may be calculated by square foot of floor space for each type of store.

The number of families required to produce the necessary sales volume depends on income levels and spending patterns. For every shopping center some minimum number of families will be required (see Figure 11–3). The proximity of competing shopping facilities will be another factor in weighing additional construction. Sometimes shopping centers are built too early. Sometimes they run into ruinous competition. Frequently there is a limit on the available land, so that investors must decide what is the right type of development and when is the right time to undertake it.

Office building development is a little more complicated because some office space is "basic" employment space and some is "service." The service space, like shopping centers, needs to be near the consumer. Space for "basic" employment is more footloose—a national headquarters may be in any of a number of cities, or in any of a number of locations within a city.

Office space development may also move in paths. For example, in Washington it moves northwest along with the high-income population. But office building space may cluster in outlying centers, including airport locations. Additionally, some small towns engulfed by urban expansion get enlarged clusters of office space.

Industrial space development is even more difficult to forecast than office space development, because much industry can be located almost anywhere. In general, however, much of the suburban land that is zoned and developable for industry will follow a path according to its type. The difficulty is in the variability of volume and location. Organization on a large scale, such as an industrial park, will influence development patterns. Transportation and access are key elements of course, and many industries will have special requirements.

All development has an orderliness, whether it be residential, commercial, or industrial. The patterns may look confused to the eye because the orderliness of a marketplace has had superimposed upon it the orderliness of a master plan. In addition, the availability of facilities has not necessarily responded to either pattern, and individual owners may not have been prodded to sell when doing so made sense for the community.

SHORT-RANGE FEASIBILITY

Market Absorption Requirements. Market absorption requirements are nothing more than a budget of the amount of land that needs to undergo conversion. The analysis of the short-term feasibility of developing a specific parcel of land is in reality an assessment of the competitive position of that site at that time.

Timing and location, as previously noted, are critical determinants of value. The location remains fixed but its developability and desirability change over time. Thus the essential question for a specific location is timing.

Investors have two ways of looking at this timing, and both are useful. One is from the top down, as in the previous long-term investment discussion. That approach emphasizes the extent of development of some market segment and indicates the location whose time has come or will shortly come. The other way is to look at it from the bottom up. That method is to examine rates of absorption of various types of land and determine their marketability according to what is moving.

The difficulty with the second method is that if the analyst uses this approach alone he will never forecast a turning point. And since lead times are so long, the tendency will be to get in on tail ends of markets. This problem is discussed in this section.

The point here is that a good indication of current absorption requirements is current sales rates. The primary method in this case is a competitive analysis of the different types of projects for which the land might be used. Table 11–5 shows analyses of sales rates for various projects, and thus indicates their relative strengths in the market at a given time.

TABLE 11–5
Subdivision Survey of Absorption, by Price Range
(1973 quarterly averages)

	1st Qtr	2nd Qtr	3rd Qtr	4th Qtr
North Fairfax and Loudoun County				
$30,000–$39,990	20	16	7	6
$40,000–$49,990	17	12	7	3
$50,000–$59,990	14	6	3	2
$60,000+	1	3	1	1
Fairfax County—The Pohick				
$30,000–$39,990	–	–	–	10
$40,000–$49,990	14	10	4	2
$50,000–$59,990	12	8	3	2
$60,000+	7	5	3	2
Prince William County				
$20,000–$29,990	30	21	3	2
$30,000–$39,990	14	7	3	3
$40,000–$49,990	17	15	5	3
$50,000+	11	11	5	2
Montgomery County				
$40,000–$49,990	9	7	3	1
$50,000–$59,990	6	5	5	8
$60,000–$69,990	7	5	4	3
$70,000–$79,990	9	3	3	2
$80,000+	4	2	1	2
Prince George's County				
$20,000–$29,990	29	21	19	16
$30,000–$39,990	11	18	7	4
$40,000–$49,990	10	5	4	1
$50,000–$59,990	9	4	3	1

Source: Metro Metrics, Inc., Washington, D.C., 1974.

The use of such sales rate data is most effective if it is part of an ongoing system. A single sales rate figure tells something about a market. But sales rate figures for similar projects in different parts of a metropolitan area tell a lot more. They tell which path is moving fastest.

Further information is provided by a series of sales rates for different market segments. Thus, changes in segments of the market show up and a particular location may be ready for upgrading to higher prices or may even best be developed by lowering the price range to compete in a better market. Many builders tend to base the price of their product upon some magic multiple of land cost. The multiple can be four or five times the price of the land in the case of a single-family residence, depending upon the metropolitan area and price range and location. In some areas it can be as little as two and a half or three times the price of the land. Historically the ratio has declined, providing more land value relative to building value. Builders who use the ratio tend to miss changing market conditions.

A look at what is moving and at the general imbalance in the market can send very strong signals. The strength may be enough to lead a builder to give up density. For example, in one case land zoned for apartments at 20 units per acre was used for condominium townhouses at about 15 units per acre with results that were exceptionally profitable. Each section sold out over a weekend.

The point of the competitive analysis is to utilize the background of the long-run forces in conjunction with the early warning signals in the market place. Long-run investors will buy before the signals. But investors who are going to take the land over the last hurdles, or who will buy or sell subject to those hurdles being surmounted, look to the current indicators.

Everything that has been said with regard to developability now comes to bear. The existence of developability problems will restrict the potential competition. Thus sales rates that are strong will ordinarily get stronger. Not all communities will open the valves even a little to permit more development, but those that do not are generally headed for court fights. Opening the valves a little means that some land will come into development. That land is the most profitable to own. It comes into development as the result of (1) market and community pressures for what makes sense, (2) political pull (some of which is illegal), or (3) court action. The short-range market absorption requirement will readily indicate which land is being undersupplied.

Market Absorption Analysis. The biggest hazard, aside from lack of developability, is too much competition. When too much competition exists, more developable land is being offered on the market than the market is prepared to take for development. Prices soften, and the time required to sell increases. Marketability dwindles.

While many local governments may protect landowners from the possibility of too much competition, that very process pushes land development farther out. The push to locations that really ought not to be developed yet, but are the only available alternatives, poses the hazard of overbuilding and thus an oversupply of developable land.

The way to analyze such potentiality is to see what is in the pipeline. In actuality, several pipelines exist, depending on the stage of development. A discussion of the various pipeline indicators follows after the discussion of various stages of construction that indicate a current market condition.

Going backward in the production process, the first indication of an oversupply aside from slower sales rates is an inventory overhang. Investors who buy land for use in order to serve a segment of the market for which a substantial overhang exists are buying for the next round. The cycle will generally have to bottom out and start up again before the absorption rates become attractive. Unless the trend reverses, the wait will be long and unattractive. The only case in which it can be worthwhile is when the price is as low as that of predevelopment land.

The next earlier measure is a forecast of competition, and before that it is construction starts. The lag from starts to completions is variable but generally predictable. Data are usually more readily available on starts. For land investment purposes, going back one more step to building permits is sufficient. Obviously, if starts are going to lead to an overhang, trouble is brewing.

Not all permits lead to starts, but in the absence of an unusual disturbing influence the relationship is consistent enough for the land investor. The two critical figures are the totals in the trends of starts and the totals in any particular market segment.

Data as to totals are generally available in one form or another. A review of past trends in construction starts, in comparison with trends in employment and market absorption rates, will give a good picture of whether building is on the upswing or not. The condition of building, of course, affects the demand for developable land.

The place to begin is with the general picture. But the key item is the number of building permits issued for competing projects. The data for a good analysis are readily available in some locations. Sometimes the data are compiled by land planning authorities, sometimes by builders associations, and sometimes by utilities. If data are not readily available, the investor can do what analysts do when they must—he can look at the official records and tabulate the activity himself.

Building permit data are not uniform throughout the country, despite the efforts of the Bureau of the Census. The dollar figures on permits are generally unreliable, but the room counts are pretty accurate. Square footages, when available, are excellent indications of the price ranges of future projects. Thus the analyst can get a picture of what will be built.

Thus far the discussion has been about building. Now let us turn to the preceding stage, that of the developability of land. Local procedures vary, but ordinarily the key act in land development is the recording of a subdivision plat indicating the creation of lots. Such data may be reported in some locations, but usually it must be sought out from local government records, or in some cases other records of transaction activities. The same is true of applications to subdivide.

The application to subdivide is the early signal that a developer is planning to create subdivision lots. A tabulation of applications pending indicates what may be coming onto the market. An even earlier indication may be transfers of land to builders or developers. That data needs to be refined by surveying developers' intentions. Indeed, a survey of intentions is an excellent way of assessing the potential supply.

Obviously, great economies are possible if such analyses are made on a large scale. At some point in the land investor needs the help of professionals. Much of the data and examples used in this chapter were drawn from a consulting firm whose principals made innovations in such analyses. The ultimate economy, of course, would be for local government to process the data and use it for guiding urban development. The author of this book conceived such a system and consulted on its implementation. The system, now in operation, is used not only by local government, but also by sophisticated inventors and developers who need to forecast market conditions.

We have seen that short-range analysis deals with current supply and demand conditions as part of a process of change. The process of change is based upon changing community requirements, which can be forecast, and assessments of what land will come into development and when.

Obviously, sophisticated urban development information systems come in very handy in such analyses. But most communities do not have them, or anything close to them, and most analysts are not accustomed to thinking in the manner just described. An astute investor can do well by getting information comparable to that generally prevailing among investors, and conducting a superior analysis. Taking the time and trouble to get superior information will provide superior rewards.

The next chapter deals with finding the land. It explains how to go about finding the parcel, how to evaluate it, and how to make the final selection. That chapter is the first in the part on investing.

Part four
Investing

12

Finding the Land

The search for land to invest in may be approached in a hit-or-miss fashion or it may be approached systematically. Many investors use the hit-or-miss pattern. They buy on the basis of what someone is trying to sell them, not on the basis of what they decide to look for. Some of these investors are successful. But investing is helped by the application of principles of good management. Investors can expect better results if they define their objectives, organize their efforts, and direct and control their activities. The first part of this chapter deals with deciding what land to look for. The second part is devoted to finding the land.

Deciding what land to look for may be only one of a larger set of decisions in an investment portfolio design. The last chapter of the book, on investment strategy, deals with how to determine what the specifications should be relative to other investments and how to handle risks. The decision here focuses on deciding what to look for in terms of rising values and parcel characteristics, without emphasizing portfolio and strategy analyses. However, the preliminaries to portfolio development are considered.

WHICH LAND?

The question of which land to look for has several dimensions: which size and price, which use and stage of conversion, and which location. Each dimension is influenced by the others.

Use and Stage of Conversion. Land may be far-out farmland, the price of which has not been much affected by nearby urbanization, or it may be farmland in the midst of rapid development, or it may be somewhere between or beyond these stages. Land may be in an interim use awaiting rezoning or development into high density and/or nonresidential uses. The permutations and combinations seem almost limitless because there is a continuum of stages in conversion and a multiplicity of types of uses, plus the possibility of interim use.

The investor who has some interim use for his land is in an enviable position. He gets all the benefits of an interim use without the nonuser management costs and problems. The use may be as a part-time farm, an old countryside restaurant, a miniature golf course, a storage yard for a wholesaling business, an office using a converted old house, a warehouse in an emerging commercial district, or a one-story store in a location that is going to go high-rise.

If the investor is in a business that could use such a location, it sometimes makes sense to move the business in order to have a real estate profit. It may even make sense to go into such a business in order to speculate on the land. Such business decisions should, however, pass the tests of appropriateness independently of the side benefits of the investment. If they do not pass, they may still be suitable provided the excess costs to the business are outweighed by the advantages of investor use.

The alternative to using the property is to take on some non-user management responsibility. In some cases the amount of management is quite minimal. What does an investor in vacant land have to do? He pays taxes and mortgage payments. It is also prudent to look at the land once in a while and see what is going on at the location. In some cases there may be occasional other activity such as clearing the brush so as to avert a fire hazard, as in an urban area, or seeing to some planting to stop an erosion problem. Such occasional care should not be a great burden.

If the investor wants to earn money providing property-management services and doesn't mind putting in some time and effort, he can buy property with multiple tenants. These, of course, assist with cash flow not only in the form of rentals but from the performance of property management or repair and maintenance functions.

At the other extreme of management/nonmanagement activities is investment in land syndication. There the use is irrelevant to the investor because the investor does not participate in management with the possible exception of some decision-making on sales or other major action, and that is shared with other persons. While a syndicate reduces the activities involved in the search for land, other activities are required for the selection of the syndicate.

Returning to the individual investor, selection of use may be made on the basis of three criteria. First, is the investor a user? If so, the decision is made. If the investor is not a user, then which use or potential use does he know the most about, and how much management responsibility is he prepared to accept? For an investor in farmland it is a great advantage to have grown up on a farm. Business people have an advantage in assessing property that is to be used for businesses. Everyone has had some experience in seeing cities grow. Thus, selection of type of land is in part a matter of personal preference. A second criterion for the nonuser is the management responsibility he is prepared to accept. This again is a matter of personal preference.

The third criterion is the forthcoming demand for the various categories of land use. Obviously, land categories in rising demand have more potential. If the investor evaluates community growth and sees a need for land for heavy industry, or office industry, or housing for families of moderate income, or more commercial use in the center city, he has identified categories within which further search may be conducted. This is the more profitable way to go about investing, and it is what much of the first section of this book was about. But the investor is best off investing in a use category he knows something about. He may start with a category he knows something about and look for opportunities within it, or he may look for opportunities and then learn whatever he needs to know. In either case he may want assistance from professionals, ranging from land economists to lawyers to geologists.

The stage of conversion that has been reached by a given property may also govern the investor's choice. For example, if local governmental decisions are pending that may involve hearings, or if community groups are pressing for some course of action or inaction, the investor can spend a lot of time looking after his interests.

It can be quite profitable to invest for that transition period. The alternative is to get in at a very early stage and get out before the transition. For example, an investor may buy and sell before the stage of zoning and facilities has been reached. The investment is made for the time during which the land was getting more valuable because of changing expectations. If the investor gets in just before the transition, or does not want to be heavily involved, he may sell subject to zoning, sewer facilities, etc. Such sales bring more money than sales without the contingencies, but less than if the investor gets the problems solved and sells the land when it is ready to be developed.

Rising expectations may endure for a long time. Land selling at around $1,000 per acre can rise in a few years to $2,000, and double again in a few more years and keep on doubling or at least increasing substantially for a long while, so that attractive profits may be made over a span of two decades or longer. Most investors do not want to wait two decades, or even one. But many will invest for five years. Some prefer to get in at $1,000 and out at $2,000; others will get in at $4,000 and out at $8,000.

Generally an investor should be able to stay with his investment through a soft market. In most cases the investor should also be able to weather a difficult impediment to development. Investors with preferences for very short time horizons should get in at the earlier stages. The staying power required may not be as much as is required in the later stages. Early investors sell out to other investors, taking the market risks but not the developability risks. Those who get in just before the developable time take the developability risk, and since land prices are usually high by that time the cost of waiting can be onerous. The paradox is that the shorter the time horizon for the investor the longer the time to development.

The most significant determinant of the timing for investment in a particular parcel of land is an underestimation of market potential. Land investors do not look for the best location, but rather for locations which will get better. Thus one may pick the market to be served in time and then work back to the present, selecting land which will be ready when there is the biggest market. The secret is in recognizing the existence of potentials more favorable than are recognized by the market.

The vast majority of land investors find themselves at the right place at the right time fortuitously. But those who saw the subdivision housing demand in the postwar era could anticipate when to buy. That was even true of the apartment house boom and the boom in shopping centers. It was also true for those who saw the need for office parks. Land investment is not nearly as scientific as it might be. That makes it relatively easy for those who can analyze expectations and are in a position to buy before everyone starts rushing in.

Location. The best location for investment is determined by the path of growth for a given type of land and the time horizon for its development.

Some communities try to time their development in order to economize on the costs of providing public facilities (or as an excuse for slow growth). Most of them, however, have not coordinated their plans well enough to know when the facilities will be there and when the development will arrive. The poorer the information, the wider the range of expectations and the greater the profit for the good guessers. If the community does a very good job of planning it reduces the risk and the profit to investors.

By assessing the path of growth as discussed in the previous chapter, the investor can pick a location for the type of property he is interested in. Fortunately, he does not have to guess the year of developability. All he needs to do is to pick a parcel that is priced according to a time and use expectation that is conservative.

As a practical matter, the investor will be able to look at comparable prices and make some judgments as to relative merits. He looks at the kind of land he is interested in and keeps going farther and farther out until the price seems in line with his expectations. The choice of where to look is a reiterative process: the investor assesses and reassesses before he selects the location and the parcel.

Size and Price. A familiarity with the market will give the investor an idea of the sort of prices he can expect to pay. He then assesses them as to relative merit. The price/location combination provides an input into size. For example, a $1,000 per acre location is far different from a $4,000 per acre location. The quantity of land to look for will vary according to the price and the purchasing ability of the individual investor.

The parcel size typically available can vary quite widely. The next section indicates how to become familiar with what is available. As a starting point the investor can compute the ideal size parcel for himself based upon the acreage price he is looking to pay and the total price he is prepared to manage. Unusually large parcels are priced lower per unit of land, unless there is some advantage in large size. Smaller parcels in heavy demand may command higher than average unit prices.

Down payments vary widely. Many properties are offered at 29 percent down because the seller enjoys a tax advantage by not accepting more than 30 percent of the sales price in down payment and principal payments in one year. Taking settlement costs and the like into consideration, one has a very wide choice at purchase prices that are three times the down payment.

Most investors would not consider a down payment that high. A more typical down payment is 20 percent. The investor who wants a lot of leverage goes no higher than 10 percent down. At 10 percent, the price is limited to ten times the down payment. The question then would probably be the size of the carrying costs.

Annual carrying costs can be as little as 10 percent of the purchase if the payments are for interest only. Then interest together with taxes may approximate the 10 percent. If, however, there are principal payments (and sooner or later there are), the carrying cost will be substantially higher. The low end of the scale would be with an amortized loan (principal and interest payments) for a long period of time such as 20 years or more. Then the carrying cost could be 12 percent, more or less. In some cases, principal payments are in equal installments over a 20- or even a 5-year period. That would run the annual carrying costs up substantially. In the case of 10 years the annual carrying cost could be almost 20 percent of the purchase price. In the case of 5 years amortization, the annual carrying cost would start out at almost 30 percent of the purchase price.

As a general guide when beginning the search process, if an investor figures on a price no higher than five times the preferred downpayment and no more than seven times the annual carrying cost, he will have a reasonable first approximation of the most appealing price range.

SEARCHING

Searching out the land one wants may be approached in several ways. The recommended procedure is first to reconnoiter and get a feel for the market, then select the area for the search, and finally seek out and inspect specific parcels.

The process usually requires the services of others. At a minimum, it will involve asking many people for information. It may also involve working through a broker who will get information for the investor and conduct part of the search process. It could involve professional assistance in the form of technical analyses. The process of searching out the land is also a process of searching out people with whom to work.

Reconnoitering. The best way to begin is by reading the real estate ads or dropping in on land brokers.

Readers of real estate ads usually go through a process of elimination. They begin with an idea of what they are looking for, turn to the section containing that category (thereby excluding the other sections), and go down the list. Then they telephone about those that interest them. In making his calls, the astute investor asks a few key questions—how much, where, what terms, and something about the physical characteristics and developability. If the answers are satisfactory, the investor is prepared to take a look at the land.

That is one way to go about looking, and many people do it that way. But consider what the real estate agent on the other end of the line is trying to do.

The agent, who may or may not be a Realtor (a member of the National Association of Realtors), is in the business of brokering real estate. Realtors get their competitive advantage in brokering land by having superior information about what is going on and by having numerous parcels of land to show prospective purchasers. The advertisement may focus on a particular parcel, but it is intended to bring in buyers for other parcels, advertised or not.

Investors should deal with only the most qualified agents if they want reliable information. In general, land sales agents who are Realtors are more qualified than those who are not, and those who are members of the National Institute of Farm and Land Brokers (an affiliate of the National Association of Realtors) are among the most qualified.

The first clue for the investor is the response to his telephone call. If the agent obviously is unable to answer questions, then time invested in talking with him or her and looking at the property offered will yield little knowledge. If the agent is a veritable storehouse of information, the call is worth following up.

An experienced sales agent will answer only enough questions to satisfy an initial inquiry, and will leave unanswered the things that might rule out the property. The agent will attempt to control the conversation, and either qualify an inquiring investor as a buyer or "talk the inquirer into the office."

Investors will be wise to give agents enough room to show their mettle. If they do their job properly, then going to see them and the land they have to offer is worth while if the land is at all appealing. If they bungle the job, going to see them or the land is not worth while. Most prudent investors would not buy the first thing they see anyway.

The purpose of the reconnoiter is not to find "the" parcel of land but to get information and establish relationships helpful in the search. Serious investors take notes and do not hesitate to ask to have further information mailed to them. By following up numerous ads over a period of time, the investor can get a feel for what is on the market, where it is, and what prices are being quoted.

Another method which may be used simultaneously or as an alternative is to visit the Realtors. A drive through the countryside where the potential investments are located will turn up signs indicating parcels of land for sale. Note the names of the Realtors and the frequency with which they appear, then visit their offices. They will usually have maps describing the area and the particular parcels. One question leads to another, and the investor may legitimately ask about sales of comparable properties. Most of the time the information will be forthcoming.

Such a reconnoiter will bring the

investor a feel of the market, an acquaintance with some of the people in it, and part of the information he will need. Investors should not start the selection process until they are comfortable with the feel of the market.

Selecting the Area for the Search. At this point the investor should have narrowed the search down to one or several parts of one or a few counties. Maps now become important.

For example, once the investor has selected a particular kind of land use, he can start with a map of the community's master plan. He may choose residential or commercial or industrial land of varying density. Next, the preliminary decision on whether to buy zoned or unzoned land is made. Assuming it is unzoned, an overlay of the two maps—the zoning map and the master plan map—narrows the range of choice. The capital improvements program will then be reviewed, along with the map of sewer lines to be extended in the next five or ten years. This may eliminate some of the farther out areas. The major road improvements programmed for the coming five years may be noted. Then, focusing on general location, the investor may rank different areas as to their desirability. Following the analyses of the previous section, he should consider where demand will be and seek out the area of greatest potential.

The result will be a map that shows the investor what he wants to buy, not what someone is trying to sell.

The most methodical way to go after these properties is to take the property tax map or other maps showing ownership and start contacting the owners. A big investor who can afford a staff may do this himself. Otherwise, the investor should tell his broker the location desired and let the broker try to find the property for him.

An investor who knows people around town may hear of events which will trigger sales. Newspapers contain a variety of notices indicating that properties may be available. Bankers and mortgage lenders and attorneys hear of situations before property reaches the market. Others do too. Who conducts the search and how is a question each investor must answer for himself.

Evaluating the Specific Parcel. Whether an investor contacts the potential seller directly or whether a property is brought to an investor's attention by a broker, the first step is to identify the parcel. Its general location may be shown on a road map.

That general location, or the size, price, and terms of sale, may be enough to rule it out. On the other hand, even if the parcel is a little too large, or overpriced, or if the terms are a little stiff, these may not be grounds for ruling it out yet. The investor may decide to compromise.

If the location is in a jurisdiction that the investor has not analyzed, he should forget it or else start the whole process over. One jurisdiction can differ significantly in some respect from a neighboring jurisdiction, so that investment in one based upon information in the other could be disastrous. For example, a developer built identical houses in two jurisdictions. The prices at which these houses sold differed by about $10,000 because one jurisdiction had low property tax rates and the other hand high rates. A land investor in the high tax rate jurisdiction who used information based on sales of land in the low tax rate area would have been misled.

Once the parcel has been identified on the map, it can be tested for location on the basis of the general demand analysis and the developability analysis already described. By way of summary, the demand analysis seeks to find out whether the local economy is satisfactory, whether the property is located in the right part of town, and whether sales data indicate that this kind of land is selling, and at what price. The potential use for the parcel should also be considered. If the market is strong and getting stronger, this is a good sign. If the market is weak, the weakness may be temporary. The investor must determine whether a long-run continued demand exists. If it does not, he can forget it. But presumably he has already made a general demand analysis, and at this point he only needs to review the situation to see whether any of the conditions have changed.

If the land qualifies on demand, then the investor checks it out for developability. His checklist should begin with zoning and/or master plans. It should go through all the utilities. And it should also consider the physical characteristics of the site.

Now we must return to subjects discussed in earlier chapters. The general assessment of zoning potentialities needs review. Does rezoning look like a good bet? If so, will the utilities be there? Public sewer and water systems may not be needed for some uses. The decision on what kind of land to look for will in part be predicated on what chances to take. Finally, is the land itself of the appropriate physical characteristics? If the land floods, it is not of much use. If it is rocky, it can be too costly to develop. If the terrain is too steep, the costs of developing it may also be too steep.

The final decision may require analysis by experts. A lawyer can check the legal aspects of the transaction, including the title, and a surveyor can determine for an investor exactly what the boundaries are. Percolation tests will reveal whether the soil is suitable for septic tanks, and tests may also be made for load-bearing capability. A market analysis may verify or negate an investor's opinion as to the merits of a particular property, and some informed opinion on the local political scene may be equally valuable. The cost of such advice is cheap compared to the cost of making a mistake. But no matter who provides the advice, the investor should make sure that the salient questions are answered.

SYNDICATION ROUTE

The alternative to doing the analyses oneself is, of course, to hire others. If an investor is going to rely on someone else for all the technical assistance, and for all the selection and negotiation process, and for the management process, he will wind up paying substantial fees. Thus he may be better off getting the whole package of services through a syndicate.

A syndicate is a group of investors who buy property together. One of the most popular forms of syndicate organization is the limited partnership arrangement, in which a general partner runs the business while the limited partners are passive investors. The selection of land for investment is likely to be made by the general partner. A potential investor is faced simply with the choice of joining or not.

This disadvantage of having to accept preselected parcels may be minimal if there are a number of syndicates to choose among. However, the fact that the investor is joining a group of investors does not obviate the need to evaluate a specific project. Many investors join a group ownership venture without knowing anything about the property to be purchased. The judgment of their colleagues, they reason, should be sufficient. Frequently it is. But such a casual approach is not for the prudent investor.

The investor may go through the same analysis when participating in a syndicate as when investing alone. If the property passes inspection, the investor examines the structure of the syndicate to see if the compensation to the general partner and to the limited partners is fair. Faith in the general partner may be warranted, but a wise procedure is to review the analyses that have been made and to come to an independent judgment on the merits of the project itself.

Syndicate Arrangements. Syndicates vary widely in form. Most land syndicates, however, are limited partnerships.

The essence of a limited partnership is that two parties, a general partner and a limited partner, divide up the ownership rights and responsibilities. The general partner takes the responsibility for managing the affairs of the enterprise and is paid a fee of some sort for these services. The general partner may be one or more persons or a business corporation. Usually, though not always, the general partner is a professional in the field who undertakes to perform the services on behalf of the partnership because he or she has superior skills, the time and opportunity to use them, and wants to be paid for them. Frequently, the services are generated as an adjunct to some other business such as a real estate brokerage or a law practice.

The limited partner or partners are investors who do not wish to be active in the management of the enterprise which employs their funds. They contract away some of the rights in order to get the benefits of someone's services. Some states have uniform partnership laws that spell out the basic arrangements. But beyond those regulations, the parties are free to contract as they wish.

The degree of decision-making authority held by the limited partner or partners as a group can be minimal or substantial. For example, the decisions may be subject to negotiation including the right to determine when to sell, sale price, terms of sale, and the right to lease property, borrow on it, or otherwise encumber it.

Under the ordinary arrangements, limited partners have a limited liability from the debt of the enterprise, much as do stockholders in a corporation. That limited liability may be jeopardized if they take part in the management of the enterprise.

Compensation. The forms of compensation to syndicate partners vary considerably. They include the following:

1. Taking the property into the syndicate at a price higher than paid for by the general partner.
2. Operating as a sales agent by selling land to the syndicate and earning a brokerage commission.
3. Receiving a management fee or expense reimbursement during the operation of the syndicate.
4. Taking some of the tax deductions on property owned by the syndicate.
5. Operating as a sales agent at the end of the holding period and earning a commission.
6. Holding an option as a property user so that the price remains fixed whether or not the current value changes.
7. Taking a percentage of the profit after the investors' capital has been returned.

Rarely does a syndicate arrangement have all or none of these forms of compensation. Frequently one or a few are sufficient.

For illustration, a real estate broker may put together a syndicate as a way of selling property. The broker may be perfectly content to do this in order to earn commissions. He may get a commission on the sale to the partnership plus a commission on the resale, or a percentage of the profits, or both.

Speculators may work with syndicates without earning any commission. They may put up some of the capital, perform substantial services during ownership, and require reimbursement of certain costs and a percentage of the profit. They may also get a disproportionate amount of the tax deduction as part payment for services.

Builders may wish to hold land needed for future projects in reserve. They may set up syndicates for that purpose, and take an option to purchase as part of their compensation. The returns to their limited partners may be both attractive and limited.

A developer-packager may acquire contracts to purchase land subject to various contingencies, and may bear the costs of holding the land and solving some of the problems. When the capital is required for settlement, or major payments on principal are called for, the developer-packager may form a syndicate. The developer does not want to get out, but he needs more capital. The project may finally be brought in at a price above the original contract cost.

The variations in syndicate deals are almost infinite. The basic questions asked by an investor should be:

1. How good is the underlying investment?
2. How responsible are the people involved?
3. What services are being provided by the limited partner?
4. What price is being paid for those services?
5. What exposure (risk) is the limited partner taking?

6. Who has what control over the major decisions (such as when to sell and at what price)?
7. What is the profit potential?

Joining a syndicate can make the finding of land much easier than operating by oneself. Investors who develop skills and a track record of their own may find that others will want to invest with them, and will pay for their services.

13

Financing the Purchase

Land is among the more difficult investments to finance because it ordinarily does not produce the income to repay the borrowed money. But it is a great candidate for highly profitable leveraged investments because it changes value rapidly and appreciably. It is also one of the better hedges against inflation, and to the extent that an investor borrows heavily on the land the profit from the hedge increases.

Few investors need to have leverage explained to them, and even fewer need to be convinced of its merits. However, to set the stage for the discussion of borrowed money, the first part of this chapter presents a few key points about leverage.

The subsequent sections deal with the reasons why the cost and availability of money changes; where to get loanable funds; and the terms of loans.

LEVERAGE

Leverage is the technique of magnifying gains and losses through the use of borrowed money. Investors who need stability of income will invest in assets with a stable income stream—for example, bonds or mortgages. The rates of interest on such assets are relatively low. But investors who, for one reason or another, expect the value of the asset to rise, may borrow on it. Thus investors who expect government bond prices to rise sharply may buy such bonds using as much as 95 percent borrowed money.

Real estate investors who want a stable stream of income may buy high-quality fully-rented properties. They may even limit their investments to properties with high-quality long-term leases. If they wish to increase their earnings, they may borrow on the property. The use of the borrowed money does two things. If the interest rate charged for the borrowed money is lower than the rate earned on the asset pledged as security, the difference will add to the yield of the investment. For example, if the asset yields 9 percent and the money can be borrowed at 8 percent, the differential of 1 percent is an increase in earnings resulting from leverage. The second thing leverage does is to provide control of assets of greater value than that which could be purchased if no borrowed funds were used. Thus any appreciation in value is magnified by the use of lesser funds. For example, an investor who receives a current yield of 9 percent on a $100,000 asset and borrows $75,000 at 9 percent may still use leverage to magnify any gain. The magnification comes when the asset sells for $150,000. That $50,000 profit can be earned with a $25,000 equity or with a $100,000 equity. That's what leverage is all about.

Investors in land are likely to be interested in capital gain as opposed to income, because land itself ordinarily does not produce income. The payment of interest on the $75,000 would thus produce a negative cash flow even though the asset is increasing in value. The more the investor borrows, the greater his negative cash flow. But if the value of the land increases enough, the eventual recovery of the negative cash flow is assured. In fact, the greater the leverage the greater the returns—not only because the investment is less, but also because of income tax treatment.

As readers will recall, interest is treated as a deduction from income when computing federal income taxes. Also, the profit from the sale of land may be treated as a long-term capital gain. So an investor can make money if all he does is to recover the interest payments (plus real estate taxes and other expenses). Thus ordinary income may be converted to capital gain by the use of borrowed money.

The concern with leverage is really two-fold—first, that the property appreciate in value more than the cost of the borrowed money, and second, that the investor can afford to hold onto the land long enough to make a favorable sale.

Earnings on Leverage. Earnings on leverage are easy to calculate when the value of the asset does not change. For example, an investor who is able to earn 12 percent on a loan of $100,000 for 1 year, and who pays 10 percent for the borrowed money, may magnify his gains by borrowing.

If an investor uses no borrowed money, the gain is $12,000 per $100,000 investment. If he or she borrows $50,000 and pays 10 percent interest, or $5,000 per annum, $7,000 is left for a 14 percent return.

Total investment	$100,000
Less borrowed money	50,000
Equity	$ 50,000
Income on total investment (.12 × $100,000)	$ 12,000
Less interest (.10 × $50,000)	$ 5,000
Income to equity	$ 7,000

Earnings on equity equal $7,000 divided by $50,000 or 14 percent.

If the amount borrowed is increased, the effect of the differential in interest rates is magnified. See Table 13–1.

The general rules are that if the cost of borrowed money is the same as the rate of earnings, leverage will not magnify the gain or loss in terms of a rate of return. (See lines 6, 14, and 20 in Table 13–1.) If the cost of borrowed money is less than the rate of earnings, obviously the gain is magnified to the

TABLE 13–1
Rates of Return for $100,000 Asset with Varying Rates of Earnings and Leverage Situations

	(1) Rate Earned	(2) Dollars Earned	(3) Dollars Borrowed	(4) Rate Paid	(5) Interest Cost	(6) Dollars to Equity	(7) Amount Invested	(8) Rate of Return
1.	12%	$12,000	-0-	-0-	-0-	$12,000	$100,000	12%
2.	12%	12,000	$50,000	8%	$4,000	8,000	50,000	16%
3.	12%	12,000	50,000	9%	4,500	7,500	50,000	15%
4.	12%	12,000	50,000	10%	5,000	7,000	50,000	14%
5.	12%	12,000	50,000	11%	5,500	6,500	80,000	13%
6.	12%	12,000	50,000	12%	6,000	6,000	50,000	12%
7.	12%	12,000	50,000	13%	6,500	5,500	50,000	11%
8.	12%	12,000	50,000	10%	5,000	7,000	50,000	14%
9.	12%	12,000	60,000	10%	6,000	6,000	40,000	15%
10.	12%	12,000	80,000	10%	8,000	4,000	20,000	20%
11.	12%	12,000	90,000	10%	9,000	3,000	10,000	30%
12.	13%	13,000	90,000	10%	9,000	4,000	10,000	40%
13.	11%	11,000	90,000	10%	9,000	2,000	10,000	20%
14.	10%	10,000	90,000	10%	9,000	1,000	10,000	10%
15.	9.5%	9,500	90,000	10%	9,000	500	10,000	5%
16.	9.0%	9,000	90,000	10%	9,000	-0-	10,000	-0-
17.	8.0%	8,000	90,000	10%	9,000	(1,000)	10,000	(10%)
18.	12%	12,000	90,000	11%	9,900	2,100	10,000	21%
19.	12%	12,000	80,000	11%	8,800	3,200	20,000	16%
20.	12%	12,000	80,000	12%	9,600	2,400	20,000	12%

(1) Assumed rate of interest on earnings.
(2) $100,000 multiplied by the earned rate from column (1).
(3) Borrowed money.
(4) Cost of borrowed money as a rate of interest.
(5) Column (3) multiplied by column (4) to get dollar interest cost.
(6) Column (2) less column (5) showing how much money is left after paying for borrowed money.
(7) The amount invested, which is $100,000, less amount borrowed, column (3).
(8) Column (6) divided by column (7).

extent the rates differ. (See lines 2 through 7 in Table 13–1.) Furthermore, the greater the amount borrowed the more the magnification. (See lines 8 through 11 in Table 13–1.)

When the borrowed money is repaid in installments, as with a mortgage, the mathematics gets a little more complicated but the principles are the same. Thus if the ratio of borrowed money to total asset value starts off at 80 percent and declines to 60 percent, the effect of leverage will be approximately the same as though 70 percent were borrowed. Most land investments involve some amortization sooner or later, and the land may well be sold before the entire debt is repaid.

The method of calculating annual earnings becomes a little more complicated when the asset value changes. An increase in value, for example, may logically be spread over the several years of the investment. Thus if the $100,000 asset increases in value to $150,000 over 5 years, the average annual increase is $10,000. That $10,000 per year can be added to the earnings to get an approximate rate of earning. The approximation may vary quite widely from reality if the time is long and the change great.

The accurate way to make the computation is on the basis of present value theory. That, simply put, consists of discounting future income to its present value. A capitalization rate is used, which is mathematically the same as an interest rate. Some investors use these techniques. But, of course, the problem is to determine the future value of the land.

Earnings from converting ordinary income into capital gains are in addition to the earnings from leverage. If an investor earns 10 percent on a $250,000 asset with a $50,000 equity, a substantial tax benefit will result even if the rate of interest is 10 percent. The $200,000 of borrowed money will cost $20,000 per year. If the investor's marginal tax bracket is 40 percent, borrowing will save him $8,000 per year in taxes. Actually, the taxes are deferred and the sale may produce a long-term capital gain. The appreciation of $20,000 per year (from the borrowed $200,000, ignoring the appreciation from the $50,000 equity) will be taxed at long-term capital gains rates. Assume that the tax rate will be 20 percent (half of the short-term rate). Then the tax bill will be $4,000 for each $20,000 of capital gain. The tax saving is $4,000 per year plus the free use of the other $4,000. The tax saving of $4,000 per year amounts to an 8 percent return on a $50,000 equity. (See Figure 13–1.)

The calculation of the tax benefits is quite complicated. But it illustrates the point that leverage may be used to convert ordinary income into capital gain.

The calculation is further complicated when the loan is amortized, because the investor's equity keeps increasing. The extent of the increase in the equity attributable to loan amortization depends upon how much of the loan is paid off by monthly payments (or whatever the period) and the number of payments. An easy way to estimate the average equity is to select a target time period—4 years, for instance—and calculate how much of the mortgage will be paid off. One half of the amount paid off plus the down payment is about equal to the average investment.

FIGURE 13–1

Tax Benefit from Leverage

Total investment	$250,000
Borrowed money	200,000
Down payment	$ 50,000

Appreciation at 10 percent per year for 4 years equals 40 percent or $100,000. Assuming a net sales price of $350,000 ($250,000 plus $100,000), the return from tax savings each year during the investment would be calculated as follows:

$200,000	borrowed money
.10	interest
$ 20,000	interest deduction

Then, if an investor pays a 40 percent tax rate, the tax saving is $8,000 per year. For 4 years the total will be $32,000.

Upon sale at $350,000, a taxable gain of $100,000 exists. Assuming the long-term capital gain rate for the investor is 20 percent, the taxes are $20,000 (20 percent of $100,000). Proceeds of sale are as follows:

Sales price	$350,000		
Less loan	200,000		
Pretax proceeds		$150,000	
Less taxes		20,000	
Net proceeds			$130,000
Less investment			
Down payment	$ 50,000		
Interest payments of 20,000 per year pretax cost, giving after-tax cost of $12,000 for 4 years	48,000*		$ 98,000
Net after-tax profit			$ 32,000

A portion of the profit is attributable to the 10 percent return earned on the $50,000 per year. That amounts to $5,000 per year pretax or a total of $20,000. Deduct taxes at 20 percent. The result is $16,000 after-tax profit for the $50,000 equity. It is an average of $4,000 per year or 8 percent after tax.

The remaining $16,000 is the gain resulting from converting ordinary income to capital gain. It averages another $4,000 per year and is another 8 percent on the equity.

* The result is the same if 4 times $20,000 is used giving $80,000 less the $32,000 tax savings.

The calculation of earnings on that equity requires a heroic assumption as to what the increase in value will be. An investor might simply assume that the value of the property will increase 10, 12, 15, or 20 percent per year. If that percentage increase is greater than the interest cost plus expenses to carry (say, property taxes at 2 percent) then leverage is working favorably. This calculation is okay for comparing rates, but does not help in computing the return on the amount of money borrowed.

An easy, but less accurate method for figuring annual rate of return from leverage for the first year is to estimate the total increase in value over five years and divide by the number of years. That annual "earning on investment" may be used as the base from which interest and carrying costs are deducted. The result is the earnings on the average equity. Figure 13–2 shows some sample calculations.

FIGURE 13–2

Leverage with Amortization

Total investment	$250,000
Borrowed money	200,000
Down payment	$ 50,000

The borrowed money is repayable at $1,667 per month for an annual total of $20,000 on 20 years amortization. At the end of 4 years the mortgage balance would be approximately $180,000. Principal payments would have totalled $20,000.

Average total investment includes $50,000 down payment plus $\frac{80,000}{2}$ total payments, or $90,000.

Assuming the property increases in value by 10 percent per year or 40 percent to $350,000, the annual average is $25,000.

The gain of $25,000 is added to the average equity build-up of $5,000 per year for a total average gain of $30,000. That gain divided by the $90,000 average investment is 33 percent pretax.

Without amortization the gain of $25,000 per year on a $50,000 investment would be 50 percent. The amortization increases the average investment.

Holding onto Land. Holding on to land until the most appropriate time for sale is a key element in investing. Leverage makes profitable investments more profitable. But it makes them more difficult to hold onto because they keep requiring additional cash investment.

Buying a parcel of unimproved land is most accurately viewed as buying an investment program. The down payment is only the first phase of the investment. Each year is another phase.

The way to use high leverage is to have the first phase small relative to the succeeding phases. When the principal payments begin, and sooner or later they must, the amount of leverage used is reduced. Thus high-leverage investors attempt to get interest-only payments for three to five years and to sell before the principal payments start. Low-leverage investors make a substantial down payment and start on an amortization of the loan right away. Low-leverage investors are typically long-term holders of land.

The key element for any investor is to be able to hold onto the land so that he can determine the time of sale. Over-leveraged properties are properties that investors cannot afford to carry.

COST AND AVAILABILITY OF MONEY

Land is more valuable the more useful and/or scarce it becomes. These characteristics of land are what make it a good investment. It is also a good investment because, as a resource that is somewhat financible, it is a great hedge against inflation.

The idea of buying something that will rise in price as the prices of other goods rise during an inflation is a fundamentally sound idea. It is also a sound idea to charge interest rates that reflect inflationary expectations. Indeed, the long-term changes in interest rates are in large measure reflective of changing inflationary expectations.

Real estate investors may hedge against inflation merely by owning the real asset, such as land. They may magnify the benefits of the hedge by borrowing to finance the purchase and paying back in cheaper dollars. This is aside from the benefits of leverage which accrue because the property earns one rate of return and the lender, in a more secure position, is getting a lesser rate of return.

Lenders are not oblivious to rising inflationary expectations, although their expectations have in the past been unrealistically low. In fact, during the post–World War II era the rise in interest rates has lagged behind the rise in the rate of inflation and thus substantially benefitted borrowers—even those who recurringly become aghast at the seemingly outrageous interest rates they pay.

The prevailing market rates change, and so does the availability of money. Land investors need to know why the rates change, and how their movement affects the ability to purchase and sell land. It is also useful to know where the loanable funds come from and where they go.

Supply of Loanable Funds. Loanable funds are obtained either directly from those who have accumulated savings and are willing to lend them directly, or from financial intermediaries that collect savings from individuals and lend them to investors.

In both cases, some people in society must save, i.e., forego spending. That is to say they must earn more than they spend. They have a claim on a quantity of goods and services. They can lend that claim to someone else, in return for getting it back plus something extra, i.e., interest.

The amount of this something extra depends upon how large a supply of savings is generally available, what the inflationary expectation is, and the risk that the loan will not be repaid. Loans with high management expenses obviously get higher interest rates, but the general level of rates is mostly related to the aforementioned conditions.

Since our economy operates with a fractional reserve banking system, the total amount of money available may be expanded and contracted by the creation and repayment of bank loans. Most definitions of money include demand deposits in commercial banks, so that banks by lending some of the money placed on deposit—i.e., creating new deposits—in fact expand the supply of money.

The system is flexible because a bank needs to keep only a portion of the money deposited with it, say one fifth. Thus it has enough reserves available to meet the requirements of those who may want their money now. The total extent of bank credit is limited by the fractional reserve requirement. In fact, the limitation is the reciprocal of the fraction. For example, a one fifth reserve means that the total supply of money can be five times the total reserves if all the banks operate fully loaned out.

Inflation may be caused by the creation of too much credit. Some expansion of credit is necessary to meet the needs of an expanding economy. That monetary expansion is the lubricant of commerce. However, when the amount of money and the rate at which it is being spent (velocity) are too great in relation to the real resources, the result will be an increase in the price level. As the saying goes, too much money is chasing too few goods.

Chapter 6, "National Patterns of Monetary and Fiscal Policy," briefly described how the Federal Reserve Board may affect the general cost and availability of money. To summarize, it does this through open market operations, reserve requirements, and the rediscount rate.

If the Fed wants to ease the money supply situation, or if the economy needs more money—as during peaks of seasonal activities—the Fed may facilitate that expansion by buying government securities in the open market. It pays for those securities with a check that is deposited in a commercial bank. The commercial bank deposits the check in its account with the Fed, thus raising its reserves. Similarly, by selling government securities, the Fed can reduce reserves.

If a greater change in the supply of money is needed, the Fed can lower or increase the reserve ratios required of member banks. For example, a change in the reserve ratio for a group of banks from 20 percent to 19 percent will permit bank credit to increase by about 5 percent. Whereas $100 million of deposits formerly required the backing of $20 million in reserves, the same $20 million with a reserve requirement of 19 percent will now support about $105,000 million of deposits. This is because $1 million that was formerly used as reserve becomes available for lending. Borrowers redepositing that $1 million somewhere give the banks receiving it the opportunity to lend out 81 percent of it (after deducting the 19 percent reserve requirement). Depositing and redepositing will eventually magnify the $1 million in reserve to about $5 million in deposits.

Since banks have to keep certain amounts on reserve the absolute dollars available to them over and above the reserve influences what they can lend out. Thus, if they want to make some loans and are short of funds uncommitted to reserves they might try to borrow money for reserves. The Fed is one source. The interest it charges the banks is called the discount rate, or sometimes the rediscount rate. Changes in these quoted rates influence the availability of reserves and hence the availability of loanable funds.

These are the ways the Federal Reserve System manages the supply of money (or mismanages it, depending on your point of view). It is a difficult and delicate process because savings rates change, and the problems are compounded by movements of money in and out of financial intermediaries.

Savings rates change because incomes and expectations change. A genuine shortage of savings may result when the economy consumes too much, or an excess of savings may develop because not enough is being consumed. Economists differ as to the nature and causes of the problems, but the variables are reasonably clear.

Changing conditions in the economy, and changes among the rates paid by various borrowers and financial intermediaries, cause savings to shift from one channel to another. At any time some portion of the pool of funds is in institutions such as commercial banks, savings banks, savings and loan associations, and life insurance companies. These are financial intermediaries. The saver has an account of some sort, or owns a cash value life insurance policy. The financial intermediary lends the saver's funds to borrowers, including business corporations and governmental bodies.

When rates change so that big high-quality borrowers pay an exceptionally attractive interest rate, many savers will withdraw their funds from the financial intermediaries and lend directly. This process is called disintermediation. When it occurs it plays havoc with the availability of loanable funds through the intermediaries.

Disintermediation occurs at high interest rates, and, as everybody knows, that compounds the problem for the mortgage market. For one thing the money is pulled away from institutions such as savings and loan associations that are heavy investors in real estate, and goes largely to non-real estate borrowers. Additionally, the high rates are more difficult for the real estate borrowers to pay because the cost of borrowed money is relatively more important to them. The result is that in inflationary periods money is exceptionally hard to get for real estate purposes, and what is available is expensive.

Sources of Land Financing. Each of the financial intermediaries has its own characteristics. Each emerged in historical development in some measure because of the functions it performed. Their policies toward real estate lending are thus pretty well set at any particular moment. In some cases, moreover, government regulations prescribe limits on lending policy.

This situation creates certain problems for the land investor. Most lenders want an income-producing security for their loan so that they can be reasonably certain of repayment. In the absence of such security they may lend on land as a resource used in production, i.e., land used for development. But these are short-term loans.

Savings and loan associations specialize in lending to home builders and owners. Most of their loans are for owner-occupied dwellings. A land investor has a chance with them if the investor is going to live in a house on the land (5, 10, or 20 acres). The developer also has a chance for a land loan, but it usually has to be for imminent development.

The story with the other major intermediaries is somewhat similar. Farm loans, of course, are not quite home loans and not quite land loans. They resemble business loans. Farming is a great way to speculate in land, not only because the income helps to carry the land but because the farming activity helps to get the financing.

While investors have numerous other institutional possibilities for financing land purchases, most of them are poor prospects. The most common method of financing land investments is through seller-provided financing.

Sellers are inclined to provide financing for several reasons. First, an all-cash sale will bring a lower price than a sale on terms. Second, the tax treatment on capital gains permits installment sales, which stretch out and reduce the tax burden. Third, finding a buyer for an all-cash sale may take a long time.

Sellers pay ordinary income tax on interest income, but capital gains rates on long-term profits. Thus, most sellers tend not to stress the interest rate as much as the sales price. However, the generally prevailing rate of interest will influence the rate of interest the seller will charge.

OTHER TERMS OF THE LOAN

Factors Affecting Cost. Mortgage lenders may use "points" to adjust their yield on mortgages. The term refers to a percentage (point) discount on a loan. It is a one-time charge by a lender when making a loan. Thus a four-point charge on a $100,000 loan is a one-time charge of $4,000. On a 25-year 8 percent loan, a 4-point charge would effectively push the interest cost up to about 8½ percent.

Points sometimes fluctuate more than interest rates. They are used to adjust the yield when the lender wishes to change the price on new loans without changing the contract rate of interest. Sellers do not charge points. But they can raise the price of the land.

The method of using borrowed money in land as a hedge against inflation is simply to buy land at a price that will in the long run rise enough to provide an attractive rate of return. To use leverage, investors may (1) borrow most of the purchase price at an interest rate below the rate of return expected from the land appreciation, or (2) borrow the money at a rate of interest based upon an inflationary expectation that underestimates the inflation to come.

Borrowing money when prevailing interest rates are 6 percent and repaying when they are 8 percent gives the borrower an edge of 2 percent. For example, suppose an investor buys land worth $100,000. Assume it increases in value by 10 percent per year, and that the carrying cost for taxes is 1½ percent. Thus the land is earning 8½ percent. Part of that is at the inflation expectation generally held when the prevailing mortgage rate is 6 percent.

On that basis, the investor putting up $20,000 on a $100,000 purchase would earn in increased values as follows:

Purchase price	$100,000
Rate of value increase	.10
Annual increment in value	$ 10,000
Less taxes (1.5%)	1,500
Net increase in equity	$ 8,500

$$\text{Property earnings rate} \; \frac{\text{increase in equity}}{\text{value of asset}}$$

$$= \frac{8{,}500}{100{,}000} = .085 = 8.5\%$$

Now, with the use of leverage:

Net increment in equity	$ 8,500
Less 6% interest paid on $80,000 borrowed money ...	4,800
Earnings on equity	$ 3,700
Equity earnings rate $\frac{\text{income}}{\text{investment}}$ $\frac{3,700}{\$\ 20,000}$ = 18.5%	

Now assume an instant change in the rate of inflation as it affects prevailing interest rates, with of course the contract rate on the purchase remaining the same.

Note that the increase in earnings amounted to $2,000 ($5,700 less $3,700). Also, note that it was attributable to the $2,000 increase in value because of inflation. The interest rate paid was fixed at 6 percent, and the land was used as a basis for borrowing the money cheaply.

Investors look to borrow money at low rates before an inflationary surge and repay with substantially cheaper dollars. Sometimes the inflationary surge drops back and then the investor is left with a large mortgage debt at high interest rates.

One way out is to refinance at lower rates. When the institutional lenders get tired of refinancing they increase the charges for prepayment, and in cases of income property loans they use "lock-ins."

Lock-ins are clauses in the mortgage that deny the borrower the right to prepay the debt during a stipulated period of time, frequently five years and sometimes longer. In addition to the lock-in, and sometimes instead of it, a mortgage may carry a penalty for prepayment. The penalty may be six months interest or it may be stated as points. For example, it may be five points in the first year, four points in the second, three points in the third, two points in the fourth, and one point in the fifth. After the fifth year, the prepayment penalty may be dropped.

Lock-ins and prepayment penalties are typical features of institutional loans nowadays. Most sellers who finance will permit prepayment in all or part at any time. They are happy to get the money. One noticeable exception is the seller who has a large taxable gain; he may limit the payment in the first year so that the total of the downpayment and other payments does not exceed 29 percent. But ordinarily, after the first year even such sellers do not care. They are generally glad to get the money.

The difficulty of paying off a high-interest rate loan if rates subside is,

Investment value	$100,000
Rate of value increase	.12 (2% more for inflation)
Annual increase in value	12,000
Less taxes	1,500
Net increment in value	$ 10,500
Less 6% interest paid on $80,000	4,800
Earning on equity	$ 5,700
Equity earning rate $\frac{\text{income}}{\text{investment}} = \frac{5,700}{20,000} = 28.5\%$	

of course, finding another lender. If the property produces no income, the sources of money are severely limited. In buying land, investors should be prepared to live with the interest rates to which they commit themselves.

Mortgage Repayment. Ordinarily the investor wants as long a time as possible to repay the loan, with the privilege of prepaying it at any time without penalty. Amortization and term arrangements are the *two* basic repayment patterns. They may also be used in combination.

Under an amortized mortgage the lender is repaid in periodic payments of principal and interest. Almost all mortgages for home purchases are amortized. In most cases the monthly payment remains constant. Each month the amount going to interest declines because the amount of the debt declined in the previous month. But, since the monthly payment remains the same, the amount going to principal increases.

For investment properties the payments on principal and interest on an annual basis are looked at in ratio to the original loan. The total annual payments divided by the original loan is called the *annual constant*. Thus, a loan for $100,000 with monthly payments of $750 which adds up to $9,000 per year has an annual constant of 9 percent. If the interest rate is 7 percent it will take 21 years 7 months to pay off the loan.

Annual constants for loans of about 20 years duration are typically 2 percentage points above the interest rate. Thus a 7.5 percent loan at 9.5 percent constant will run for 20 years and 11 months. Similarly, an 8 percent interest

TABLE 13–2
Annual Constants, Selected Amortization Periods and Interest Rates

Number of Years	Rate of Interest: 7 Percent	8 Percent	9 Percent
20	9.31	10.04	10.80
21	9.11	9.85	10.62
22	8.93	9.68	10.46
23	8.76	9.53	10.32
24	8.62	9.39	10.19
25	8.49	9.27	10.08

Source: Constructed from *Financial Constant Percent Amortization Tables*, Boston: Financial Publishing Company, Publication no. 187, 1969, pp. 148–49.

loan with a 10 percent constant will run for 20 years and 3 months.

Table 13–2 shows how annual constants vary for 7, 8, and 9 percent loans with terms of 20 through 25 years.

An alternative way to amortize a loan is with level principal payments. For example, a purchase of land for $100,000 with a $20,000 down payment leaving a balance of $80,000 might be paid for over 10 years with 40 quarterly payments of principal. In this case each payment would be $2,000 of principal plus interest. Assume interest is 8 percent. Then quarterly interest is 2 percent, so the first payment would be $2,000 principal plus 2 percent of $80,000 or $1,600 for a total of $3,600. Each payment would decline as interest declined. See Table 13–3.

Some amortized loans are quite short. For example, a land purchaser might call for the mortgage balance to be paid over five years. In that case the investor might make 5 annual payments of principal or 10 semiannual, 20 quarterly, or 60 monthly payments.

If the loan is going to last only a few years, perhaps up to five or in a few

TABLE 13-3
Amortizing a Loan with Level Principal Payments

Loan Balance	Interest at 2% Per Quarter	Principal Payment	Total Payment
$80,000........	$1,600	$2,000	$3,600
$78,000........	$1,560	$2,000	$3,560
$76,000........	$1,520	$2,000	$3,520
$74,000........	$1,480	$2,000	$3,480
.			
.			
.			
$ 6,000........	$ 120	$2,000	$2,120
$ 4,000........	$ 80	$2,000	$2,080
$ 2,000........	$ 40	$2,000	$2,040
-0-...........	-0-	-0-	-0-

Source: Table constructed by author.

cases longer, the seller or lender may be willing to take interest only for that period of time. That type is called a term loan. Thus, for example, the $80,000 quarterly interest of $1,600 would be paid for say 5 years or 20 payments, but then the entire balance would be due and payable.

This kind of loan makes sense if the land is going to be developed within the time frame. It will be difficult, to say the least, to refinance the property unless development is close. If it is about to start, a developer could get a land loan from an institution. But that is part of the development and construction financing process.

Some seller-lenders are unwilling to take interest only but will take amortization for say five years and then the payment of the balance. Such seller-lenders may give amortization terms that would run 20 to 25 years (but most are shorter, say 10 years), provided there is a lump sum payment of the balance in full at the end of 5 or 8 years. So they will give a partially amortized loan, i.e., a loan with an amortization schedule that would take a long time to repay in full; however it calls for a balloon payment when only part of the loan has been paid off. In the example of a loan for say $10,000 with a constant of 9.5 percent and an interest rate of 8.0 percent, the terms of the loan would be 23 years, 2 months. The balloon payment in 10 years to pay off the loan balance would have to be $7,710. Or, to take another example, a loan of $10,000 with a 9 percent constant (payments of $75 per month per $10,000) would with an interest rate of 7 percent run 21 years 7 months. The loan balance after 5, 10, and 15 years would be as follows:

	5 Years	10 Years	15 Years
Loan Balance	$8,910	$7,110	$4,720

This type of loan is useful if the investor can reasonably expect to pay the balloon when it falls due.

Such a balloon may be paid off in three basic ways. One is through resale to a developer who will use a land loan to pay all cash. The second way is to sell for a downpayment big enough to pay off the loan and carry back the balance as a mortgage. The third is to come up with the money from other sources.

The third alternative may not be attractive. That is why the analysis of when the land will be ready for sale to a developer is especially important. The analysis should indicate the time at which the seller could expect to get the all-cash sale, or at least when the value should be high enough to set a favorable sale that would produce enough cash to pay the loan.

Other Mortgage Features. The salability of land to developers is affected by some features of mortgages other than cost. These may be incorporated into the mortgage at the time of the purchase by the investor. Thus the investor may transfer the mortgage along with the real estate if the mortgage is attractive to someone else, and of course if the terms of the mortgage do not prohibit such a transfer.

Land bought in large parcels is frequently developed in stages—a part at a time. A developer who purchases 160 acres may want to subdivide only 40 acres at a time. The seller carrying back a mortgage will have all 160 acres for security. The seller can relatively easily include *release clauses* providing that for payment of part of the mortgage balance part of the land will be released. Suppose that a seller holds a $480,000 mortgage on the 160 acres. The pro rata share per acre is $3,000. The release provision may call for 120 percent of a pro rata share payment. Thus, for every acre to be released, the principal must be reduced by $3,600. So if the developer wants 40 acres he pays a total of $144,000 to the lender to free the land of debt. When buying land an investor may ask for the same type of release provisions, and then in selling have the new buyer take over the loan. In buying land, an investor does well to get a loan good enough to pass on to the next purchaser.

The mortgage with a subordination clause has a really good feature for the buyer-developer. Subordination means that the priority of claim on the mortgage is adjusted to make a first mortgage become a second mortgage.

The owner of real estate may borrow and pledge the property as security for the debt. If the owner later wants to borrow again, this time from some other party, he may (as long as someone will lend). Now he has pledged the same property as security for both loans. This he may do. But suppose he does not pay, and the lender forecloses. Who gets paid off first? The lender who gets paid first is the one who lent first.

If the investor wants to reverse that priority of claim so that the seller who has a first mortgage will have a second mortgage when the developer obtains a land loan from the institutional lender, then the seller's loan has to be *subordinated.* The institutional lender generally requires that it have a first claim. And this requires that the lender on any existing loan agree to subordinate his priority of claim.

Obviously subordinated loans can be risky for the party that subordinates his interest. But because it makes development financing easy, the developer will pay an attractive price for subordination. With good enough terms the developer does not really have to put up much, if any, cash.

Personal Liability on Mortgage Borrowing. Certainly mortgage loans carry some repayment risk, and institutional lenders may ask for security beyond the property. Investors ordinarily should not agree to be personally liable for seller-provided financing; they ordinarily cannot get away from it on institutionally provided financing. But in some cases the property may be given as the sole security for the loan and the investor should so state in the mortgage.

The normal presumption is that when one borrows one promises to repay, and the addition of collateral is not in and of itself a relief of the liability. In some states a "purchaser money mortgage" may limit the purchaser's liability, but the safest way is an explicit statement of sole security.

Once a borrower has liability on the mortgage, the lender or lender/seller may not want to let the loan stay on the property if the borrower/buyer sells. For this reason the mortgage may contain an *acceleration clause.* It provides that if ownership is transferred the loan becomes due and payable at the option of the lender.

Even if a lender does not prohibit passing the loan on to another purchaser, the borrower is not automatically off the hook if the property is sold. A new purchaser may assume and agree to pay the mortgage, but the original borrower will still remain liable, although secondarily liable.

When buying land under an existing mortgage, an investor preferably would take title "subject to" existing encumbrances (mortgage). That means that the buyer acknowledges the existence of the mortgage but does not take on the personal liability for paying it. Certainly, if the mortgage is not paid, the property can be sold to satisfy the debt.

Types of Mortgages. The discussion has thus far proceeded as though only one type of mortgage existed, with variations in features. What has been described is really a "lien theory" mortgage where the note is deemed to be included by reference.

Actually, in borrowing money on the security of real estate two separate instruments are used. One is the note, which is the promise to pay. The other is the mortgage, which is the pledge of the property to secure the debt. The term "mortgage" has been used to refer to both instruments as though they were one.

In some states the borrowers pass title to the property to the lender to make foreclosure easier for the lender if it become necessary. These are "title theory" states. The foreclosure procedure is different and may not involve an auction sale on the courthouse steps.

In some states in which the foreclosure process is especially difficult, the use of deeds of trust has developed. In that case the "title" for the property for the purpose of securing the loan is held by a third party called a trustee. This facilitates foreclosure if the debt is not paid. The earlier reference to mortgages includes the deed of trust, commonly called *trust deed.* Thus these trust deeds can have the same features as discussed under mortgages.

In some states with difficult foreclosure procedures and little use of trust deeds, low downpayment purchasers of real estate, especially land, use what is known as a *land contract* or *contract for deed.* This instrument may also be used in low downpayment purchases even when trust deeds are common. But they so favor the seller in bypassing foreclosure that their use is quite limited where trust deeds are common.

The big difference between these *land contracts* (or *contracts for deed*) and mortgages and trust deeds is that in the former the title remains with the seller, who agrees to pass title when all or a predetermined portion of the purchase price is paid. But until then the title remains with the seller. As a result, the buyer who defaults is less protected than under a mortgage or trust deed and the equity built up may be lost.

Land contracts have their appropriate uses, but they should be employed with great care. The seller's position, although strong, may not be trouble free. Defaulting purchasers may later offer to cure their default and attempt to establish their claim by suing for specific performance. Even when the seller wins it can be expensive.

Options. The investor who buys with a low downpayment subject to an existing mortgage and gives the seller a purchase money mortgage for the balance of the purchase price with the property as sole security, stands only to lose what he has put into the property. That is one way to buy. Frequently the idea is to gain control of a piece of property in the expectation that something will happen to make it much more valuable. The reward is worth the risk of the loss of the investment, but the extent of the risk is limited to the cash invested.

An alternative way to finance control of the property is to use an *option.* An option is a contract in which a buyer purchases the right to buy from a seller. The seller is obligated to sell if the buyer chooses to exercise the option. The buyer is, however, not obligated to buy.

Obviously an option is an excellent way in which to control property using a great deal of leverage. The purchaser pays a fee for the option. The price can be high or modest. Usually the option price is low if the selling price is high. That is, if some crazy investor is willing to pay an outlandish price then the seller is only too happy to give an option. If the buyer gets the zoning or whatever is needed, then the price may not be so crazy after all.

Expensive options are those in which the price is close to market value. Then the seller really needs to be compensated for taking the property off the market.

In any case, investors who use options limit their potential losses. They can lose only what they have put up, plus the expenses incurred in working out whatever they are trying to do.

14

Negotiating the Purchase

Once the investor has found a parcel of land to acquire and has determined the desired financing arrangements, the next step is negotiating the purchase. Such negotiations are delicate and technical.

Good salesmen are good negotiators in that they are able to work out compromises. Not all such salesmen, however, are good technicians, and some of them may need technical support in negotiating a satisfactory agreement.

Much of the technical problem is legal. The rights in the land may be limited by regulation, or the seller may not actually have title, or other persons may have claims against the property.

Legal counsel is useful for these problems. But legal counsel should not control the negotiation because the counsel may so protect the client on legal aspects that the client will lose what would have been a fine purchase. Instead, the investor should use legal counsel as staff support to inform him what the legal problems are.

Technical support may also be needed from geologists and engineers in determining the usability of the land. These technical specialists likewise should advise as to what can be done with the land and what the potential problems are.

Appraisers and market analysts serve similar functions. They may advise on value and markets, but the investor must determine what price to pay and how to negotiate the terms.

The first part of this chapter deals with information that the investor needs in negotiating a purchase. That it may be drawn from a variety of professionals is incidental. Indeed, in some cases little professional help is needed. The investor must make that determination based upon the complexity of the situation and his own experience.

Having acquired the necessary information to begin negotiations, the investor starts a process. The process ordinarily requires a document or documents that spell out the intended agreement. The process itself is a very sensitive matter. That is, the acceptability of an offer to a seller is in part determined by who presents it and how it is presented.

Skilled brokers can help in this because their objective is generally to make a sale. The usual arrangement is for the broker to act as the agent of the seller. Technically, a fiduciary relationship exists in which the broker is supposed to represent the seller. But since the broker's compensation is usually a commission, it is a fair bet that he is also representing his wife and children.

If the seller's attorney is negotiating on behalf of the seller, then the negotiation may be made difficult because the attorney's tendency is to protect the seller rather than to take the initiative in working out a sale. Some lawyers, however, are skillful negotiators and excellent at doing business; they are worth retaining for those services.

Negotiation, as we have said, involves a process. The second part of the chapter deals with the content of the relevant documents used in the process.

INFORMATION REQUIREMENTS

The Market. Market information is the first kind of information to use in negotiating the purchase. The discussion throughout the earlier chapters has dealt with getting superior information about the future of the market in order to select land for investment. Having found such land, the objective is to buy it.

One wants to pay the lowest price possible, with one exception. If the land is significantly underpriced, the question is not one of getting it as cheaply as possible but rather of being sure to make the purchase. If the land is really priced right, it may be more advantageous to negotiate a sure sale than to press for a lower price and risk losing out to another buyer or having difficulty reaching an agreement.

If the property is far overpriced, which often happens, then hard negotiations are in order. Surprisingly, sometimes an offer to purchase at 20 percent below the asking price is accepted. Seldom is the asking price realistic. It may even be 30 percent over market value.

Information on market value can be obtained in several ways. One is by shopping. A second is through the broker, and the third is by checking sales from public records. In many cases information may be verified by talking to the parties to the transaction.

Shopping, as the term implies, means seeing what is available on the market. The process is simply to follow up with the agents, owners, and other contacts that were made during the search process. By keeping a set of notes, a diligent investor can have a great deal of market information on prices. If the search process takes a long time, and it may, the investor will have a chance to check back to find out what properties from all those he has seen were sold—and at what prices. If the investor specializes in a particular area, he can over a period of time amass a great deal of information which will be of use to him in his negotiations.

Realtors who specialize in land, especially members of the National Institute of Farm and Land Brokers, are veritable storehouses of information. Many such professionals keep a full set of records on ownership and sales.

Owners of record are frequently shown on tax maps, i.e., maps prepared by the tax assessor. Sales records are usually based upon information received by the county recorder when a sale takes place, although sometimes the brokers' records may be updated from other sources. The information may be recorded on a master map or in a card file. Additionally, property that is offered for sale may be noted on the map or in the file.

In a small community such records are easy to keep if pursued with diligence. Most brokers will have some of the information in some sort of order but will rely heavily on their own recollections and scattered files. Therefore the investor who wants information would do best to find a broker who is organized in collecting and handling it. Such a broker should be anxious to provide a potential purchaser with a list of properties available for sale. When the investor has selected one or more for serious consideration, the broker should be willing to compile a list of similar properties that have been sold recently. He may say that nothing quite like it has been sold. But the investor, undaunted, should insist upon information on whatever has been sold, similar or not.

In any event an investor can always get the information from the county recorder, who maintains files on ownership transfers and numerous other matters affecting title. Picking up the information is a chore, but appraisers do it all the time. In fact, if an investor has difficulty in getting satisfactory information, he can obtain help from a professional appraiser.

The two major professional appraisal organizations from whom potential appraisers may be selected are the American Institute of Real Estate Appraisers and the Society of Real Estate Appraisers. Both provide designations that attest to professional competence.

An investor can get the land appraised and ask for a complete appraisal report, including the list of comparables and the reasoning behind the conclusion. Such a report is much more suitable than an unsubstantiated opinion. If anyone is going to form an unsubstantiated opinion it had best be the seller, not the buyer or the buyer's counsel.

The whole idea of market information is to get facts. Superior information on what others will pay for the land is critical in negotiations. If the price asked is less than what the investor thinks it should be, based upon his expectation of the market, he has found an opportunity and should buy. If the seller has reasonable expectations, the price will not be a problem. If the seller is not attuned to the market price, and is asking for too much, the investor's information will be useful in negotiating a sale.

Most sellers who live on their land know what has been happening, but not all of them. Absentee landowners have difficulty keeping up with local activity. That is why prices asked may be far from realistic market prices.

The Property. During the various

stages of negotiations the investor needs to know what land he will actually get title to and what he will be able to do with it. The details are generally provided in stages as the negotiations proceed and the sale is consummated.

The investor will require an identification of the property being purchased. The first identification is likely to be a loose description, such as somebody's farm, a street address, or the lot next to a building. While the offer to purchase document may include some further identification, at some point a complete identification is necessary. That may be provided by a legal description.

The legal description may be based upon one or more location identification systems. If an area has been subdivided the subdivision plat will be recorded in the county offices. The parcel of property will be identified on the map by a subdivision name or number and a lot number. In some jurisdictions the subdivision may be divided into blocks, and the blocks into lots. The details may vary. For example, some areas may be divided into squares and lots. But the essential idea is that a map is recorded and the parcel is identified on the map. The map also shows streets and street markings. Anyone may take a map, go out to the location, and find a permanent marker imbedded in the street, curb, or ground. The map shows where the property is located in reference to the marker. (See Figure 14–1.)

Most land not subdivided is identified by the quadrangular survey system. That system uses a series of townships that are located by survey lines running north/south, identified as meridians, and additional survey lines running east/west, identified as parallels. The township is thus located by meridians and parallels that resemble longitude and latitude. (See Figure 14–2.)

The township, which is generally a 6-mile square, is further divided into 36 one-mile squares. Each square is numbered. (See Figure 14–3.) Each square can then be identified by township and range number, and physically located by a marker in the ground.

A 1-mile square is 640 acres, and since smaller portions of the land than 640 acres are sold, the description of those portions may simply be as fractions of the total. For example, a sale of the northwest quarter of section 7 of township 2 north and 5 west of some principal meridian would accurately identify the parcel. That quarter section would be 160 acres. One might further sell the northwest quarter of the northwest quarter of section 7. That would be 40 acres. The north half of the northwest quarter of the northwest quarter of section 7 is 20 acres. The system works well down to 10 acres or 5 acres of even $2\frac{1}{2}$ acres, as long as the parcels are of rectangular shapes. Irregular shapes require another system.

An alternative system is that of metes and bounds. Metes are measures. Bounds are directions. All that is needed for a metes and bounds description is a known point of beginning plus measures and directions. "Starting at the northern tip of the big rock next to the old oak thence north for a distance of 4,000 feet then east for a distance of

FIGURE 14–1
Subdivision Plat

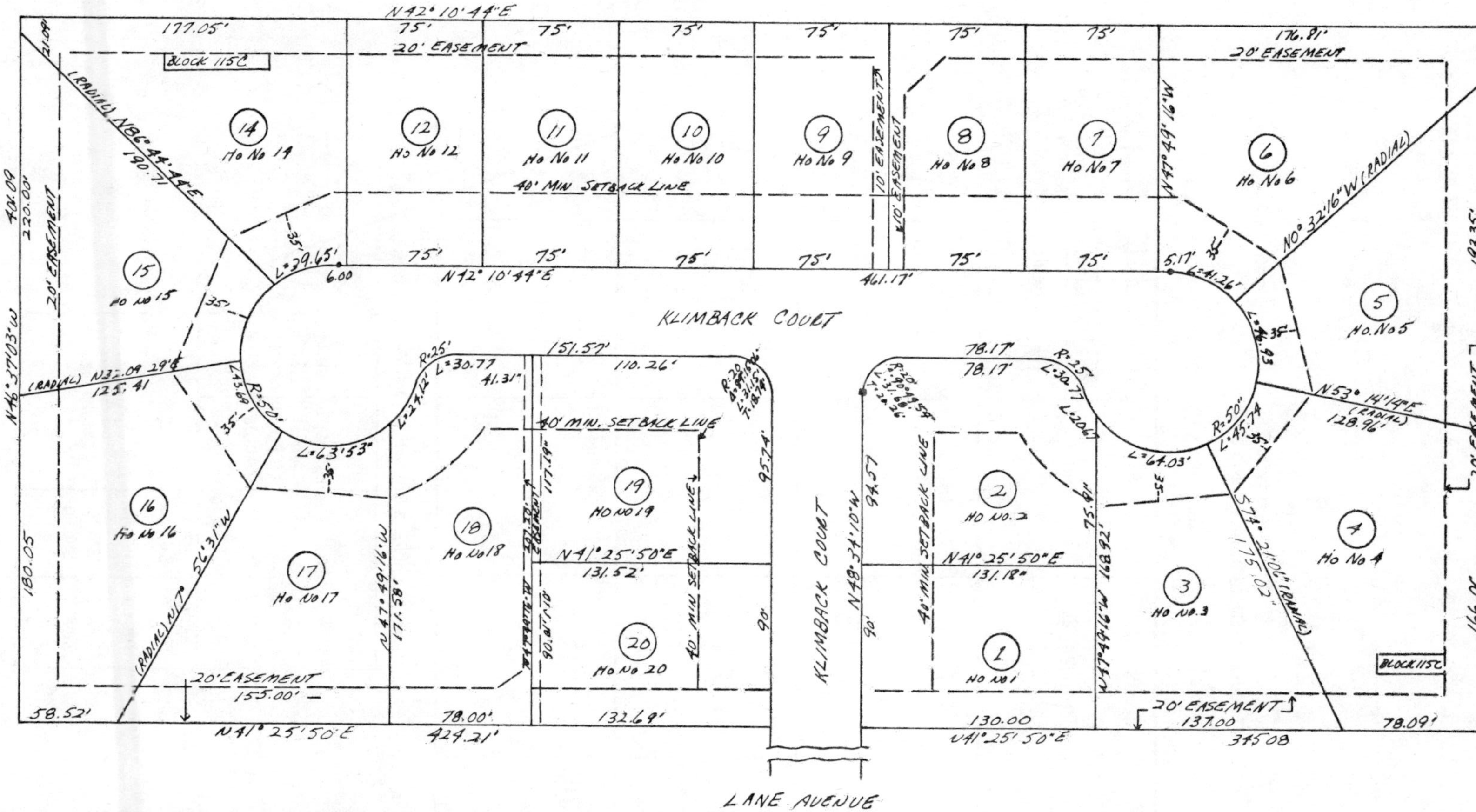

Source: Final map of Lane Avenue Estates, Borough of West Caldwell, Essex County, N.J., Nov. 23, 1968, George C. Stuart Assoc., Inc., Engineers and Surveyors.

FIGURE 14-2
Township System: Meridians and Parallels

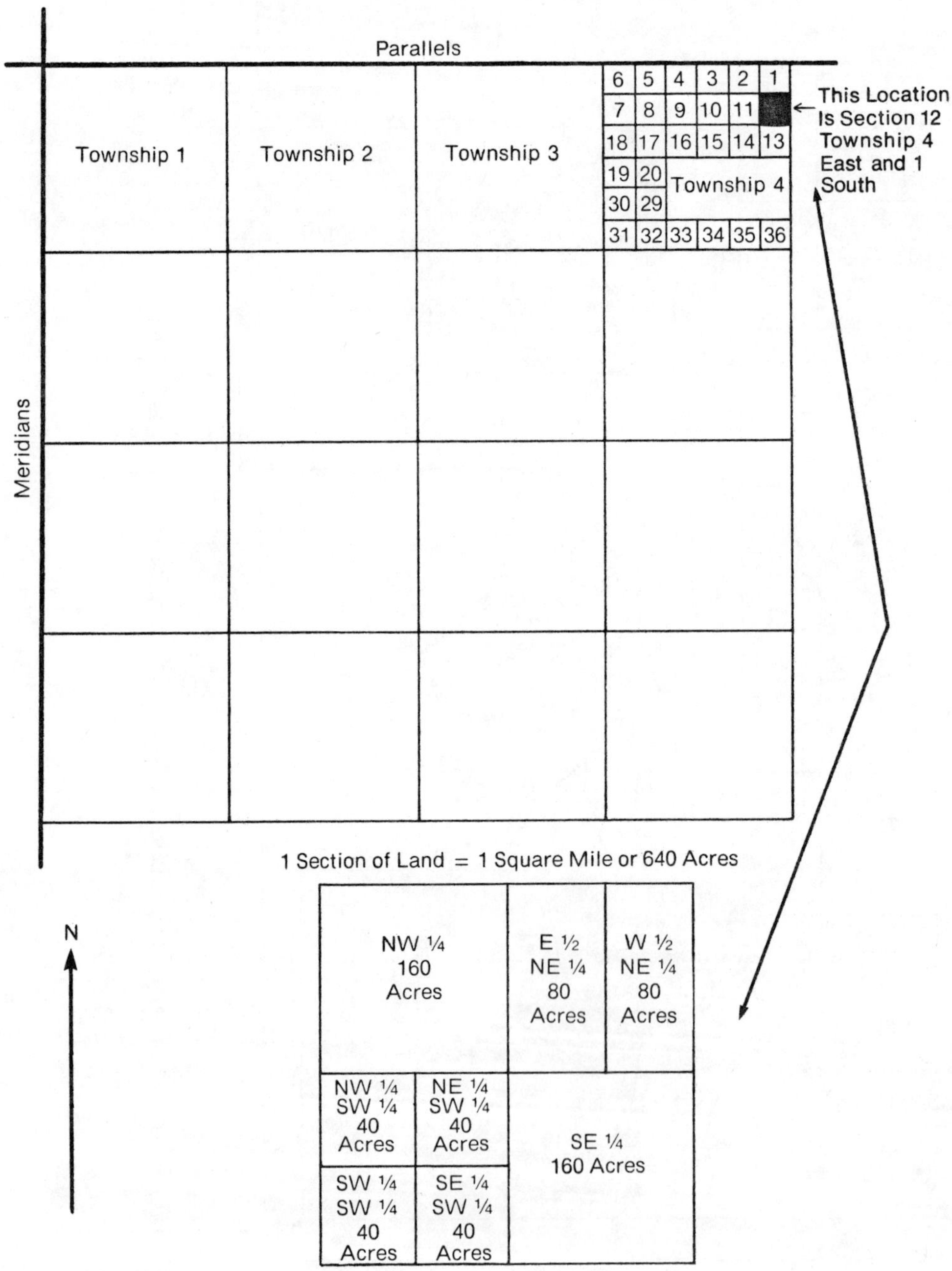

2,000 feet then south for a distance of 4,000 feet, then west for a distance of 2,000 feet to the point of the beginning," is a metes and bounds description. Natural monuments or markers can serve as reference points but they do have problems. Metes and bounds may, however, be used in combination with the quadrangle survey system or the subdivision system. Thus the reference point can be the northwest corner of lot 22 of some named tract or subdivision.

These legal descriptions refer to the parcel of land, not the ownership rights. Investors may acquire widely varying interests in real property. Ownership is an ambiguous word.

An investor may purchase a lease on land and, though not owning the land, may build a building and own the building. The investor therefore owns property but that ownership is subject to other claims, not the least of which is likely to be the rights of the landowner from whom the land was leased.

An investor may acquire ownership rights in a leasehold interest, which is like being a tenant, or ownership rights that are "freehold." The freehold estate, in contrast to the leasehold estate, is one in which the greatest array of rights of ownership is possible. The most complete degree of ownership is known as fee simple. That is the kind of title an investor wants to get.

A lesser freehold estate, by way of example, is an estate for life. The seller of such an estate conveys only his or her interest, and when the seller dies the purchased ownership of the land comes to an end.

The fee simple estate may be, and usually is, encumbered. It may be encumbered by a lease, easements, mortgages, or taxes and other liens. The only rights sellers can convey are those that they have. So investors need to know what rights they are buying and what rights the seller has the power to convey.

Rights in property are created by law, enforced by law, and limited by law. The limitation by law includes zoning regulations. If the zoning changes, so do the rights and usually the value.

The rights may also be limited by private contract. If the seller has, as an owner, agreed with other owners that none of them will subdivide their property with parcels less than 2 acres in size until 1985, one may be reasonably assured that this will affect the purchaser's use of the property.

The way in which purchasers receive notice of such agreements, unless they happen to hear about them, is through the county records. Such restrictive covenants are recorded in

FIGURE 14–3
Township Squares

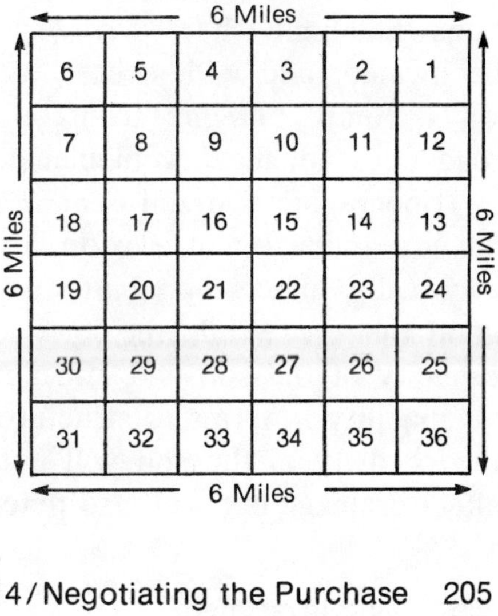

the offices of the county in which the land is situated, so that any interested person, especially prospective purchasers or lenders, can look them up.

Aside from the ownership rights and the legal description, an investor needs to know about the physical developability of the site. This information may include the availability of utilities, limitations of access, building regulations, and soil conditions.

The timing of availability of utilities is, as already discussed, critical to the timing of development. Additional detail may be required depending upon particular circumstances. A brewery, for example, rejected a potential site because the water quality was variable. The water came from different sources so that the brewery could not count on a consistent blend of impurities. Requirements for utility services vary with the potential uses. An investor needs to know what service is available, and perhaps its quality and cost, in addition to knowing the expectations for future provision of such services, especially if they will be necessary for development.

Information on access has to do with local building and zoning regulations that limit where driveways may be located, and with access to highways. Simply having frontage on a road does not mean vehicular access.

Topographic and soil conditions influence drainage and erosion, and will eventually affect the ability to build upon the site. While the load-bearing capacity of the soil will affect its developability in terms of structure size, the porosity of the soil will not only affect drainage but will also determine the feasibility of a septic tank field for low-density development.

Obtaining all the necessary information about the property may be expensive. It may also be impractical before going to contract, i.e., before signing the initial agreement to purchase. Some of these information requirements can be written into the contract.

DOCUMENTS REQUIRED

The Contract. The contract is a paper instrument used to identify what ownership rights are to be conveyed, what contingencies will affect the completion of the sale, and who gets stuck with what problems, if any. Of course it also states the price, terms, and other elements of the agreement.

The purchaser needs to know that it is a valid contract. The legal requirements for an enforceable contract affecting title to land are that it be between parties who are legally competent, that an offer be made and accepted, for a valuable consideration such as money, and that each party be obligated to do something. In addition, the object of the contract must be legal, the contract must be in writing, and it must be signed by the parties who are to be bound.

Typically the contracting procedure is for the purchaser to submit a written offer to purchase. The offer may be prepared by the broker, the purchaser's attorney, or the purchaser. It may be labeled "Deposit Receipt" or "Offer to Purchase" or even "Agreement to Purchase." Until it is accepted by the seller, however, it is not a binding contract. If an investor is going to get legal counsel on the contract, the time to get it is before it is submitted to the seller, not after it has been accepted.

The "Offer to Purchase" is a negotiating document even if it is called by some other name. It is a presentation to the seller of the buyer's offer, which:

1. Identifies what is being purchased as to:
   a. Property address and legal description.
   b. Ownership rights.
2. Submits the financial terms, including:
   a. Price.
   b. Down payment.
   c. Arrangements for the balance.
3. Notes the timing and actions such as:
   a. The amount of deposit.
   b. Additional payment required before settlement.
   c. When settlement will be made.
4 Specifies any contingencies such as:
   a. Seller delivery of clear title.
   b. Buyer being able to obtain financing.
   c. Property being suitable for intended development.

The buyer submits the offer with a check (made out to the broker, escrow agent, title company, or seller). When that offer is accepted an enforceable contract exists.

Contingencies. In negotiating the sale the buyer may want to make the offer contingent upon some event. One or more contingencies may weaken the negotiations or possibility of acceptance. Yet contingencies may be essential.

The buyer may make the offer contingent on approval of the covenants, conditions, and restrictions of record. This gives the buyer a chance to review the limitation on use before going to settlement, and a chance to back out if the land cannot be used for the intended purposes. The contingency is sometimes removed well before settlement time by ordering a preliminary title report and accepting the existing covenants, conditions, and restrictions of record within say 10 or 15 days of the receipt of the report. This clause is frequently used as a general escape clause for buyers. But if the buyers are not really bound, neither are the sellers.

If development is the objective, the purchaser may make the offer to purchase contingent upon satisfactory percolation tests, engineering tests for load bearing capacity, or even upon an engineering study to determine lot yield and preliminary development costs.

The offer may also be subject to the buyer being able to obtain a rezoning and/or a utility connection. In these cases the time element could be substantial.

Another contingency may be the availability of financing of a particular amount and at specified terms. In these, as in the other matters, the more specific the details of the contingency the smaller the area for potential dispute.

Process. The process may entail some verbal negotiations which could lead to an understanding. The understanding without the writing is not legally enforceable. Thus if price or other terms are being negotiated, the process may be more effectively handled with a written offer that can be accepted by the parties. Otherwise, a lot of testing and possibly some revoking may occur.

The probability of misunderstanding an offer to purchase can be lessened by use of a letter of intent, but usually the most effective method is the written offer with a substantial check. If the offer to purchase is not acceptable, the negotiations may proceed with a counter offer. An agent is particularly helpful in this process. A counter offer constitutes a rejection of the original offer. Also, offers may be withdrawn prior to acceptance. The process has high hazards.

An investor must determine what elements in the contract are important to him. The most important element may be a contingency and not the price. The terms may also be more important than the price, especially if no personal liability is involved and the whole investment is quite speculative.

The seller may also have strong preferences. He may want a sure sale. Or he may want a high price and be willing to put up with rezoning contingencies, subordination, and/or an interest-only contract for many years.

Negotiating the sale requires discovering what the most important items are to the respective parties and working out the trade-offs. The best trade-offs are those in which one party gives up something of minor importance and the other parties gain something of major importance.

Subsequent Documents. In many states an *escrow* arrangement is used. A set of escrow instructions will be drawn, which provide a lot of detail about the sale. They may also be used to change some of the negotiated points. Usually, however, the instructions spell out how some things not previously covered are to be handled. In the absence of prior agreement, local practice usually prevails.

The purchase itself is consummated either by the escrow agent transferring the money to the seller and the deed to the purchaser, or by the settlement attorney or title company fulfilling that function.

The title itself passes with the delivery of the deed. The buyer records the deed, or has it recorded, to let the world know of the claim. By that time the investor has probably started on the management of his investment by monitoring the community development that he expects to make the land more valuable.

15

Investment Strategy

Astute real estate investors are concerned with two types of risk-reward relationships. One is the risk-reward relationship in a particular investment. That is, how good a bet is the investment? What is the reward relative to the risk?

The other type of risk-reward relationship is the suitability of an investment for personal objectives. Some investors are concerned with whether they can personally handle the risks. They are not mesmerized by the hope of fantastic rewards. They want as good a return as they can get, but within the risks they can afford to take. Investors have made fortunes by ignoring the risk situation. The strength of their desire for profit pushed them to take chances that few prudent investors would consider. Many have been successful, but many have not. Such aggressive strategies may be best for some people, but most investors would prefer a more prudent approach.

The purpose of this chapter is to explain how an investor may develop his or her own strategy for land investment, one that will be suitable both for the property and for the person.

SPECIFYING OBJECTIVES

Investment strategy is an aspect of management. Fundamentally, management involves choosing objectives, organizing resources to get certain things done, and exercising some control to see that the things that should get done do in fact get done.

In the case of investment management the objectives relate to making money through the use of capital but without inordinately risking loss of the capital itself. The analysis of objectives thus specifies the kinds of rewards (such as cash flow, tax shelter, and proceeds of sale) and the kinds of risks that are to be considered.

Risks. The specification of the risks in a statement of objectives is one of minimizing selected hazards. As discussed in chapter 3, no investment will be free of all chance of loss. The investor seeks to develop a portfolio of investments that in the aggregate provide a set of acceptable risks.

The acceptability of risks varies widely from individual to individual. Some people will buy an option on land with nearly their last dollar, and will press to "make it big" while they are having trouble putting food on the table. Most investors, however, will allocate their income and assets so that they may first be sure that they can operate at some desired standard of living.

A typical investment profile would be that of a person who earns more than he or she spends, and seeks to put the surplus to work. Some of the surplus works to provide the security of a contingency fund. An old rule of thumb was to keep cash on hand, in checking or savings deposits, equal to six months income. That may be okay for some people some times, but many investors find it much too simplistic. They meet their liquidity needs with some cash, but supplement it with U.S. Savings Bonds (which are highly liquid), the cash value of their life insurance (which is also liquid), and short-term government obligations (notes and bills), or even savings certificates. On that basis, cash in checking accounts and/or savings accounts (which as a practical matter are available for withdrawal on demand) may amount to the equivalent of only 1 or 2 months income, while the total holdings in the broader range of liquid assets may be equal to a year's income.

Variations occur because people differ in the uncertainty of earned income from employment and in their attitudes toward cash and security. Salaried people with secure positions (and wealthy relatives) may run their finances with meager liquid reserves. Professional people with variable fee income may run their finances with meager liquidity from time to time, but they usually try to maintain substantial reserves to take care of gaps in income or occasional demands for large cash expenditures.

Beyond the first line of liquidity (which includes demand and savings deposits, U.S. Savings Bonds, short-term marketable securities, and the cash value of life insurance) two more general degrees of liquidity exist. Second-line liquidity includes long-term bonds and listed common stocks. The stock market conditions of recent years have created some question about including these investments in secondary liquidity. Yet an organized market exists, with quoted prices; a sale can be consummated quickly (within minutes), and settlement obtained within days. These are also assets which are traditionally financible with ease. So if the investor has a portfolio of stocks and bonds and desires cash, the securities are excellent collateral for a loan even if stock and bond prices are depressed. This second line of liquidity is recommended not because stocks and bonds have such a great record as investments (for most people they really do not) but because they serve a very useful purpose—to provide a secondary reserve with better earnings, usually, than the more liquid assets.

The third level of liquidity—or really the first level of illiquidity—is real estate, and a variety of other investments ranging from mortgages to unlisted common stocks, and including syndicate interests in oil, cattle, or real estate. Investors get paid for giving up liquidity, and they get paid well. To the extent that the investor's circumstances permit illiquid investments, the risks of lack of liquidity are acceptable.

Land, of course, is in the third category. In fact it is the least liquid of the real estate investments. But it is potentially the most profitable. The relevance of all this is simply that the investor may specify his or her objectives as including some degree of liquidity, and may meet that liquidity in a variety of ways. When it is met and investable funds are left over, the objectives may include high profits from land or other illiquid investments.

Rewards. The specification of objectives on the reward side will also vary with the individual investor. Youthful tycoons, prepared to risk all (some haven't much to risk) may go for accumulating wealth. The wealth may be accumulated by investing in nondividend-paying stocks (hoping for appreciation) or in real estate which carries itself (produces no cash flow) but has a great deal of potential. Young professionals with high taxable incomes will invest in almost anything that reduces their income-tax bills. They evaluate the risk-reward potentials on an after-tax basis, figuring that they have to pay half of their incomes in taxes anyway. Thus the benefit they seek is tax shelter, with perhaps some hope of recovering their investment and even more.

Seasoned investors tend to be somewhat more prudent, and not only put great store in being able to get their money back but also in getting it when they need it. Thus investors with college-age children may have carried back mortgages from prior sales of real estate, or accumulated bonds, with the intent of paying for their children's education out of interest and principal from these investments. They may also have accumulated other investments that will be sold off to meet the needs of a period of high cash requirements.

Investors who have retired typically opt for high cash flow investments. Mortgages provide such cash flows, but the principal eventually gets paid off. Income-producing real estate, however, produces cash flow for an indeterminate but long time. It becomes an excellent investment for retired persons, especially if they have owned it for many years and paid down the mortgage, which is then recast to low monthly payments. The cash flow is even higher when the property is free and clear of debt.

These examples are obviously contrived to illustrate single-purpose benefits. They are suitable for the situations depicted. But most potential land investors have much more complicated situations. What they need to do is build a mix of benefits suitable to them. That mix of benefits changes over time, not only because their objectives change over time but because their ability to take risks changes.

DESIGNING STAYING POWER

Investing in land is an excellent choice for those who can bear the risk and wait for the rewards. The question may then be posed, how does one put oneself in that position?

Capital Requirements. Accumulating cash for investment is obviously the first step. Some land investment enterprises can be managed without too much money. Syndicators do it all the time. But the question is not what a syndicator does, but what an investor does.

The investor has to accumulate enough cash to meet liquidity needs and an initial down payment on a piece of property. Then he or she has to be able to generate enough to carry the land. Beginning investors may do this out of income. Such a starting program is reasonable for aggressive young investors. Hopefully they can buy the land without any personal liability on the mortgage, which may be greater than their total net worth. And hopefully their income is sufficient in size and stability to carry the investment. The results of such a program are likely to be a sharp increase in wealth.

If an investor has only enough money for one shot, and the time it has taken to build up the cash is so long that he or she will not get another, land may well be the wrong kind of bet. The risk would be inappropriate. But for an investor to try more than once is reasonable even if it means starting over.

It is better, however, when accumulated wealth allows multiple investments, some of which are in land. The diversification provides greater opportunity for profitable investment, and in most cases the question is not how big a winner it is but whether it is in the big winner class. If one of several investments is, the overall benefits will be exceptionally attractive.

Some investors looking to make it big are against diversification because diversification dilutes the big winnings. That argument has merit, especially if one is looking at investments that yield about 8 percent and is hoping for a return of 12 percent or more as a winner. If one is successful in getting a 12 percent return, it may spread rather thin over the rest of the portfolio. But that is not typical of returns in land investment. Winners in land may get returns of 20, 30, or 40 percent or more per year. Even mediocre investments should produce 10, 12, or more percent per year. At this writing 20 percent is a reasonable expectation. Without that expectation, an investment in land may not be attractive. Even if inflation reduces it to 12 percent in real terms, it's not all that bad.

A diversification in land investment may produce a number of projects which average about 12 percent, and one or two that reach a 20 or 30 percent return or more. These would drive the average up substantially. But 12 percent should not be dismissed cavalierly.

Investors in common stock who on the average have earned 6 percent on their money have done well. That has been typical over long periods of time for a broad segment of the market. Many investors have fared much worse. Real estate on the whole has done much better than 6 percent—probably from 8 to 9 percent, depending on the sample structure and time covered. Many investors, of course, have done substantially better, and while some lose these are very few in number. The rates of return are built upon inflation, which has historically run at annual averages of 2 to 3 percent. The 8 to 9 percent return is a counterpart to interest rates on savings accounts and on the highest grade securities of about 5 percent. The recent inflation has added 3 to 5 percentage points to most of the above figures.

In real terms the rate of interest has hovered around 3 percent per year before inflation, financial risk, and liquidity. Thus, the investor in a time of stable inflation at about 2 percent can expect about 5 percent from a very secure loan to the U.S. government or from a savings account. A mortgage investment with less liquidity will buy a couple more interest points return, and so will a stock investment. These may yield say 6 to 7 percent. Income-producing real estate will buy a little more, say 8 to 9 percent. Bear in mind that these are minimal rates for the vast majority of such investments. They are not empirically measured, numerically averaged rates of return, including all incomes and offsetting all losses, although those rates could be about the same. They are minimal model rates, the rates most frequently achieved in the market.

On a basis unadjusted for inflation or income taxes, a 12 percent annual rate of return compounded will double the investment every 6 years. Or, if the real rate adjusted for a minimal inflation of 2 percent is 10 percent, it will double the investment in a little over 7 years. If another 2 percentage points per annum is taken off to compensate for the effective federal income tax rate (considering tax shelter and tax deferral), the resulting after-tax rate is 8 percent. An 8 percent rate will double the investment every 9 years. These are reasonable minimal objectives considering that a straight 6 percent return for an investor in a 33 percent tax bracket would mean 4 percent before inflation. Subtracting 2 percent for minimal inflation, that would bring the real after-tax return down to 2 percent. At 2 percent it would take many years for the money to double.

Increasing inflation worsens the position of investors in monetary assets (mortgages, bonds, savings deposits). As inflation increases the market rates of interest also increase, but in a rapidly rising inflation the rates do not increase fast enough. Those who owe money get a windfall gain and those who own real estate or other real goods get a hedge against the inflation plus the benefit of repaying their debts with cheap dollars. The effect of the income tax regulations is to give a preferential rate to holders of real estate as the inflation proceeds. They pay most of their taxes when the sale is made, at preferred rates and with depreciated dollars.

Investors who want to sell their monetary assets (bonds or mortgages) can do so only at prevailing prices. The prevailing price in the market for such assets is dependent on the prevailing interest rate. Thus when interest rates rise, say for bonds, the price of existing bonds drops, and so investors in these assets get losses if they attempt to sell before maturity. The choice is between a capital loss and an even lower real rate of interest.

A reasonable investment strategy is one in which real estate of some sort is built into a portfolio as soon as the cash position permits. Then land investment is added when the carrying ability permits. The bonds and other assets suitable for secondary liquidity should be kept for that purpose. But the best returns are in real estate, especially land.

FUNDING CAPITAL REQUIREMENTS

A major consideration in funding the capital requirement for land investment is being able to continue to make the payments. A major constraint in developing a portfolio of investments is to be able to get at one's invested capital when one needs it. Investors who put all their money in land and fund the continuing costs out of income are taking an exceptional risk. If their income drops they may be pressed to sell the land, not only because they can no longer keep up the payments but because they also need the capital.

The timing of the land sale is critical. The investor should be able to base the timing of sale on the merits of the investment, not on his personal needs. In order to build in that choice it is preferable to fund the carrying ability of the land from a nonearned income source, i.e. from an investment income source.

A prudent strategy is to accumulate investments in income-producing real estate with whatever cash flow they generate. An initial real estate investment might well be in rental property that produces some modest positive cash flow. Over the years income will rise and the equity will build up. Sooner or later even a modest investment can produce substantial cash flows, either from the mortgage having been paid off or from a combination of increasing rents and possibly a recasting of the mortgage (reducing mortgage payments by lengthening the term). Or the built-up equity can be traded for property that produces a cash flow. However the investment is handled, at some point it will have the capability of producing a flow of cash. That flow of cash may be used to carry the payments in a land investment.

Another variation is to invest in a piece of real estate that produces enough income to carry itself, or perhaps provide a cash flow. When it is sold, a part of the profit may be taken back as a mortgage. Carrying back the mortgage will help in making the sale and in getting a top price. The mortgage can be paid out over a relatively short period of time. It is a high cash flow item and a good source of income for making payments on land. The tax treatment is also pretty good. The gains from the sale of the real estate are taxed at capital gains rates. The payments for carrying land are deductible to the extent that they are for interest and property taxes (plus a few other minor expenses). Only the amortization is not deductible. On the whole, the tax deduction on the land should exceed the taxable income from carrying the mortgage.

Additional sources of cash for carrying land such as sales of stocks and bonds, or withdrawals from savings accounts, are reasonable alternatives. The main thing to guard against is a situation in which forces adversely affecting the income to pay for the land will also affect the salability of the land. In the extreme case, a land sales person who puts all his or her savings in land investments really goes for broke. The forces that cause commission income to decline are the same as those that reduce the marketability of the land. If payment for the land is financed by a mortgage from a previous sale of land, the position is a little better as long as the buyer of the land from the previous sale keeps making payments.

The strongest way to carry land is to own it free and clear of debt. Then property taxes are the only expense, and they may not be much of a problem. That is a reasonable approach for very-long-term investors, but most investors want leverage. It is well worth having, but the risks of leverage need to be protected against. Being able to carry the property is a protection. It may be achieved by simply having a diversified portfolio of income-producing assets such as rental or leased property, mortgages, or even stocks and bonds. Those assets will keep the investor from having to sell the land at an unfavorable time.

SELL DECISIONS

The preliminary decision to sell should be made at the time the decision to buy is made. The decisions are made at the same time because they are part of a single plan.

That plan is to buy low, sell high, and use someone else's money. The buying low means that the prevailing price is below what it should be, predicated on more realistic expectations of events that will make the land more valuable. The idea is to anticipate these events so that when the time to sell comes, the price will be high.

Selling high means expectations are at the peak of optimism. To know what the expectations are, an investor must monitor the situation.

MONITORING THE SITUATION

Monitoring the situation requires monitoring community development. The two areas to watch are the demand for land and its developability.

In watching demand, the critical indicators are employment and other numerical guides. Fortunately for the lay investor, these data are reported and analyzed in the bank and utility company newsletters. Newspapers also contain reports, but they are frequently short on analyses.

All that is usually necessary to keep abreast of the general trends is an annual outlook and a quarterly update. Development firms may provide this internally by relying on multiple sources for data. Or they may get reports from their economic consultants. Individual investors can get in the habit of periodically making such assessments through sources which they become accustomed to watching.

The more localized changes, of course, are not conveniently available from published data. If the investor lives near his investments, it is wise to periodically drive to the area to see the new construction moving out toward the land. That will give him a feel for what is developing. Obviously the feel will be more precise if the new subdivisions are charted on a map and dated, or if a population map is constructed and updated. Such information may be readily available from the office of the local government planning division. Monitoring the awarding of contracts for new sewer lines, road widening, and other facility development activity is also advisable.

The idea is to find out if the expected progress is occurring. An investor may need to obtain detailed information as to increases in sewer capacity, development of roads, and other facilities that will affect developability as well as demand. This information on what is happening should be compared with what was planned.

Sometimes qualitative changes in demand and development cause markets to shift. These changes are discernible from the numbers or by simply seeing what is being built and where. If the kind and location of the changes taking place are in accord with anticipations, then the investor's decision to hold is reinforced. If, however, the expectations are not turning out, a reconsideration of the sell date is in order.

Changes in the wind are also reflected in changes in community attitudes. In recent years the mood has been anti-growth. But some of the no-growth advocates have modified their position to that of slow growth. Also, the mood is now shifting toward controlling growth as to location.

Depending upon the location of an investment, the changing mood may reflect changing market prices because prices affect anticipated developability. The buy low-sell high approach is to buy when others are not buying and to sell when others are not selling.

That approach means that the investor takes advantage of the low expectations in the market. Obviously, one does not buy as soon as growth possibilities begin to look bad. It is best to wait for the darkest hour. Then the investor can make a deal, and being a little late is better than being a lot early.

The worst thing, however, is to be a lot late. Investors who wait for all the problems to be solved will buy at the height of expectations. That is the time to sell, not to buy. And the more evidence keeps building up that this is the time to sell, the closer the market is to its crest. It happened with housing subdivisions after World War II; it happened with garden apartments, bowling alleys, and neighborhood shopping centers. It will also happen with town houses and condominiums.

The land investor, of course, is interested in the end-use market because that affects the price of land. And just before the end use gets overbuilt, the developers pay more for the land than they should. The land really becomes overpriced.

Then an investor must watch and wait. When the flurry of sales begins he or she must carefully determine the timing of a sale. An investor should not try to squeeze too much out of it because the first $100,000 profit is important, not the last $10,000. If the market is missed it can be anywhere from a few years on up until the time is right again.

The traditional cycles in land investment have been moderated by difficulties in providing sufficient developable sites. The cycles are still there when money gets very tight or the employment situation gets difficult. But real changes in volume are more often associated with the availability of sewer capacity.

Other factors that affect the land market are the mood of the public and changes in local government. The local government may cause cycles by its action and inaction. Changes in who is elected and in administrative effectiveness will open up or shut down development.

The recurring change in the ability of government to cope with problems presents opportunities because developable land is scarce. The problems with which local government has to cope also change. Whether the change is in the *ability* to cope with the problems or the *magnitude* of the problems, an impact will be generated. To an investor in the short run, it makes little difference as to what the cause is. If an administration is going to do nothing for four years, then the development of the land may have to wait. Pressures may build up and the values of developable land may become fantastic. Then, after the courts and the voters straighten out the officials, the supply of land will be adjusted. In the meantime, investors in land not currently developable must wait until their land is expected to be developable. (Of course, investors who own land which is developable during the era of great shortage will reap great profits.)

If local government suddenly opens up development sufficiently to permit a competitive situation, it may spur such an increase in the supply of homes that land values will soften. Efficient management of urban development can destroy much of the monopolistic advantage to land investors. Inefficient management will make opportunities for great profit and then, with dramatic adjustments, make opportunities for loss.

Sooner or later society will demand better management of land development, and that will make land investment less profitable. Investors should watch for signs of this, because that is the time to start unloading the land, especially if it has already reached the developable stage.

According to the Property. Monitoring influences the sell decision according to the changing potentials of the property. That decision to sell should have tentatively been made in a preliminary plan. For example, a target date of say four years may have been set when the land was purchased. That time horizon may be adjusted by a year or two either way according to how rapidly growth actually takes place.

Additional considerations on the timing of sale according to the property itself include financing: financing for the purchase and financing for the sale.

The use of other people's money, i.e., highly leveraged financing, is built into the purchase. Frequently an investor obtains an interest-only period or a low-amortization period. Investors who use this leverage when they buy are prodded to sell when high principal payments start to come up.

When possible, the land investor should get financing that is not only good for the purchase but also good for the next investor. It not only should be transferrable but it should also have a period in which amortization is low. So if the target time is four years, obtaining interest-only payments for eight years will be highly desirable. If that is not possible, then low amortization for a long time is the next best alternative.

To buy with an agreement for a balloon payment of the balance of the principal in five years, even with a four-year time horizon, may not be wise because the payoff on the balloon payment may be more than the downpayment on the resale.

Financial markets at the time of resale are of great importance if the land is being sold to developers. If interest rates are high, the market will be slow and prices soft. Thus a land seller should be prepared to wait a year or even two beyond his target for a better capital market.

Sales can usually be made when desired, without having to wait. The sale may take a few months to make and a few more months to settle. That is what is meant by lack of liquidity. Sales prodded by individual circumstances rather than property considerations may not be the most desirable for the seller.

According to Personal Objectives. In order to avoid these exigencies, the timing of the sale should be in the original plan with some allowance for contingency.

By way of example, young investors who want to send their two children to private universities will find that having $50,000 available about the time the youngsters start college will be of substantial assistance. A land purchase to finance that expenditure should have a planned sell date a couple of years before they need the money. With a target time for investment of say five years, investors should be looking for the land investment when their oldest child is ten years old.

Some may think that this timing is conservative. But one could argue that the land acquisition should be made even earlier. An earlier purchase and sale would allow for a reinvestment of the funds and possibly a gift to the children so that they could reinvest some of the funds. The idea is to use land to make money before one needs to spend it.

A couple could sell their land just before retirement and live on the mortgage payments. But if that were their major source of income, the program would be quite hazardous. It is better to sell the land five years before retirement. Then the cash can be reinvested and provide some diversity. In either case, a delay in selling because of a difficult market would not be catastrophic.

DEVELOPING A STRATEGY

Most investors want to have a big winner. Astute investors want to avoid a big loser. To make up for a substantial loss of capital requires a lot of other investments that succeed. That is why astute investors, although willing to take risks, take only calculated risks.

The calculation of risks starts with their classification. Holding all of one's money in cash or other monetary assets out of fear of loss is foolish. Inflation will steal it as surely as if it had been lent and not repaid.

Diversification is a reasonable way to meet some risks. But it should only be used as part of a process to provide an investor with protection. A strategy for protection is best developed in an ordinal sequence which may at some point include diversification.

The first investment is in liquid assets. The returns will be lower in percentage rates but the purpose of liquidity will be served. Once liquidity needs are met, then diversification for financial risk is a next logical step. Most investors are not content with the rates paid by so-called riskless investments. A reasonable diversification of stocks or bonds will protect against the danger of having all of one's eggs in a single basket.

When diversification permits giving up liquidity, then the investor is ready for real estate. The first real estate may well be some kind of income-producing property. But when an investor is ready for some really big money, and can afford to wait, then he or she is ready for land. This is a different kind of diversification.

An investor does best to build staying power into his investment. If the land mortgage payments do not exceed the cash flow from various property holdings, time is not going to force a poor sale. When the land is sold, the stage is set for another round of investment.

SELLING THE LAND

A lot of profit is available in land. The investor can take some and leave some. He does not have to sell at the very top price. But an investor who wants the very top price can get it by sharing some of the next round of risk.

When one land investor sells to another, the terms will also affect the price. If an investor is still bullish on the investment but is making changes for portfolio reasons, then a sale at a top price with a low down payment is in order.

If the sale is to a developer the inclusion of subordination will greatly increase the price. The investor is in effect becoming a money partner with the developer, and can expect to be paid for it. And if the venture succeeds the rewards will usually be handsome.

If the sale is to a developer, the developer will want to know that the land is usable. That will require a contingent contract or an option. From the seller's point of view, it may be quite satisfactory for the developer to do all the work to get the land developable. Certainly the price will be higher than it would be with no contingency in the contract.

One of the best ways of selling from a tax point of view is not to sell but to trade for other vacant land, and simply postpone the capital gain. Or the original land may be traded for income-producing property. An additional variation is to build on the property. In all these cases the investor may get a new investment and a source of cash for further investment without paying taxes.

Land is not the only mechanism for saving on income taxes. But since it is highly leverageable, it gets a reasonable tax treatment. Also, since it may be traded or developed, it can be converted from one investment to another without there being a taxable event. Thus investors who wish to accumulate wealth will find land an excellent vehicle.

Land really is for living. But people in government are doing a very poor job of managing it. And the worse job they do the more profitable it is for an astute investor. To an investor, land is for making money. Understanding what is happening is the first step to a successful strategy.

APPENDIX: Typical Finished Lot Price by City

	1960	1964	1969	Percent Change 1960-1969
ALABAMA				
BIRMINGHAM	3,582	3,938	5,451	52.2
DECATUR	2,500	3,400	3,800	52.0
DOTHAN	1,650	2,083	3,242	96.5
SHEFFIELD	1,900	2,483	4,666	145.6
HUNTSVILLE	2,681	3,650	5,800	116.3
MOBILE	3,050	3,750	4,507	47.8
MONTGOMERY	3,240	3,707	5,356	65.3
TUSCALOOSA	2,850	3,750	3,625	27.2
	2,681	3,345	5,068	89.0 **
ALASKA				
ANCHORAGE	3,500	5,166	7,909	126.0
	3,500	5,166	7,909	126.0 **
ARIZONA				
PHOENIX	2,766	4,657	4,852	75.4
TUCSON	2,727	4,145	5,900	116.4
	2,746	4,401	5,201	89.4 **
ARKANSAS				
LITTLE ROCK	2,769	3,859	4,933	78.2
FAYETTEVILLE	1,700	1,758	2,825	66.2
FORT SMITH	2,250	2,891	4,885	117.1
PINE BLUFF	2,560	3,260	4,891	91.1
	2,319	2,942	4,763	105.4 **
CALIFORNIA				
BERKELEY	4,455	6,942	8,216	84.4
FRESNO	1,620	2,480	4,508	178.3
LAFAYETTE	5,090	7,893	10,751	111.2
MODESTO	3,005	4,009	7,368	145.2
SACRAMENTO	3,190	4,485	5,798	81.8
SAN BERNARDINO	3,675	5,959	6,233	69.6
SAN DIEGO	5,396	7,339	7,671	42.2
SAN FRANCISCO	6,303	10,648	10,478	66.2
SAN MATEO	10,972	15,468	14,987	36.6
SANTA CLARA	5,268	9,700	9,805	86.1
	4,916	7,752	8,577	74.5 **
COLORADO				
COLORADO SPRINGS	2,559	3,338	4,544	77.6
DENVER	4,106	5,094	5,877	43.1
PUEBLO	1,850	2,040	2,650	43.2
	2,838	3,490	5,324	87.6 **
CONNECTICUT				
NEW LONDON	2,285	6,413	5,980	161.7
WEST HARTFORD	4,098	5,954	9,515	132.2
WESTPORT	6,282	8,753	13,803	119.7
	4,221	7,040	10,937	159.1 **
DELAWARE				
WILMINGTON	3,730	5,833	8,875	137.9
	3,730	5,833	8,875	137.9 **

Typical Finished Lot Price by City (Continued)

	1960	1964	1969	Percent Change 1960-1969
DISTRICT OF COLUMB				
WASHINGTON D C	4,352	7,034	9,267	112.9
	4,352	7,034	9,267	112.9 **
FLORIDA				
DAYTONA BEACH	2,775	4,050	3,880	39.8
DELAND	1,000	2,000	1,925	92.5
FORT MYERS	1,716	2,937	6,000	249.7
GAINESVILLE	2,332	2,910	4,320	85.2
JACKSONVILLE	2,576	3,212	4,926	91.2
LAKELAND	3,425	3,498	6,907	101.7
MIAMI	3,368	3,967	7,828	132.4
ST.PETERSBURG	2,783	3,360	5,154	85.2
ORLANDO	2,453	3,389	4,896	99.6
PALM BEACH	2,676	4,010	4,914	83.6
PENSACOLA	2,290	3,075	3,869	69.0
FORT WALTON	2,050	2,703	3,300	61.0
SARASOTA	2,185	3,933	4,000	83.1
TALLAHASSEE	2,110	2,678	4,700	122.7
TAMPA	2,650	3,258	4,371	64.9
TITUSVILLE	2,150	2,980	3,500	62.8
VENICE	1,500	3,500	3,000	100.0
WINTER HAVEN	2,475	3,975	3,750	51.5
	2,361	3,302	5,324	125.5 **
GEORGIA				
ALBANY	3,360	4,280	4,300	28.0
ATHENS	2,500	3,087	5,000	100.0
ATLANTA	3,642	5,026	7,281	99.9
AUGUSTA	2,480	3,596	5,225	110.7
COLUMBUS	1,981	2,852	4,378	121.0
MACON	3,138	4,464	4,525	44.2
ROME	2,071	2,614	4,250	105.2
SAVANNAH	2,427	3,510	4,706	93.9
	2,699	3,678	6,046	124.0 **
HAWAII				
HONOLULU	6,946	10,888	15,826	127.8
	6,946	10,888	15,826	127.8 **
IDAHO				
BOISE	1,666	2,183	3,200	92.1
	1,666	2,183	3,200	92.1 **
ILLINOIS				
AFTON	2,650	3,230	3,995	50.8
BLOOMINGTON	4,500	4,250	6,000	33.3
CHAMPAIGN	3,937	5,141	6,350	61.3
CHICAGO	4,769	6,227	9,847	106.5
DANVILLE	2,500	4,200	7,166	186.6
DECATUR	7,633	9,548	5,290	30.7-
GALESBURG	1,900	2,500	2,875	51.3
KANKAKEE	2,950	3,075	7,000	137.3
ROCK ISLAND	3,512	5,300	5,587	59.1
PEORIA	4,328	5,533	5,666	30.9

Typical Finished Lot Price by City (Continued)

	1960	1964	1969	Percent Change 1960-1969
ROCKFORD	2,710	3,150	5,062	86.8
SPRINGFIELD	4,500	3,300	5,705	26.8
	3,856	4,560	7,728	100.4 **
INDIANA				
ANDERSON	2,130	2,937	3,362	57.8
BLOOMINGTON	2,400	3,835	5,792	141.3
EVANSVILLE	2,500	3,533	5,750	130.0
FORT WAYNE	2,963	3,652	4,791	61.7
GREENSBURG	2,300	2,600	3,850	67.4
INDIANAPOLIS	3,010	5,055	5,897	95.9
LAFAYETTE	3,300	4,291	5,650	71.2
MARION	1,500	3,250	5,250	250.0
MUNCIE	2,600	2,125	3,245	24.8
NEW ALBANY	2,100	3,170	3,866	84.1
RICHMOND	2,720	3,016	4,280	57.4
	2,502	3,405	5,189	107.4 **
IOWA				
AMES	3,600	3,885	6,000	66.7
CEDAR FALLS	2,700	3,068	4,880	80.7
CEDAR RAPIDS	2,876	3,917	4,379	52.3
CLINTON	2,400	2,850	3,900	62.5
COUNCIL BLUFFS	2,450	2,814	3,650	49.0
DAVENPORT	3,116	3,528	4,655	49.4
DES MOINES	3,158	3,773	4,911	55.5
FORT DODGE	1,500	3,500	3,333	122.2
IOWA CITY	2,675	3,900	5,653	111.3
MARSHALLTOWN	2,800	3,200	4,500	60.7
SIOUX CITY	2,000	1,850	4,291	114.6
	2,661	3,298	4,836	81.7 **
KANSAS				
HUTCHINSON	3,841	4,906	6,700	74.4
SALINA	2,025	2,200	3,150	55.6
TOPEKA	3,422	4,086	4,122	20.5
WICHITA	1,880	3,104	3,376	79.6
	2,792	3,574	3,709	32.8 **
KENTUCKY				
COVINGTON	2,233	3,765	4,764	113.3
HOPKINSVILLE	1,375	2,083	2,733	98.8
LEXINGTON	3,344	4,471	5,812	73.8
LOUISVILLE	3,507	4,401	6,543	86.6
OWENSBORO	2,948	3,120	3,175	7.7
PADUCAH	2,466	3,200	3,937	59.7
	2,645	3,506	5,612	112.2 **
LOUISIANA				
ALEXANDRIA	3,133	4,112	5,690	81.6
BATON ROUGE	3,210	3,960	6,972	117.2
LAFAYETTE	2,733	3,733	4,500	64.7
LAKE CHARLES	3,200	4,500	5,812	81.6
NEW ORLEANS	4,350	5,652	7,021	61.4
SHREVEPORT	2,687	2,959	4,784	78.0

Typical Finished Lot Price by City (Continued)

	1960	1964	1969	Percent Change 1960-1969
WEST MONROE	2.040	2.725	4.061	99.1
	3.050	3.948	6.017	97.3 **
MAINE				
PORTLAND	1.650	2.783	5.500	233.3
	1.650	2.783	5.500	233.3 **
MARYLAND				
BALTIMORE	2.895	4.342	5.931	104.9
CUMBERLAND	1.940	2.650	2.850	46.9
FREDERICK	2.733	3.900	5.750	110.4
	2.522	3.630	5.654	124.2 **
MASSACHUSETTS				
ATTLEBORO	2.125	3.000	3.500	64.7
BOSTON	3.694	5.723	9.210	149.3
FALL RIVER	2.250	2.650	4.375	94.4
LOWELL	2.050	3.343	5.355	161.2
LAWRENCE	4.000	4.750	7.157	78.9
SPRINGFIELD	2.306	3.122	5.113	121.7
WORCESTER	2.837	3.446	4.850	71.0
	2.751	3.719	7.560	174.8 **
MICHIGAN				
ANN ARBOR	3.700	4.562	9.583	159.0
BATTLE CREEK	2.733	3.057	4.066	48.8
DETROIT	4.154	5.764	8.172	96.7
FLINT	2.157	2.943	5.157	139.1
GRAND RAPIDS	2.912	4.327	4.500	54.5
JACKSON	2.685	3.525	5.409	101.5
KALAMAZOO	2.628	3.677	4.147	57.8
LANSING	3.161	4.300	5.333	68.7
MIDLAND	3.000	3.800	5.383	79.4
MUSKEGON	2.225	2.137	3.642	63.7
SAGINAW	2.700	3.112	5.455	102.0
	2.914	3.745	6.147	110.9 **
MINNESOTA				
DULUTH	3.900	4.262	4.050	3.8
MINNEAPOLIS	3.079	4.295	7.240	135.1
ROCHESTER	3.833	9.225	5.377	40.3
ST.PAUL	2.550	3.737	5.796	127.3
	3.340	5.379	6.584	97.1 **
MISSISSIPPI				
GREENVILLE	1.830	2.425	3.585	95.9
HATTIESBURG	1.933	2.216	8.800	355.3
PASCAGOULA	2.192	2.938	4.000	82.5
JACKSON	2.645	3.428	4.875	84.3
	2.150	2.751	5.215	142.6 **
MISSOURI				
COLUMBIA	2.400	3.166	5.905	146.0
KANSAS CITY	3.171	4.398	5.101	60.9
SPRINGFIELD	2.383	2.970	3.713	55.8

Typical Finished Lot Price by City (Continued)

	1960	1964	1969	Percent Change 1960-1969
ST. LOUIS	4,877	6,376	7,027	44.1
	3,207	4,227	5,888	83.6 **
MONTANA				
BILLINGS	2,150	2,150	5,875	173.3
GREAT FALLS	2,455	3,100	4,250	73.1
HELENA	1,400	1,200	3,500	150.0
	2,001	2,150	4,888	144.3 **
NEBRASKA				
LINCOLN	2,625	3,815	5,876	123.8
OMAHA	3,070	3,751	4,918	60.2
	2,847	3,783	5,225	83.5 **
NEVADA				
LAS VEGAS	2,791	4,711	4,775	71.1
	2,791	4,711	4,775	71.1 **
NEW HAMPSHIRE				
NASHUA	2,500	3,500	3,812	52.5
KEENE	1,000	2,500	8,300	730.0
MANCHESTER	1,866	2,350	4,400	135.8
	1,788	2,783	4,973	178.1 **
NEW JERSEY				
ATLANTIC CITY	1,987	3,162	6,500	227.1
BERNARDSVILLE	3,823	7,000	12,310	222.0
CAMDEN	3,051	4,210	5,604	83.7
UNION	6,635	9,345	14,770	122.6
POINT PLEASANT	3,877	5,786	9,536	146.0
TRENTON	5,583	7,385	10,333	85.1
	4,159	6,148	10,184	144.9 **
NEW MEXICO				
ALBUQUERQUE	2,805	4,234	4,066	45.0
LAS CRUCES	2,183	2,528	4,021	84.2
	2,494	3,381	4,052	62.5 **
NEW YORK				
BUFFALO	2,929	3,866	5,231	78.6
ELMIRA	2,857	4,022	4,260	49.1
HEMPSTEAD	4,978	7,871	12,150	144.1
JOHNSON CITY	2,916	3,837	6,542	124.3
ALBANY	2,771	3,500	5,268	90.1
STATEN ISLAND	2,866	5,560	10,400	262.9
ROCHESTER	3,729	4,897	6,793	82.2
SCHENECTADY	2,688	3,562	4,625	72.1
SYRACUSE	3,178	4,861	5,487	72.7
	3,341	4,884	7,707	130.7 **
NORTH CAROLINA				
CHARLOTTE	2,578	3,057	5,990	132.4
DURHAM	2,407	2,842	4,366	81.4
FAYETTEVILLE	1,750	2,136	4,188	139.3
GREENSBORO	3,296	3,835	6,776	105.6

Typical Finished Lot Price by City (Continued)

	1960	1964	1969	Percent Change 1960-1969
RALEIGH	2,990	3,677	5,015	67.7
ROCKY MOUNT	2,750	3,257	5,659	105.8
SALISBURY	1,800	1,900	3,000	66.7
WINSTON SALEM	2,648	3,557	6,210	134.5
	2,527	3,032	5,764	128.1 **
NORTH DAKOTA				
FARGO	1,862	2,290	4,361	134.2
	1,862	2,290	4,361	134.2 **
OHIO				
AKRON	4,026	5,005	8,380	108.1
ASHTABULA	2,000	2,750	3,100	55.0
ASHLAND	4,000	4,600	10,700	167.5
CANTON	2,523	3,000	4,410	74.8
CHILLICOTHE	2,866	3,933	4,500	57.0
CINCINNATI	4,190	5,931	7,781	85.7
CLEVELAND	4,442	6,172	8,730	96.5
COLUMBUS	3,560	4,732	6,947	95.1
DAYTON	3,589	4,709	8,227	129.2
ELYRIA	2,691	4,055	5,020	86.5
LANCASTER	2,600	2,750	2,800	7.7
LIMA	3,083	3,481	4,371	41.8
MANSFIELD	2,930	3,145	4,061	38.6
SANDUSKY	3,066	4,340	4,000	30.5
SIDNEY	2,400	1,916	9,400	291.7
SPRINGFIELD	2,850	2,975	4,975	74.6
TOLEDO	3,461	5,082	8,222	137.6
GREENVILLE	2,000	2,833	3,525	76.3
TROY	2,462	3,550	4,940	100.6
WINTERSVILLE	2,750	3,400	4,166	51.5
	3,074	3,917	7,149	132.6 **
OKLAHOMA				
BARTLESVILLE	2,240	3,360	5,357	139.2
ENID	2,200	2,587	3,666	66.6
LAWTON	1,650	2,250	2,563	55.6
MOORE CITY	2,025	2,413	3,833	89.3
NORMAN	2,328	2,841	3,271	40.5
OKLAHOMA CITY	2,694	3,555	5,307	97.0
PONCA CITY	2,562	3,433	9,300	263.0
TULSA	2,914	4,070	5,275	81.0
	2,326	3,064	5,073	118.1 **
OREGON				
EUGENE	2,475	3,222	5,347	116.0
PORTLAND	2,603	3,611	5,515	111.9
SALEM	2,158	3,212	3,625	68.0
	2,412	3,348	5,317	120.4 **
PENNSYLVANIA				
ALLENTOWN	2,475	3,440	4,893	97.7
ALTOONA	1,500	2,000	1,200	20.0-
CHAMBERSBURG	3,500	3,833	2,950	15.7-
ERIE	2,133	2,762	4,220	97.8

Typical Finished Lot Price by City (Continued)

	1960	1964	1969	Percent Change 1960-1969
HARRISBURG	2,401	3,185	4,557	89.8
JOHNSTOWN	2,350	2,025	4,025	71.3
KINGSTON	1,757	2,500	3,642	107.3
LANCASTER	2,040	2,216	4,195	105.6
PHILADELPHIA	3,063	4,463	7,068	130.8
PITTSBURGH	3,931	5,508	7,441	89.3
STATE COLLEGE	2,642	3,771	5,333	101.9
YORK	2,209	2,523	3,713	68.3
	2,500	3,235	5,413	116.5 **
RHODE ISLAND				
PROVIDENCE	1,745	2,585	4,858	178.4
	1,745	2,585	4,858	178.4 **
SOUTH CAROLINA				
CHARLESTON	2,472	3,425	4,577	85.2
COLUMBIA	2,383	3,581	4,550	90.9
GREENVILLE	1,879	3,185	4,520	140.6
SPARTANBURG	1,881	2,750	3,186	69.4
	2,153	3,235	4,209	95.5 **
SOUTH DAKOTA				
SIOUX FALLS	2,533	3,627	4,842	91.2
	2,533	3,627	4,842	91.2 **
TENNESSEE				
CHATTANOOGA	2,167	4,065	3,520	62.4
JACKSON	1,500	3,200	2,500	66.7
KNOXVILLE	2,209	2,613	3,117	41.1
MEMPHIS	2,960	3,805	5,072	71.4
NASHVILLE	2,215	2,583	4,384	97.9
JOHNSON CITY	2,933	4,250	2,666	9.1-
	2,330	3,419	4,096	75.8 **
TEXAS				
ABILENE	1,890	2,190	4,500	138.1
AMARILLO	1,960	2,305	2,992	52.7
AUSTIN	2,311	3,200	5,225	126.1
BEAUMONT	2,309	2,572	5,293	129.2
CORPUS CHRISTI	2,490	3,354	4,301	72.7
DALLAS	3,200	4,486	6,410	100.3
EL PASO	2,542	3,055	3,188	25.4
FORT WORTH	2,797	3,471	3,546	26.8
HOUSTON	3,425	4,471	5,428	58.5
LONGVIEW	2,025	2,216	3,175	56.8
LUBBOCK	3,400	2,412	5,141	51.2
LUFKIN	2,166	2,400	3,500	61.6
MIDLAND	3,000	3,000	3,300	10.0
SAN ANGELO	1,491	2,133	4,000	168.3
SAN ANTONIO	2,294	3,667	3,757	63.8
TEXARKANA	1,875	2,300	2,575	37.3
TYLER	2,200	2,625	3,093	40.6
VICTORIA	1,821	2,398	3,958	117.4
WACO	1,591	1,935	3,700	132.6
WICHITA FALLS	2,583	2,683	2,900	12.3
	2,312	2,790	4,876	110.9 **

Typical Finished Lot Price by City (Concluded)

	1960	1964	1969	Percent Change 1960-1969
UTAH				
OGDEN	2,310	3,241	3,925	69.9
SALT LAKE CITY	2,635	3,992	7,034	166.9
	2,472	3,616	6,205	151.0 **
VIRGINIA				
CHARLOTTESVILLE	2,928	6,200	4,740	61.9
LYNCHBURG	1,766	2,333	3,785	114.3
NEWPORT NEWS	2,977	3,975	5,391	81.1
NORFOLK	2,505	3,530	5,388	115.1
RICHMOND	2,750	4,376	5,663	105.9
ROANOKE	1,825	2,412	4,308	136.1
	2,458	3,804	5,243	113.3 **
WASHINGTON				
KENNEWICK	1,600	1,975	4,500	181.3
LONGVIEW	2,620	3,375	4,500	71.8
OLYMPIA	2,231	2,993	4,000	79.3
SEATTLE	2,687	3,909	6,274	133.5
SPOKANE	2,643	2,775	3,666	38.7
TACOMA	2,147	2,697	3,786	75.3
YAKIMA	3,250	3,940	4,085	25.7
	2,454	3,095	5,004	103.9 **
WEST VIRGINIA				
CHARLESTON	3,675	5,375	5,000	36.1
HUNTINGTON	2,875	3,550	5,437	69.1
MORGANTOWN	3,533	3,700	5,214	47.6
	3,361	4,208	5,217	55.2 **
WISCONSIN				
APPLETON	3,133	3,833	4,150	32.5
GREEN BAY	1,783	2,200	3,490	95.7
MADISON	6,250	8,153	7,343	17.5
BELOIT	1,653	2,022	3,287	98.9
MILWAUKEE	4,100	5,713	8,711	112.5
RACINE	2,883	4,116	4,496	55.9
WATERTOWN	2,150	2,200	2,700	25.6
	3,136	4,033	6,699	113.6 **
WYOMING				
CHEYENNE	2,100	2,600	3,000	42.9
	2,100	2,600	3,000	42.9 **
	2,851	3,852	6,217	118.1

Source: Michael Sumichrast and Sara A. Frankel, *Profile of the Builder and His Industry,* Washington, D.C.: National Association of Home Builders, 1970, pp. 43–50.

Selected References

Ina S Bechhoefer and Janice T. Stango

Alonso, William *Location and Land Use: Toward a General Theory of Land Rent.* Joint Center for Urban Studies Publications Series. Cambridge, Mass.: Harvard University Press, 1964.

A theoretical treatise of the relation of land values to land uses within an urban area. Mathematical analyses of agricultural rent and land use, residential bid price curves, and market equilibrium. Who uses what land for which purposes and why.

American Institute of Real Estate Appraisers, Sixth Edition Textbook Committee *The Appraisal of Real Estate.* 6th ed., Chicago: AIREA, 1973.

Basic theory and principles of real estate appraisal. Particular emphasis on capitalization techniques, as well as indepth treatment of the three traditional approaches to value—the income, cost, and market data approaches.

Andrews, Richard B. *Urban Growth and Development: A Problem Approach.* New York: Simmons-Boardman, 1962.

An introductory work on the problems of adjustment to urbanization. Deals with basic questions such as, the CBD, city-suburban frictions, zoning, and urban design.

Atteberry, William *Modern Real Estate Finance.* Columbus, Ohio: Grid, Inc., 1972.

Introductory text on the fundamental concepts of financing real estate. Basics of mortgage markets, condominiums, sale-leaseback, and government involvement.

Babcock, Richard F. *The Zoning Game: Municipal Practices and Policies.* Madison: University of Wisconsin Press, 1966.

Examination of local legislators and developers' biases in the zoning process. Principles underlying zoning law and suggestions on restructuring this system of land use regulation.

Babcock, Richard F., and Fred P. Bosselman *Exclusionary Zoning: Land Use Regulation and Housing in the 1970's.* New York: Praeger Publishers, 1973.

Detailed analysis of land use controls that can be restrictive. The social and economic costs of land use controls to the developer and community, how local governments can promote a balanced housing supply, and regional, metropolitan, and state agencies' role in land use regulation are among topics covered. Recommendations for improvements within the system.

Beaton, William R. *Real Estate Finance.* Englewood Cliffs, N.J.: Prentice-Hall, 1975.

Basic and up-to-date text on principles and practices of real estate finance and mortgage lending written in nontechnical language. Discusses the various traditional and innovative sources and uses of funds. Emphasizes residential mortgage finance including construction and permanent financing.

———. *Real Estate Investment.* Englewood Cliffs, N.J.: Prentice-Hall, Inc., 1971.

Basic text of particular interest for the investor, broker, developer and lender. Explanations of depreciation, installment sales, capital gains and methods of creative financing. Case examples.

Bogue, Donald J. *Principles of Demography.* New York: John Wiley & Sons, Inc., 1969.

Comprehensive introductory text detailing the basics of population study. Explanation of demographic differentials such as household formations, residential mobility, economic status, and income analysis will be of particular interest to the investor.

Bosselman, Fred, and **David Callies** *The Quiet Revolution in Land Use Control.* Washington, D.C.: Council on Environmental Quality, 1972.

Outlines some of the changing approaches to land use controls that could be of interest to the investor in development planning for the future.

Boyd, Orton W. *Atlas' Tax Aspects of Real Estate Transactions.* 5th rev. ed. Washington, D.C.: Bureau of National Affairs, Inc., 1971.

Detailed analysis of real estate taxation. Spells out the tax effects of real estate transactions enabling the investor to plan accordingly.

Burchell, Robert W., with **James W. Hughes** *Planned Unit Development: New Communities American Style.* New Brunswick, N.J.: Center for Urban Policy Research, Rutgers University, 1972.

Definitive text on the evolutionary and revolutionary aspects of planned unit development. Explains what developers need to know to convince local jurisdictions that a PUD will pay for itself. PUDs can yield more profits than standard subdivision development. Case studies.

Campbell, Angus, and **Philip E. Converse,** eds. *The Human Meaning of Social Change.* New York: Russell Sage Foundation, 1971.

A book of readings dealing with the psychological aspects of economic and social change. Utilizes data such as consumption patterns, population trends, and labor force distribution in its analysis.

Chapin, F. Stuart, Jr. *Urban Land Use Planning.* 2d ed. Urbana: University of Illinois Press, 1965.

Considered the authoritative text on theoretical and practical aspects of comprehansive land use planning. Special attention given to market analysis and amount of land development required for various land use functions.

Clawson, Marion *Suburban Land Conversion in the United States: An Economic and Governmental Process.* Baltimore, Md.: Johns Hopkins University Press, 1971.

Deals with dynamics of population migration to metropolitan areas and the resulting suburbanization process. Emphasis on land use determinants and complex processes of change involving suburban land use.

Eichler, Edward P., and **Marshall Kaplan** *The Community Builders.* California Studies in Urbanization and Environmental Design. Berkeley: University of California Press, 1967.

Profit and idealogical goals involved in the new-town development process. Emphasis on a study of the motives of James Rouse, Columbia, Maryland, developer, and Robert Simon, Reston, Virginia, developer.

Franklin, Herbert *Managing Urban Growth But for Whom.* Washington, D.C.: Potomac Institute, 1973.

Case study and analysis of Ramapo, New York's successful attempt at development timing. Vital reading for developers facing jurisdictional no-growth controls. Particular emphasis on staged development as tied into capital improvement programs.

Goodman, William I., and **Eric C. Freund,** eds. *Principles and Practice of Urban Planning.* 4th ed. Washington, D.C.: International City Managers' Association, 1968.

A basic text covering both concepts and principles of the urban planning process as well as a guide to the local government administration of planning. Historical perspectives, the current state of the art, and future trends in urban planning are presented. Methods and techniques of planning are stressed.

Graaskamp, James A. *A Guide to Feasibility Analysis.* Chicago: Society of Real Estate Appraisers, 1970.

Contemporary view of the multidimensional feasibility analysis and development of a methodology with which an appraiser and/or investor should approach the subject. Market trends, constraints and alternatives.

Haar, Charles M. Land Use Planning: *A Casebook on the Use, Misuse, and Re-use of Urban Land.* 2d ed. Boston: Little, Brown and Co., 1971.

Although intended primarily for law students and planners, the book contains much of interest for those who wish to develop a comprehensive understanding of the legal framework within which land use decisions are made. Topics included are public control of land use, public role of private land arrangements, and the sources of decision making for the urban environment.

Hagman, Donald G. *Urban Planning and Land Development Control Law.* St. Paul, Minn.: West Publishing Co., 1971.

Legal aspects of planning and development. Case studies regarding incorporation. Zoning, subdivision regulations, building and housing codes. Also analyzes private land use controls, PUDs and new towns.

Hoagland, Henry E., and **Leo D. Stone** *Real Estate Finance.* 5th ed. Homewood, Ill.: Richard D. Irwin, Inc., 1973.

Introductory text dealing with all phases of real estate financing. Covers basic legal concepts, origination, and servicing procedures and roles of the federal government.

Hoyt, Homer *Changing Principles of Land Economics.* Washington, D.C.: Technical Bulletin 60, Urban Land Institute, 1960.

Explanation of the revolutionary changes in land use over the century as a guide in understanding present day problems.

Kinnard, William N. *Income Property Valuation.* Lexington, Mass.: D. C Heath and Co., 1971.

Beginners text on appraisal principles and techniques for income properties for the person with existing knowledge of real estate market operation. Particular emphasis on income capitalization. Topics include market and site analysis, sales comparisons, improvements analysis, as well as income estimating and forecasting.

Kratovil, Robert *Real Estate Law.* 6th ed. Englewood Cliffs, N.J.: Prentice-Hall, Inc., 1974.

Basic principles of real estate law for use by brokers, builders, land developers, financiers, and planners. Explanation of the legal process from listings to easements to contracts to closings.

Lynch, Kevin *Site Planning.* 2d rev. ed. Cambridge, Mass.: M.I.T. Press, 1971. An introduction to the art of site planning. A behavioral approach to the principles of placing buildings and structural systems in harmony with each other and the surrounding environment.

McKeever, J. Ross, ed. *The Community Builders Handbook.* Anniversary Edition. Washington, D.C.: Urban Land Institute, 1968.

A guide to sound community development practices. Includes site selection, market analysis, construction, maintenance, and sales techniques for residential and shopping center development.

Masotti, Louis H., and **Jeffrey K. Hadden** *The Urbanization of the Suburbs.* Urban Affairs Annual Reviews, vol. 7. Beverly Hills, Calif.: Sage Publications, 1973.

Collection of readings that critically analyzes contemporary suburbanization. Historical perspectives are followed by a presentation of the current state of the art that focuses on political, social, and economic problem conceptualization as well as defining issues that need further attention in the 70s and beyond.

National Association of Home Builders *Land Development Manual.* Washington, D.C.: National Association of Home Builders, 1974.

"How to" guide outlining the basic principles for environmentally sound and aesthetic land planning. Covers the entire process of development from planning controls, site selection, design functions, construction, utilities, financing, marketing, and tax considerations.

Nourse, Hugh O. *Regional Economics.* New York: McGraw-Hill Book Company, Inc., 1968.

Introduction to location theory and regional economic development, including systems of land use and the impact of growth on regional structure. Government's role in the region's spatial growth.

Perloff, Harvey S., and **Lowden Wingo, Jr.,** eds. *Issues in Urban Economics.* Baltimore, Md.: The Johns Hopkins Press, 1968.

A book of readings handling the economic growth and stagnation of cities, local impact of national policies and expenditures, transportation, public facilities, and urban development policies. Attempts to uncover the elements of change in urban environments.

Ratcliff, Richard U. *Real Estate Analysis.* New York: McGraw-Hill Book Company, Inc., 1961.

Explanations of problems of real estate with particular emphasis on the investor's point of view. What to buy, when to sell, when to replace or modernize, and whether and how to lend are among the topics covered.

———. *Urban Land Economics.* New York: McGraw-Hill Book Company, Inc., 1949.

Principles dealing with the utilization of urban land as part of the market system. Rights in land, land values, demand factors, market functions, and economics of urban land policy are discussed.

———. *Valuation for Real Estate Decisions.* Santa Cruz, Calif.: Democrat Press, 1972.

Comprehensive study of the appraisal processes of real estate. Goes beyond the standard appraisal techniques and develops a valuation method using probability qualifications as well as other contemporary tools of analysis.

Real Estate Research Corporation *Costs of Sprawl.* Washington, D.C.: U.S. Government Printing Office, April 1974.

Study funded by HUD, CEQ et al. develops a model of alternative methods of residential development and concludes that suburban sprawl has been overly costly on both economic and environmental terms. Comprehensive literature reviews and annotated bibliography.

Ring, Alfred A. *The Valuation of Real Estate.* 2d ed. Englewood Cliffs, N.J.: Prentice-Hall, Inc., 1972.

Introductory text on appraisal principles and practices. Stresses the traditional appraisal approaches. Case study appendices with demonstration appraisal problems. Topics include techniques of capitalization, political, social, and economic forces upon property value, and importance of cost, price, income, and market approaches to value.

Seldin, Maury *Selections from Seldin.* Washington, D.C.: The American University, 1972.

Collection of articles dealing with the urban development system and its forces for change. Stresses understanding the operation of the urban system as a guide in the formation of an urban development strategy. Land costs, the location of residential development, development planning, and market information systems.

———, and **Richard H. Swesnik,** *Real Estate Investment Strategy.* New York: Wiley Interscience, 1970.

Risks and rewards of real estate investment. Develops a methodology for selecting an investment strategy. Profit potentials and tax considerations for single and multifamily residential, office buildings, retail centers, industrial, and special uses. Selecting the form of investment and the availability of borrowed money.

Semenow, Robert W. *Questions and Answers on Real Estate.* 7th ed. Englewood Cliffs, N.J.: Prentice-Hall, Inc., 1972.

Some 4,000 questions and answers on real estate topics such as brokerage, legal documents, financing, valuation, appraisal, and landlord-tenant relations.

Siegan, Bernard H. *Land Use Without Zoning.* Lexington: Lexington Books, 1972.

Case study of Houston, Texas, to illustrate patterns of development without the restraint of zoning regulations.

Smith, Halbert C.; Carl J. Tschappat; and **Ronald L. Racster** *Real Estate and Urban Development.* Homewood, Ill.: Richard D. Irwin, Inc., 1973.

Introductory text that focuses upon the investment decision approach as a tool in the understanding of the principles of real estate and urban development. Emphasis is placed upon the interrelationships among investment decision making, city growth, and social problems.

Smith, Wallace F. *Housing: The Social and Economic Elements.* California Studies in Urbanization and Environmental Design. Berkeley: University of California Press, 1970.

Introduction to the economic elements of the housing market. Investors and developers will find the concepts of resource allocation systems, aspects of housing prices, entrepreneurial behavior in the housing market, and characteristics of the housing stock of particular importance.

Thompson, Wilbur R. *A Preface to Urban Economics.* Baltimore, Md.: John Hopkins Press, 1968.

Economics of income, land use, and growth patterns. Topics of interest to investors include income analysis, local productivity, local service sector efficiency, and business cycles. Problems and policies of the urban economy.

Tiebout, Charles M. *The Community Economic Base Study.* Supplementary Paper no. 16. New York: Committee for Economic Development, 1962.

Explains basic underlying factors in economic base studies including how to undertake and analyze such a study to evaluate income-earning opportunities. Illustrates the principle with data collected from Los Angeles Metropolitan Area.

Unger, Maurice A. *Real Estate: Principles and Practices.* 5th ed. Cincinnati, Ohio: Southwestern Publishing Company, 1974.

Introductory text on theory and practices of real estate. Discussions of the economic, social, and legal aspects of real estate are followed by sections on property ownership, financing real estate, real estate brokerage, property evaluation, and planning for the future.

Weimer, Arthur M.; Homer Hoyt; and **George F. Bloom** *Principles of Real Estate.* 6th ed. New York: Ronald Press, 1972.

Widely acclaimed introductory text on real estate. Problems of administrative decision making with emphasis on real estate resources as well as functions of the industry. Economic characteristics of real estate, business conditions, and local trends. Identifies the areas of decisions for investors.

Wendt, Paul F., and **Alan R. Cerf** *Real Estate Investment Analysis and Taxation.* New York: McGraw-Hill Book Company, Inc., 1969.

Investment analyses and decision making with emphasis on internal rate of return analysis. Case examples. Still a useful text despite the outdated tax information.

Whyte, W. H., Jr. *Cluster Development.* New York: American Conservation Association, April 1964.

Explains the rationale for the cluster development concept and its environmental, political, legal, social, and economic implications.

Wingo, Lowdon, Jr., ed. *Cities and Space: The Future Use of Urban Land.* Baltimore, Md.: Johns Hopkins Press, 1963.

Essays which consider space as a finite resource to meet growth and development requirements. Management of space leading to optimum allocation for competing land uses.

Index

Index